HCI RELATED PAPERS OF INTERACCIÓN 2004

T0191755

HCI related papers of Interacción 2004

Edited by

RAQUEL NAVARRO-PRIETO

University Pompeu Fabra Fundation,
Estació de la Comunicació, Barcelona,
Spain

and

JESÚS LORÉS VIDAL

University of Lleida, Spain

 Springer

A C.I.P. Catalogue record for this book is available from the Library of Congress.

ISBN-13 978-90-481-7071-5
ISBN-10 1-4020-4205-1 (e-book)
ISBN-13 978-1-4020-4205-8 (e-book)

Published by Springer,
P.O. Box 17, 3300 AA Dordrecht, The Netherlands.

www.springer.com

Printed on acid-free paper

TABLE OF CONTENTS

Editors' Introduction

The present book contains a collection of the best papers presented at the *5th International Conference* on *Interacción Persona Ordenador* (IPO) (which is Human Computer Interaction in Spanish), which took place in Lleida on May 5th-7th, 2004. This conference was co-organised by the *Universitat of Lleida* and the *Universitat Oberta de Catalunya*.

Each year this conference is promoted by the *Asociación para la Interacción Persona Ordenador* (AIPO), the Spanish Human Computer Interaction Association, in collaboration with the local group of ACM-SIGCHI (CHISPA). In its fifth edition this conference has become a multidisciplinary forum for the discussion and dissemination of novelty research in Human Computer Interaction.

The main goals of Interacción 2004 were:
To expand the conference scope with internationally recognised invited speakers. The plenary talks were presented by Alan Dix, Yvonne Rogers, Geritt van der Veer, and Angel Puerta.
To open the participation to Spanish speaker worldwide in order to be a point of reference of this discipline not only in Spain but also in the wider Spanish speaking community. This goal was reached through a very diverse program which included panels and posters sessions, where many different aspect of the Human Computer Interaction (HCI) were presented. All through the program, research from outside Spain was reflected through the contributions from people of other countries.
To enrich the relationship between industry and academia through the organisation, for the first time, of a day of the Industry-Academia Collaboration. During this day's diverse activities, round tables and panels were conducted, and numerous practitioners of HCI joined our conference specifically for that event.
To increase the multidisciplinary nature of the contributions to the conference. Towards this goal a great effort was made to involve researchers from disciplines close to HCI.
To help in the development of doctoral dissertations of high quality, a doctoral consortium was held for the first time.

This book is organised according to the main areas of both basic and applied research that were presented at the conference. These areas were:

- Usability and Accessibility
- Ubiquitous computing and context aware systems
- Interaction with learning recourses
- User Centred design methodologies
- Cooperative systems
- Models of interactive systems
- Applications of User Centred design
- Information of Visualization
- HCI methodologies
- Semantic web
- Group learning and work

Regarding the reviewing process, our program committee, reviewers and meta-reviewers (integrated by recognised researchers both from Spain and from the international community), made a great effort in selecting the best papers for the conference and later on for this publication. The success rate for submitted papers to be part of this publication was 54%. We will like to acknowledge the effort of the program committee of this publication: Julio Abascal, Xavier Alamán, Josep Blat, José Cañas, Pablo Castells, Alan Dix, Miguel Gea, Jesus Lores, Roberto Moriyón, Raquel Navarro, Manuel Ortega, Mari Carmen Puerta and Yvonne Rogers. We will like to also thanks the two universities that co-organised this conference, namely, the *Universitat de Lleida* and the *Universitat Oberta de Catalunya*.

We hope that you enjoy your reading and find this book useful.

An Expert-Based Usability Evaluation of the EvalAccess Web Service

Julio Abascal, Myriam Arrue, Inmaculada Fajardo, Nestor Garay

Laboratory of Human-Computer Interaction for Special Needs
UPV/EHU.
Manuel Lardizabal 1. E-20018 Donostia
{julio, myriam, acbfabri, nestor}@si.ehu.es

1. Introduction

The activities developed by means of Internet have rapidly increased in the last years. Most of the Internet success is due to the proliferation and popularization of information and services provided through web sites. However, many web pages have been designed without having in mind that there may be people, devices and even browsers that can not access them. A number of initiatives have been developed to prevent web accessibility barriers, including the accessibility laws promulgated by diverse coun-tries-such as the Section 508 in the USA-. There are also independent institutions that have compiled accessible design guidelines, some of them with great influence in the design of accessible web pages. In particular, the best known ones are the guidelines compiled by the Web Accessibility Initiative (WAI), which is part of the World Wide Web Consortium (W3C) [1]. All these initiatives specify and regulate the characteristics that universal accessible web sites must have. However, these efforts are not enough if developers are not provided with tools that support universal design.

Evalaccess is a tool that automatically evaluates the accessibility of web pages. It is an evolution of the EvalIRIS tool that was developed within IRIS European project [2]. EvalAccess allows verifying whether a web page -or a web site-satisfies a particular set of guidelines in order to determine its accessibility. WAI accessibility guidelines are habitually used, but EvalAccess can evaluate the compliance with any other set of guidelines if they are specified using a specifically designed XML schema. This automatic evaluation tool has been implemented as a web

1

R. Navarro-Prieto and J.L. Vidal (eds.), HCI Related Papers of Interacción 2004, 1-17.
© 2006 Springer. Printed in the Netherlands.

service[1] in order to be used from any web application. In this way, accessibility evaluation can be performed from any tool and can be included in the development life cycle.

Even if EvalAccess was designed as a web service to be used not by human beings but by other applications, a user interface application was developed in order to allow people to directly make use of EvalAccess. Its main aim was to let web developers and evaluators to access the services provided by the web service. Subsequently, it was found that the interface was also useful for users interested in directly performing web accessibility evaluations. Therefore, this user interface was made publicly accessible. The original interface was simple and straight because it was oriented to the own developers needs. When the Laboratory of Human-Computer Interaction for Special Needs decided to provide a public interface, the need of a deep usability evaluation and a subsequent redesign was recognized.

2. Characteristics of the evaluation

Among the frequently obviated metrics criteria[2] that any evaluation tool should accomplish such as Validity, Reliability, Sensibility, Diagnosticity, etc. Usability is one of the most relevant. We adopted this criterion as the primary requirement of the EvalAccess user interface in order to provide a Usable and Accessible way to the application.

The main purpose of this paper is the application of this criterion in a usability testing exercise, that is, the evaluation of the usability of EvalAccess interface itself. For this purpose two Expert-based Usability Inspection Methods were used: Revision of Guidelines and Heuristic Evaluation. The second step, the Empiric Method (controlled experiment with real users), is currently under development. In the next section the main methods of Usability Evaluation are summarized and the advantages and disadvantages of Expert-based Evaluation are discussed.

---

[1] A web service is an application that allows communication with other applications through Remote Procedure Calls (RPCs) in a distributed environment (for example, a remote or local network) [3]. The main advantage of web services is that they are platform-independent. Normally both, inputs (parameters) and outputs (results), have an XML format [4].

[2] O'Donnell & Eggemeier provide more information on metrics criteria [5].

3. A brief revision of usability evaluation methods

There are many taxonomies for classifying Usability Evaluation Methods (UEMs) according to different dimensions or categories. In this study we used the taxonomy of Andre [6] which classifies UEMs into three categories: (1) Empirical Methods, (2) Expert-Based Usability Inspections and (3) Analytic or Model-Based methods.

In this exercise, we utilized two techniques classified into Expert-Based Usability Inspections: Guideline Reviews and Heuristic Evaluation. Expert Inspections consist of the exhaustive examination of those specific aspects of an interface which are related to the effective, efficient and satisfactory interaction of users, carried by experts in the field. According to Mack and Nielsen [7] in the Guideline Reviews method experts analyse the conformity with a comprehensive, and frequently extensive, list of usability guidelines. Its main advantage is that, due to its easiness, it allows experts to perform structured evaluations avoiding formal training [6]. There are numerous sets of guidelines proposed for different types of interfaces. The most adjusted to our objective are Nielsen & Tahir sets of Homepage Usability Guidelines [9]. Its features will be explained in the next section. Nevertheless, Guideline Reviews has also disadvantages: guidelines are frequently vague, and sometimes contradictory, and lacking empirical support. In addition, according to Abascal and Nicolle [8], when the number of design guidelines is too large their application may result tedious.

On the other hand, according to Andre [6], Heuristic Evaluation uses a reduced number of experts that examine the interfaces according to recognized usability principles or general rules which describe common properties of usable interfaces. The main advantage of these techniques is that they are easy to use and they help to find several usability problems with low cost. However, the results of the heuristic evaluation are influenced by the subjective experience of the experts and can produce "false alarms". The list of heuristics proposed by Molich, R., & Nielsen [10] and Nielsen [11] are among the most used and validated. They are based on a factorial analysis of 249 usability problems. In the next two sections, we describe our experience with these two techniques used to evaluate the usability of the Web Service EvalAccess

4. Guideline Review of three Web Services: EvalAccess, Wave and Bobby.

As previously mentioned, the Nielsen & Tahir List of Homepage Usability Guidelines
[9] was selected with the aim of evaluating and contrasting the usability of EvalAccess. We also selected two tools, similar to EvalAccess, Wave [12] and Bobby [13], which provide their services through the Internet by means of a web interface. Four usability experts, members of the Laboratory of Human Computer Interaction for Special Needs (University of the Basque Country), took part in this study. Each expert evaluated the homepage of the three Web services: EvalAccess, Wave and Bobby. The order of the evaluation was balanced between experts for preventing the sequence effect.

Before performing the guideline review, we analysed the degree of agreement between experts with regard to the applicability of the selected guidelines, since the web pages evaluated were not strictly homepages. Therefore, two evaluation objectives were agreed:

• To analyze the applicability of the Nielsen's web page usability guidelines to the selected web sites and to select the most adequate ones and

• To assess the compliance of each web page with the selected guidelines.

4.1. Applicability and Agreement among Experts

The list of Nielsen & Tahir Homepage Usability Guidelines classifies them in 26 categories: (1) Communicating the site's purpose, (2) Communicating information about your company, (3) Content writing, (4) Revealing content through examples, (5) Archives and accessing past content, (6) Links, (7) Navigation, (8) Search, (9) Tools and task shortcuts, (10) Graphics and animation, (11) Graphic design, (12) UI widgets, (13) Window titles, (14) URLs, (15) News and press releases, (16) Popup windows and staging pages, (17) Advertising, (18) Welcomes, (19) Communicating technical problems and handling emergencies, (20) Credits, (21) Page reload and refresh,

(22) Customization, (23) Gathering customer data, (24) Fostering community, (25) Dates and times, and (26) Stock quotes and displaying numbers.

	>50%	<50%	U	Z	P level
EvalAccess	285.000	66.0000	0.00	4.28	0.00
Wave	284.500	66.5000	0.5	4.26	0.00
Bobby	285.000	66.0000	0.00	4.28	0.00

Table 1. Results of the Mann-Whitney U Test used to compare applicable and non applicable categories of guidelines for each Web Service Interface.

The task of the experts was simply to decide if a guideline was applicable to evaluate de usability of the proposed interfaces. We calculated the proportion of guidelines applicable for each category and each interface. The result was used like an index of category applicability in each interface. We performed a Kendall's Concordance Test to analyze the agreement between experts about the applicability of each category. This test provides a coefficient of concordance which ranges between 0 and 1, where 0 means lack of agreement and 1 means total agreement. The coefficient of Kendall's Concordance for the three web service interfaces was 0.8 (Aver. rank r = 0.77) which means that experts agreed on category applicability in an 80%. To know if there were differences in the applicability index for each Web service interface we applied the non parametric Kruskal-Wallis Test. We introduced the Type of Web Service Interface (EvalAccess, WAVE and Bobby) as independent variables and the global index of applicability as dependent variable. The differences between Web Service Interfaces were not significant. Finally, the indexes of applicability were used to divide the categories of guidelines between applicable (>0.5) and non applicable (<=0.5). The Mann-Whitney U Test (see Table 1), showed that the difference between applicable and non applicable categories was significant for all Web Service Interfaces. This result allowed us to remove the categories of guidelines which were not applicable enough (categories 2, 8, 9, 14, 15, 19, 22, 23, 24, 25, 26).

4.2. Results of Guidelines Review

The same experts who performed the applicability test participated in the Guideline Review. The task of the experts was to decide which of the fifteen guidelines selected in the previous phase were fulfilled by each Web Service Interfaces.

We calculated the global percentage of guidelines fulfilled by each interface and the percentage of guidelines fulfilled per categories for each interface. According to Nielsen & Tahir [9] the values above 90% mean that the web page evaluated is usable; web pages with values between 90% and 80% could be considered moderately usable; for web pages with values between 80% and 50% the redesign is recommended; and web pages with values below 50% are intractable and the redesign is absolutely recommended. In the case of EvalAccess interface, the 87% of guidelines were fulfilled. The analysis per categories showed that the categories 3, 5, 11, 12, 16, 18, 20 and 21 were fulfilled to the 90%; the categories 6, 7, 10, 13 y 17 were only fulfilled to the 80% approximately; the category 1 to the 60% and the category 4 to the 30%. Therefore, according to Nielsen & Tahir, the global redesigned of this interface would not be necessary and it could be enough to redesign the aspect related to the guidelines of the categories 1 and 4 (respectively, Communicating the site's purpose and Revealing content through examples). The global fulfilment score of Wave Interface and Bobby Interface was respectively 82% and 75%. With the aim of contrasting if the guidelines fulfilment of EvalAccess Interface was significantly higher than the fulfilment of the other two interfaces, we performed a non parametric Kruskal-Wallis Test. The results showed that EvalAccess Interface was significantly more usable than Bobby Interface $(H (1, N = 8) = 5.33 p = 0.020)$ but not more usable than Wave Interface.

5. Heuristic Evaluation of EvalAccess

Heuristics set proposed by Nielsen [11] were chosen in order to carry on this evaluation: 1. Visibility of system status, 2. Match between system and the real world, 3. User control and freedom, 4. Consistency and standards, 5. Error prevention, 6. Recognition rather than recall, 7. Flexibility and efficiency of use, 8. Aesthetic and minimalist design, 9. Help users recognize, diagnose, and recover from errors and 10. Help and documentation.

The user profile selected was "a novice user accessing EvalAccess website for the first time". Performing the accessibility evaluation of a web page was selected as the main use case, which was divided into eleven use scenarios. The following list summarizes the objectives of these use scenarios: 1. Read the using instructions, 2. Specify the web page to evaluate, 3. Configure the evaluation options (priority levels), 4. Acces the evaluation results, 5. Analyze the evaluation results, 6. Save/Print the evaluation results, 7. Perform a new evaluation, 8. Go back to homepage from the evaluation results web page, 9. Go back to evaluation results, 10. Contact the organization which offers the service, 11. Search for related links.

5.1. Procedure

The same four experts who carried on the guidelines review participated in this process. Each expert familiarized with the EvalAccess user interface before performing individually the Heuristic Evaluation. The experts contributed with a brief description of errors found in each scenario. Then, they decided on the heuristics applicable to each encountered error, sorting them according to their applicability order. Finally, the four evaluators produced a report, discussed the different evaluations and synthesized the results.

5.2. Results and Discussion

A table showing the number of found errors and the number of not fulfilled heuristics in each scenario was produced by each expert. This allowed us to quantitatively sort and summarize the obtained data. Firstly, the average (M) of the found errors in each scenario and each evaluated web page was calculated (see Figure 1a). As can be seen, scenarios 2 and 5, Specify the web page to evaluate (M = 2) and Analyze the evaluation results (M = 3.75), gave the highest average value of errors. The next highest average value was produced by the scenarios Configure the evaluation options (M = 1.75) and Access the evaluation results (M = 1.75). The average of errors for the remaining scenarios was 1.

According to the data analysis by heuristic (Figure 1b), the highest average values for heuristics not fulfilled were produced by heuristic 10 (M = 0.77) and 6 (M = 0.66). Therefore, considering the totality of scenarios the less fulfilled heuristics were Help and documentation and Recognition rather than recall.

The heuristics not fulfilled in the scenario where the highest errors average values were obtained (Specify the Web Page to evaluate (2) and Analyze the evaluation results (5)) were also analyzed. The heuristics that gave an average value for found errors higher than 1 were the following: 8 (Aesthetic and minimalist design), 7 (Flexibility and efficiency of use), 6 (Recognition rather than recall), 5 (Error prevention), and 10 (Help and documentation).

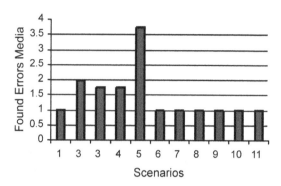

Fig. 1a. The figure shows the Average values of found errors in each EvalAccess use scenario.

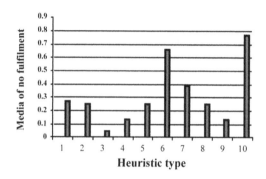

Fig. 1b. The figure shows Average values of found errors by heuristic in all EvalAccess use scenarios.

6. General Discussion of Experts' Usability Evaluation

Both the result of Guideline Review and Heuristic Evaluation reveal that EvalAccess interface provides not sufficient help and documentation of the system which allow the users to understand the propose and functioning of the EvalAccess Service. Errors which experts connect with "Help and documentation" heuristic describe situations as: poor description of the service is provided, help is not provided, the user does not know how to use the service, etc. On the other hand, Heuristic Evaluation shows some important usability problems not revealed in the Guideline Review, for example the interface produces excessive memory charge. According to the heuristic "Recognition rather than recall", the situation is described in this way: the buttons for performing the accessibility evaluation task are not explicit enough, configuration features of the priority of the evaluation are not visible and are not available in every part of the interface, the title of the results is not visible (the user has to remember which web page she/he has evaluated), etc. Therefore, descriptions of these errors have to be considered when improving the usability of the interface.

Additionally, Heuristic Evaluation allows us to evaluate diverse scenarios, which make possible to refine the diagnostic of usability problem. Regarding the scenario that obtained the highest average value of errors, Analyze the evaluation results (5), the errors that could mainly cause usability problems were related to: providing extra and redundant information, lack of visibility of the information summarizing tables, inexistence of direct accesses to parts of information (as hyperlinks), lack of errors prevention (for instance, absence of any explanation of results meaning). Therefore, this data has to be considered as a main concern when redesigning EvalAccess interface since this scenario is the one which could cause major usability problems.

7. Redesign based on the results of Evaluation by Experts

EvalAccess web service was redesigned based on the results obtained in this analysis. This redesign process was divided into two phases: homepage redesign and accessibility evaluation results page redesign.

7.1. Homepage redesign

The original homepage is shown in Figure 2. As can be seen in the figure, the homepage contained the following elements: logo and links to the entities or organizations involved in the development of the tool, several links to related information, two alternative text boxes –one of them for introducing the URL of the web page to evaluate, and the other one for introducing the HTML code to evaluate–, and a button close to each text box. Clicking any of these buttons will start the accessibility evaluation process.

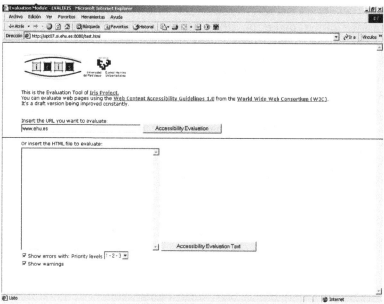

Fig. 2. Original EvalAccess Homepage.

By using the elements mentioned above, different tasks can be performed:

• Accessibility evaluation of an on-line web page. This task can be performed by introducing the URL of the web page in the first text box and clicking the correspondent button.

• Accessibility evaluation of HTML code. Copying and pasting the HTML code into the second text box and clicking the associated button is enough in order to perform this task.

In addition to the previously described tasks, it is possible to configure some options of the evaluation process, for instance, it can be selected the priority of the accessibility guidelines that are going to be used to evaluate the on-line web page or HTML code.

As a result of the review of design guidelines, experts concluded that the redesign of the following categories was crucial.

• Communicating the site's purpose (Category 1)

• Revealing content through examples (Category 4) The problems and their solution related to Category 1 are the following:

• There was not any logo of the tool. A logo was designed and introduced in the left top of the web page as it is stated in [9].

• There was not any description of the purpose of the tool. A brief description was incorporated in the top of the page, under the logo of the tool.

• The most important tasks the user can perform with the tool were not clearly presented. A navigation bar was included in the web page, so the user can easily access to the different services offered, more information about the tool and help and using instructions. In addition, the navigation bar informs the user about the option or service which is currently performing (associating a different style to the active link). According to category 4, the main problem was the inexistence of any graphical examples that helped the user to have a better understanding of the existing content in the web page. The incorporation of these examples would cause conflict with the minimalist design heuristic, so the experts decided to prioritize this heuristic. Therefore, the solution adopted consisted of the help and instructions section and the brief tool description inserted on the top of the web page.

Issues detected in the evaluation of heuristic 10 and heuristic 6 were our priorities when solving the problems arisen from the heuristic evaluation, as these problems affected generally to all the described scenarios.

The detected problems and implemented solutions related to the heuristic 6 were the following (see Figure 3a y 3b):

• The action performed by each button on the web page is not clear and the text they contain is not consistent. Implementation of a navigation bar was agreed in a previous step of the redesign. This action also is a solution for the correspondence between the service and the button that performs it. The texts of the buttons performing the same action were homogenized. Moreover, the implemented navigation bar maximizes the conformance of this heuristic, as it makes possible access to the instructions or any other option from any web page or section of the interface.

• The configuration options of the evaluation were not visible enough as they were on the down part of the web page and it was not clear which services they affect to. These options were placed below each service when dividing the services in different web pages, so the use of this feature was facilitated.

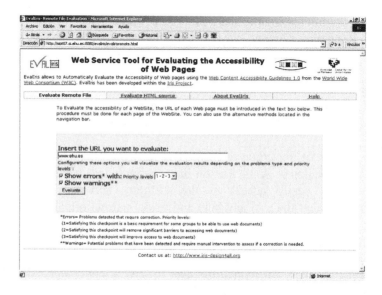

Fig. 3a. Redesigned EvalAccess Homepage. The shows the option of inserting the URL.

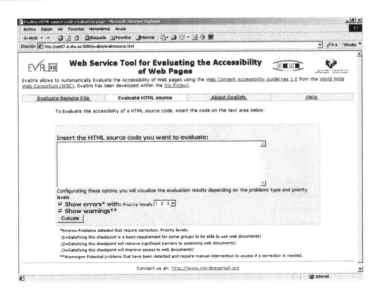

Fig. 3b. Redesigned EvalAccess Homepage. The figure shows the option of inserting the HTML code.

The problems detected when evaluating the heuristic 10 were solved by the implementation of the help and tool using instructions section.

7.2. Accessibility Evaluation Results Page Redesign

As it is shown in Figure 4, the original results page was formed by the evaluated web page, a summary table of all found accessibility errors and the complete report consisting of detailed information of each error, and a link to a web page where more information can be obtained.

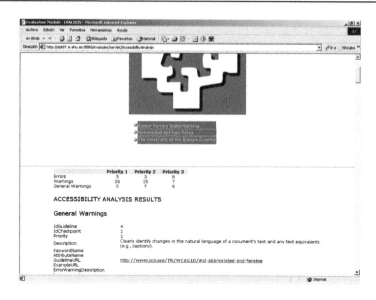

Fig. 4. The figure shows the Original EvalAccess evaluation results web page.

As a result of the heuristic evaluation, the scenario where most errors were obtained was Analysis of the Evaluation Results. This led us to completely redesign this web page. Although some detected errors affected heuristic 5, Error prevention, they were not taken into account in the redesign as their solution required changes in the implementation of the tool itself, as well as, modifications in the interface. Therefore, the redesign was focused on the following heuristics: 8, 7, 6 and 10.

The detected errors and the implemented solutions, in order to maximize the conformance of heuristic 8, were the following (see Figure 5):

• Excessive information was presented in a lineal and no-ordered way. The results web page was structured on several tables, one of them showing the global data of the evaluation and others reporting the found accessibility errors in detail. The information was shown formatted in columns in order to minimize the number of rows required for reporting one and therefore reducing the need of using the scroll.

• In the original results page, the evaluated web page was shown before the report of found accessibility errors. This was irrelevant to the user. The solution was to remove the evaluated web page from the results page showing only the important information, the errors report.

• Unusable information was shown in the report, such as empty fields. The solution taken was to remove these empty information categories.

Regarding heuristic 7, the main problem detected was the lack of efficiency when visualizing the detailed information provided in the report. This problem was solved incorporating links from the global resume table to the related detailed information in the report.

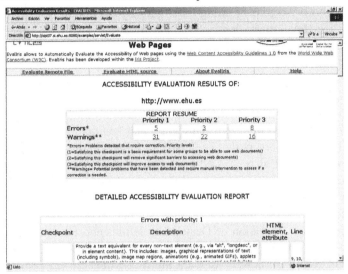

Fig. 5. The figure shows the redesigned version of the evaluation results web page.

Detected errors and their solutions in order to conform to heuristic 6 were the following:

• There was not any explanation about the meaning of the configuration options defined for performing and showing results of the accessibility evaluation. The meaning of these options was incorporated below the global resume table of results.

• In the results page shown after an on-line web page accessibility evaluation the URL of the evaluated page was not shown in an appropriate place, so the user could not easily identify the results of the evaluation of which web page she or he was viewing. The URL of the evaluated on-line web page was moved to a highlighting position in the redesigned results page. Regarding heuristic 10, previously described help and tool using instructions section has been designed and implemented. The description of the results' format and each part of the resulting report were included in this section.

8. Conclusion

The goal of this study was performing a usability evaluation of the EvalAccess web service interface. Initially, this user interface was designed with the aim of being used only by accessibility experts and by the service developers themselves. However, its use was spread out to incidental or inexpert users that do not know accessibility tools. For this reason, it has been necessary to evaluate the usability of the interface for this new user profile in order to achieve an efficient, effective and satisfactory interaction.

With this objective in mind, we made a study based on expert-based usability evaluation methods. This approach has demonstrated its validity for finding design errors that can cause problems in the use of the interface by novice users. It also showed a number of design errors that may make the interface impractical. One of the used techniques, the Revision of Design Guidelines, showed that EvalAccess interface was significantly more usable than the interface of other similar web service (Bobby). Both used techniques (Revision of Design Guidelines and Heuristic Evaluation) provided us some diagnostic data about the causes of the usability problems. Some of these causes are the following: missed communication about the purpose of the site, lack of specification of the tool functionalities that can be used via web, user memory overload due to the presentation of redundant and irrelevant information, etc.

This data set allowed us to redesign EvalAccess user interface. The comparison between the two versions of the interface (pre- and post-redesign) will serve on the secon d phase of the study, which is currently b eing made, to contrast whether the expert-based evaluation results really express the usability problems detected by users. Furthermore, it will be used to evaluate the efficiency of the design solutions that are implemented in order to overcome the problems of the redesigned interface.

References

1. Web Accessibility Initiative (WAI). Available at http://www.w3.org/WAI/.
2. IRIS European Project [http://www.iris-design4all.org/].
3. Galbraith B, Tost A, Irani R, Basha J, Hendricks M, Modi T, Milbery J and Cable S. (2002). Professional Java Web Services. Wrox Press Ltd.
4. XML Available at http://www.w3.org/XML/.

5. O'Donnell, R. D. & Eggemeier, F. T. (1986). Workload assessment methodology. In Boff, K., Kaufman, L. & Thomas, J. (Eds.): Handbook of Perception and Performance (vol. II). New York: Wiley, ch. 42.
6. Andre, T. S. (2000). Determining the effectiveness of the usability problem inspector: A theory-based model and tool for finding usability problems. PhD Thesis. Blacksburg, VA: Virginia Polytechnic Institute and State University.
7. Mack, R. L., & Nielsen, J. (1994). Executive summary. In J. Nielsen & R. L. Mack (Eds.), Usability inspection methods (pp. 1-23). New York: John Wiley & Sons.
8. Abascal J., Nicolle C. (2001). Why Inclusive Design Guidelines. In C. Nicolle, Abascal J. (eds.): Inclusive Design Guidelines for HCI. Taylor & Francis.
9. Nielsen, J. & Tahir, M. (2000). Homepage Usability: 50 Websites Deconstructed. New Riders Publishing, Indianapolis
10. Molich, R., & Nielsen, J. (1990). Improving a human-computer dialogue. Communications of the ACM, 33(3), 338-348.
11. Nielsen, J. (1994). Heuristic evaluation. In Nielsen, J., and Mack, R. L. (Eds.), Usability Inspection Methods. John Wiley & Sons, New York, NY.
12. Wave (Pennsylvania's Initiative on Assistive Technology (PIAT). http://www.wave.webaim.org/index.jsp.
13. Bobby (Watchfire Corporation) http://bobby.watchfire.com/bobby/html/en/index.jsp.

Adaptive and Context-Aware Hypermedia Model for Users with Communication Disabilities

M. Gea, M.J. Rodríguez, M.L. Rodríguez, N. Medina, R. López-Cózar,

P. Paderewski, F.L. Gutiérrez

Dpt. Lenguajes y Sistemas Informáticos, ETSI Informática, Univ. Granada

1 Introduction

Technological advances improves our every-day life, and should be beneficial for all, and mobile technology gives new opportunities to user with special needs [2]. Augmentative and Alternative Communication (AAC) Systems [10] provide devices and techniques to improve the communicative ability of a person whose disability makes it difficult to speak. The causes may vary from one person to other for different reasons (sensorial, physical or psychical disabilities), it can be a temporal or permanent disorder and the population is very heterogeneous. There are several AAC systems, which are being used by different communities: sing languages (deaf people), pictorial languages, templates and communicators (e.g. Alphatalker using the Minspeak language [1]).

One of the collectives demanding such systems is children diagnosed as having autism. Autism is considered a lifelong neurological disorder characterized as follows [7]:

- These children have difficulty with social relationships and with verbal and non-verbal communication.
- The pathology and its manifestations vary from one child to another. Each child manifests different behavior, capabilities and expectations.
- The child is strongly influenced by his environment, preferring predictable situations. Changes in environment could provoke unpredictable changes in the child behavior.

Difficulty in communication causes many problems to these children, provoking fears and anxiety crisis. The crises often occur when the situation/activity is new, frustrating, uncertain or difficult. In this field, therapeutic researchers have focused on reducing the behavioural

R. Navarro-Prieto and J.L. Vidal (eds.), HCI Related Papers of Interacción 2004, 19-28.

symptoms, anticipating future events and creating controllable situations [4] and elicitation methods [6].

One of the main objectives of an AAC system should be adapting to different kind of users and user needs. However, current AAC systems do not cover these requirements. The communicators are far too general to be used by a broad community, or they are created for a concrete context and individual, which leads to many difficulties to be modified for new situations or changes. A successful design might cover the following features: Portable, easy of use and recall, used in different context (class, house), for different purposes and as learning aid (for educators).

This paper focuses on the development of a communication architecture suitable for children with non-verbal disabilities based on user adaptation and context aware as a key goal to overcome their communication barriers. The next section shows the proposed architecture. Section three describes the user modelling technique. After that, section four shows the evolving and adaptation mechanism. Section five describes the context aware mechanism, and finally, conclusions and future works are described in section six.

2 Architecture

Sc@ut is our AAC proposal based on a extension of previous works [8] on adaptive hypermedia technology. Symbolic pictorial templates are the basis for knowledge representation. Although several pictorial standards have been proposed such as Bliss Symbols, from our experience, working and mixing these symbolic pictures with other meaningful images (e.g. the mother's image, everyday objects, etc.) improves the communication by affective motivations. Images are set on templates depending on user needs and context. The user directly selects these images by pointing. Changes for different reasons can evolve the underlying user knowledge, translating these changes to the pictorial templates. A general view of the underlying model is explained below.

The children use the hypermedia model to express their desires, navigating through the templates and selecting items.

The user profile and knowledge domain (communication context) are represented and considered in the hypermedia design.

The user interaction and navigation depends on his location.

The communicator evolves, adapting to each child and to the changes in the scenarios.

Figure 1 shows a typical template and the proposed two-tier architecture of Sc@ut. The communicator is a handheld device for the child communicative capabilities (the sound is attached to each picture), whereas the metacommunicator is a meta-tool which allows the educator adapt the communicator to the user needs and to new contexts. It also acquires knowledge from the child interaction. The meta-communicator architecture includes components responsible for specifying: the user profile, the knowledge domain, the user interaction, the hypermedia model, the learning and evolving process. This architecture is implemented in different devices. The meta-communicator is running on a PC and the communicator is implemented in a PDA device. This artefact is small enough to be portable, the speed of power-on minimises the child anxiety, and its display allows us to select an object by direct pointing with the finger. The benefit of this architecture is the separation of concerns. First of all, there are two kinds of users which use this architecture with different purposes. Secondly, the cognitive, interaction, design and learning aspects have to be differentiated to avoid the coupling. Thereby, evolution/adaptability can be done more easily and safely because the architecture components are independent [5].

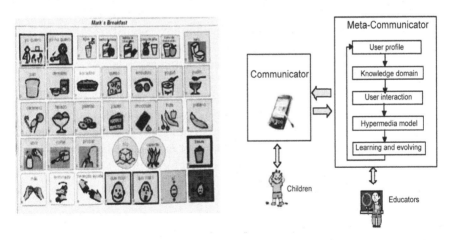

Figure 1. The Sc@ut Architecture

3 User Modelling

Up to now, educators create static templates describing different scenarios for the child as shown in figure 1. The creation of a scenario includes different interrelated concepts needed for the communication: desires (I want/I don't want, yes/no), domain objects (cheese, water, ...), qualifiers (more, finished, heat, cold), feeling (good, bad), and context (go to the bath). The user model contains three important steps: identification of user features (the user profile), an explicit representation of the context (knowledge domain) and specific goal requirements from educators to create templates of concepts on a hypermedia model.

3.1 User Profile

These templates contain information of different nature, some is specific for a particular child while other is generic to the group. The best strategy for information management is the separation of the user profile in different categories. Our approach considers the following categories.

- *Communication habits.* These aspects describe personal behaviours and general knowledge. For example, Mark is shy and has difficulties with complex scenarios (he prefers structured activities step-by-step and familiar images). However, he is capable of constructing easy sentences correctly.
- *Domain specific* (Scenario). This information is related with specific contexts (preferences). For example, Mark likes cake and ice cream a lot, and he drinks water only in his cup.
- *Educator's goals.* This information identifies educator goals for a child on a particular scenario. For example, Mark should learn that his hands have to be cleaned before eating.

3.2 Knowledge Domain

This knowledge domain is represented by means of a semantic network to capture relevant features of each user. This information is posted as a set of concepts and meaningful relationships between them (figure 3 shows a semantic network). *Feelings* denotes the child emotions whereas *Activities* are situations in which the child knows/learns how to act. Depending on the child profile, different activities will be proposed (e.g. *Nutrition, Hygiene*, etc.). Two kinds of concepts are showed in the network: complex concepts such as *Activities, Nutrition* or *Drinks*, and basic concepts, such as *Water, Milk* or *Juice.* Every concept, has an associated meaningful information (called Item) composed of audio, text, image, etc

Complex concept are represented by a circle (e.g. *Drinks*) and basic concepts with rectangles (e.g. *Water*). A bidirectional relationship (labelled "influences") between *Activities* and *Feelings* concepts reflects the repercussion that an activity has in the child's feelings and vice versa. The "kind_of" conceptual relationship is used to specify the division in parts of a complex concept. The "prerequisite" relationship establishes a mandatory relationship between two complex concepts. For example, has to wash his hands (*Hand Wash)* before eating the food (*Nutrition*).

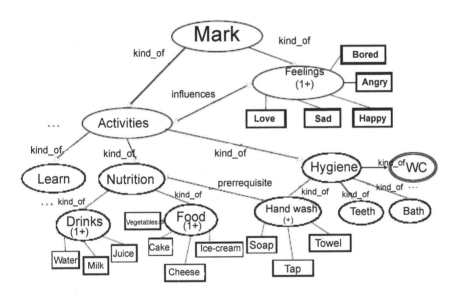

Figure 2. Mark's Knowledge Domain

Basic concepts describe structures or instances of complex concept. For example, *Feelings* has a basic concept for each considered mood: *Angry, Happy, Sad,* etc. Basic concepts are leafs in the semantic network. The decision about whether a concept is complex or basic will depend on the detail level at which the knowledge domain is represented. Part of the semantic network should be always accessible to the child (called permanent concepts). This is the case of the *WC* concept (go to the WC), which appears surrounded by a double circle. Besides, the type of association between a complex concept and its basic concepts must be specified. denoting a choice (1), a multiple selection (1+) or a specific ordering (1*). Also, **grammatical** and **contextual** models can be attached to activities and fixing rules for its correct use. Figure 4 shows the knowledge domain, and different locations can be attached to the same activity (i.e. *Nutrition* can be done in *Class*, in *House* or in *Restaurant*). These relationships (labeled as "perform") link activities with available locations in which they can be executed.

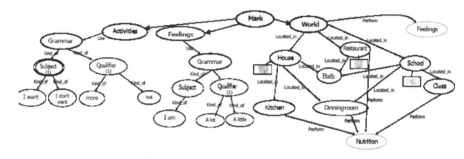

Figure 3. Mark's Model

3.3 User Interaction and Hypermedia Model

The hypermedia model is generated from the knowledge model. It consists of templates, items and links, and it will be implemented on the PDA device. Hand-held devices impose size constraints to the number of visible cells at the same time. In our experience, we have used a maximum of 4x3 cells distributions for guaranteeing usability and easy of use with the finger directly pointing the screen. This restriction may no be longer a true problem because all the information is not always necessary at the same time. Following, we translate from knowledge model (described in the semantic network) to hypermedia model on a straight forward way (taking into account prerequisites, permanent concepts, etc.). Hypermedia structure may be based on one or more of these scopes (grammar, activities and context) depending on the child profile or interaction preferences. Figure 5 shows a set of activities in *School* (a) the selection of *Nutrition* activity (b), the steps (c) and after that the food (d).

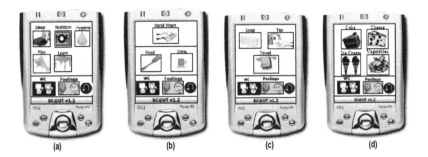

Figure 4. Hypermedia Templates

Some of the rules applied for the hypermedia creation are the following:

• Each complex concept is implemented as a template (figure 5.a) and items must be included in another template (on hierarchical way).

• If the concept is divided into other complex concepts (e.g. Activities in 5.a), the template shows the pictures of the higher-order concepts.

• If a concept has a prerequisite, this concept will be added on the template as mandatory activity (in the first row) such as Hand *Wash* when the user selects *Nutrition* (5.b)

• If the concept has associated basic concepts, the template includes an image and text-description for each item (figure 5.d shows the *Food* template).

• Permanent and associated concepts are always visible on each template (*WC* and *Feelings*).

• A *Back* item is added to navigate through templates.

4 Evolving, Adaptation and Context Aware

The meta-communicator detects user tasks and changes in the scenario in order to adapt the hypermedia model. Collecting measurable information about child navigation through the hypermedia. These modifications are propagated through the hypermedia model, guaranteeing its consistency and integrity. The adaptation and evolution process (shown in figure 6) has several steps: it is necessary to represent and update the user model with meaningful information from the child interaction (e.g. feeling history, activities performed, error rates, etc.)

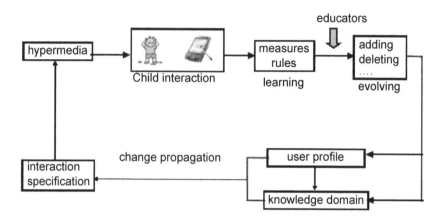

Figure 5. Learning and Evolving Process

The *transition matrix* allows us to evaluate the child activity, capturing the conceptual relationships followed by the child during the navigation. For example, taking into account the matrix shown in figure 7, it is possible to deduct that after having food the child usually drinks something, and after having a bath the child is not very willing to learn. Then, the educator can identify conceptual relationships that are needed (or not) in the knowledge domain. For example, if *Food* and *Drinks* are related in the semantic net, the child will be able to access faster the template *Food* from the template *Drinks* and vice versa. In [9] we have presented robust mechanisms to evolve the semantic network [9].

	Learn	Drinks	Foods	.....
Learn		10	12	
Drinks	7		21	
Foods	5	(47)		
Bath	(0)	14	34	
.....				

Figure 6. Transition Matrix

An important issue of our proposed system is concerned with context-awareness for adaptation [3]. We are working on child's house, school (class, dinningroom) and other specific scenarios (e.g. an Italian restaurant). Activities depend on child location; therefore, we may adapt the device to each context. Location is an important issue for child autonomy Handling location-awareness implies carry out several activities for evolving actions and user adaptation. Some of these activities are shown below:

- Load the suitable template for such scenario. If dynamical changes have been produced on the scenario (e.g. it does not contain an Ice Cream item), these changes must automatically update and prune concepts from the child's template.
- Meta-Communicator also obtains meaningful information from user location and intentions. If Mark goes too much frequently to the Kitchen, it may denote an anxiety crisis for any reason (e.g. he does not find something there, he is not sure about what to do now, etc.).

5 Conclusions and Future Work

This paper presents our research on adaptive hypermedia models for children with autism. We have presented a two-tier architecture based on mobile devices, wireless technology, a mechanism to represent knowledge, user modelling and user adaptation, and have instantiated the knowledge domain to a case study for simplicity. The result of our work suggests the architecture can be benefit for other potential users with (temporal o permanent) disabilities, with no changes in it conceptual model. Thus, a possibility for future work is the application and comparison to different collectives in order to measure the evolution in the user performance and knowledge acquisition.

References

1. Baker, B.: Minspeak. Semantic Compaction Systems, http://www.minspeak.com/
2. Bertini, E., Kimani, S.: Mobile Devices: Opportunities for Users with Special Needs: Mobile HCI 2003, LNCS 2795, pp. 486-491, Springer 2003.
3. Ciavarella, C., Paternò, F.: Design Criteria for Location-Aware, Indoor, PDA pplications. L. Chittaro (Ed.): Mobile HCI 2003, LNCS 2795, pp. 131-144, Springer-Verlag, 2003.
4. Dautenhahn, K.. Design Issues on Interactive Environments for Children with Autism. Humans and Automation Seminar Series, 2002.
5. García, L., M.J. Rodríguez and J. Parets, "Evolving Hypermedia Systems: a Layered Software Architecture", Journal of Software Maintenance and Evolution: Research and Practice. Wiley. 14, (2002), 389-406.
6. Hayes, Gillian R., Kientz, Julie A. et al: Designing Capture Applications to Support the Education of Children with Autism. In the Proceedings of Ubicomp 2004, September, Nottingham, England, 2004.
7. Koegel, L.K., Interventionsto Facilitate Communication in Autism, Journal of Autism and Developmental Disorders, 30, No. 5, 2000.
8. Medina N., L. García, M.J. Rodríguez, and J. Parets, "Adaptation in an Evolutionary Hyperpedia System: Using Semantic and Petri Nets", AH 2002. LNCS, 2347, (2002).
9. Rodríguez, M.J., Paderewski, P., Rodríguez, M.L. and M. Gea, "Unanticipated adaptation of a communicator for autistic children". 1st Int. Workshop on Foundations of Unanticipated Software Evolution (FUSE), in ETAPS'04, Barcelona (2004).
10. Schlosser, R.W.Y Braun, U. Efficacy of AAC interventions: Methodological issues in evaluating behavior change, generalization and effects. AAC Augmentative and Alternative Communication, 10, 207-223. (1994).

Decoupling Personalization Aspects in Mobile Applications

Arturo Zambrano[1], Silvia Gordillo[1,2], and Luis Norberto Polasek[1]

LIFIA, Facultad de Informatica, Universidad Nacional de La Plata 50 y
115 1er Piso

1900 La Plata, Argentina

1 {arturo, gordillo, pola}lifia.info.unlp.edu.ar

2 CIC, Provincia de Buenos Aires

1 Introduction

Mobile computing is constantly evolving and it is evident that with the
advance of technological issues this trend will grow. Mobile software,
executing in small devices such as Personal Digital Assistants (PDAs) and
cell phones, must provide the user with a great variety of information and
services that will be even more complex in the future to come. In this
context and, as explained in [10], efective use of information and services
can only be carried out by using adequate personalization mechanisms to
present the information and services in a way that is better suited to the
user. Research on personalization issues has been quite important for Web
software, but personalization on software running in mobile devices is still
premature. In this direction we propose to address behavioral adaptation
for mobile applications by using the Aspect-Oriented Programming
paradigm, following the ideas presented in [11] to introduce adaptation and
in [6] to identify concerns. In this paper we present an architecture in
which components implementing functional applications' requirements are
completely decoupled from those implementing personalization features in
order to obtain independent evolution of both. Separation of those
concerns is achieved by using aspects that model adaptation components,
isolating them from the base application. This paper is organized as
follows: In Section 2 the basic personalization concepts using throughout
the paper are presented and related work in this subject is discussed. In
Section 3 we describe the most important issues when realizing adaptation
in mobile software. In Section 4, the basic concepts of Aspect Oriented

R. Navarro-Prieto and J. L. Vidal (eds.), HCI Related Papers of Interacción 2004, 29-40.

Software are introduced. Section 5 presents our architecture and in Section 6 we show how to map a concrete application onto the presented architecture. Finally, some concluding remarks and further work are discussed.

2 Personalization

According to [1] personalization is understood as the process that adapts functionality, interface or information contents to make it more relevant to a particular user. For an application to be personalized it must know the user's context, i.e. all those features that characterize the execution environment including user information and preferences. Personalized software should maintain models of the objectives, characteristics, preferences and knowledge of the intended user. These models are used to keep up-to-date information on each user (usually called user profile) to adapt services to his preferences, in order to satisfy his needs [8]. This adaptation will also consider usually other contextual elements and will involve presentation or management issues. The adaptation process consist usually in three tasks depicted in Figure 1.

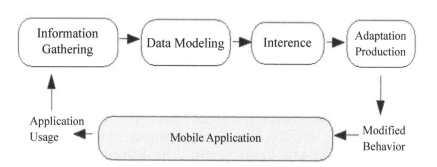

Fig. 1. Adaptation process for personalization

User data acquisition. In this process we identify available user data, such as his characteristics, behavior and environment. With this information, initial models of the user preferences are built.

User proþle representation and secondary inference. That is, presumptions on the user and/or group of users, behavior and environment are elaborated.

Production or Adaptation. It generates content, presentation or behavior adaptations that are then introduced in the application.

It is interesting to note that, due to the previously mentioned characteristics, when an application is modified in order to support personalized behavior, code must be added in diferent modules of the application. This makes the task of application evolution difcult and error-prone. Among most usual actions, to adapt the information presented to the user, we can mention:

- Filtering: It consists in removing information or services that are not interesting to the user.

- Ordering or Priorization: It is achieved by reorganizing information according to the user preferences Suggestion It consists in giving spontaneous suggestions to the user, presenting information or suggesting tasks that are assumed of his interest.

3 Adaptation for Mobile Devices

Nowadays, mobile devices such as cell phones and PDAs allow the user to access information and services according to his geographical position and current activity. Changes in the geographical position and the situation where the device is used are inherent characteristics of such systems.

The information delivered through mobile devices is bound to the usage context, the activity in which the user is involved, and user preferences. On the other hand, the minimal resources available in mobile devices impose constraints regarding information processing. Wireless communication is expensive and not reliable. Storage capacity is very limited and processing is not powerful (typically less than 200MHz). Furthermore, graphics displays are not always available, or they are low resolution ones. In this context adaptation is a fundamental tool needed to cope with these issues.

Furthermore, these non-functional requirements must be envisaged from the early design phase. But they have a negative effect on the design and implementation. The inclusion of such non-functional concerns tends to complicate the design making application modules hard to understand.

At the same time it is very diffcult to trace where those requirements are implemented, since they are spread along several modules.

Then, the resulting designs and implementations of functional and non-functional requirements are coupled. In the worse case, depending on the cou-pling level, the final implementation of non-functional requirements can be em-bedded into the functional requirements' implementation.

4 An Overview of Aspect Oriented Programming

In the application development process, it is common to find a set of concerns that affect many objects beyond their classes which constitute (in object-oriented programming) the natural units to define functionality. They are called crosscutting concerns. A crosscutting concern is one that is spread along many of the modules of a system. Typical crosscutting concerns are persistence, synchronization, error handling. etc. As it is said in [3]: "...existing software formalisms support separation of concerns only along a predominant dimension neglecting other dimensions... with negative effects on reusability, locality of changes, understandability...". These secondary dimensions correspond to crosscutting concerns. In our case, secondary dimensions are represented by context-awareness related concerns.

Aspect-Oriented Programming (AOP for short) [5] is one of many technologies resulting from the effort to modularize crosscutting concerns. The goal of AOP is to decouple those concerns, so that the system's modules can be easily maintained, evolved and seamlessly integrated. To do that AOP introduces a set of concepts:

- Join Point is a well-defined point in the program flow (for instance a method call, an access to a variable, etc)
- Point-Cut selects certain join points and values at those points.
- Advice: Advises define code that is executed when a point-cut is reached.

The program whose behavior is affected by aspects is called base program. A join point specifies a point in the execution of the base program that will be affected by an aspect. One or more of these join points (from one or different classes) are identified by a pointcut in the aspect layer, associating it with an advice. In this way, when one join point, referred in a pointcut, is reached in the program execution, the additional code, defined in the proper advice is executed. The aspect's code is composed of advises and the pointcuts where those advises must be applied.

5 Our Approach

Considering the negative effects of embedding adaptation code into the core application code, it is necessary to define an architecture which enables the separation between system modules and those that realize the adaptive personalization functionality. At same time, this separation is useful as it allows a correct integration of the different system's views, ideally in a transparent manner from the core application point of view.

Such an architecture will provide a set of advantages, among them we found:

- Extensibility: since each view of the system is independent from one another, they can evolve independently.
- High abstraction level: since the personalization features are isolated from the rest of the system, it allows the designer/programmer to focus in the core application, regardless secondary views such as personalization features.

In this work we propose the use of aspect oriented techniques in order to properly separate the core application components from those aimed to personalization. In order to get such a separation we have identified the main components, their roles and relationships, and defined the foundations of a software architecture that combines both objects and aspects.

5.1 Architecture's Main Components

A personalized mobile application can be divided into two dimensions or views. The first one is where the base application belongs to, that is to say, where the functional requirements are implemented. The second one comprises the non-functional requirement of personalization and its implementation. More views can be modelled as needed but, as far as this work is concerned, two views or dimensions will be enough.

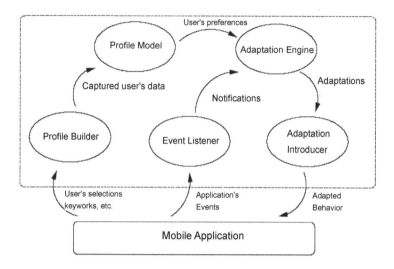

Fig. 2. Separation between the two main dimensions, base application and personalization

Figure 2 presents a layout of these components, the mobile system is divided into two parts. The core mobile application itself which is operative, independently from the personalization layer, it implements the functional requirements of the system. Modules located at this layer provide the main system functionality.

The second layer corresponds to a metalevel, where the personalization feature is reificated. This metalevel is the part of the system in charge of gathering user preferences, storing them in a proper way for later retrieval, and instrumenting the execution of the underlying mobile application, adapting its behavior to meet those preferences.

It is important to note that, since the base mobile application is completely functional and independent from the personalization metalevel, there is no interaction from the application towards the personalization level. This independence is a benefit that starts at the design phase, since it allows the designer to concentrate in the core functionality, abstracting him from those details related to personalization.

It is worth to note that in our approach we suggest to settle the personalization functionality on the client side, that is, in the mobile device. This characteristic makes this approach different from other works on personalized services for mobile devices. Client side personalization makes the system *network failsafe*, since it does not rely on the server to provide the personalized behavior. Due to instability of wireless connections in mobile contexts it is common to face situations where there is no connectivity. That's why we argue that personalization should be located at the client side. Since information gathering, storing and adaptation mechanisms regarding personalization are implemented at the client side, it is possible to cope with offline situations, and keep providing personalized response to the user.

Back to the architecture, the personalization dimension is formed by the following components:

- Profile Model: This component is in charge of storing user preferences.
- Adaptation Engine: The engine is responsible for inferring the kind of adaptation that should be done, it is done using the information stored in the profile model.
- Profile Builder: This component is in charge of intercept certain application execution points in order to feed the profile model with information about the user,
- Event Listener: This component comprises a set of aspects that detect the occurrence of certain application events. These events can be seen as triggers of adaptive actions.
- Adaptation Introducer: Once an interesting event has been detected, and the proper kind of adaptation identified, this component controls the application behavior adding the planned adaptation. This is done through aspects that can introduce behavior in the application.

Figure 3 shows the mapping between architecture components and a potential application design. Graphical notation is an UML variant [7], which denotes aspectual concepts through stereotypes. Advised methods are pointed by <<pointcut>> relationships. As it is shown in Figure 3 the base application is intercepted in those methods related with the user interaction by using the proper pointcuts. This interception is performed by the ProfileBuilder component, which gathers information about the user profile and passes it to the ProfileModel component. At the same time, the EventListener catches those events that can trigger some kind of adaptive behavior, and notifies the AdaptationEngine, which decides the adaptation type to be done. These adaptations are introduced in the application by the AdaptationIntroducer, where pointcuts are defined on those application parts where adaptation make sense to be done. Generally, suitable joint points are user interface events.

5.2 On the application and the personalization model

The link between the application model and the personalization one is done transparently by an aspectual layer. Aspects located in this layer are responsible for three key personalization activities:

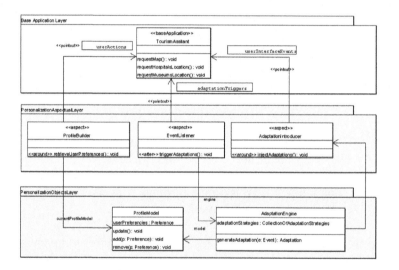

Fig. 3. Object-Aspect Oriented Architecture

1. Interception of user actions in order to gather information regarding his preferences, usual actions and so on.

2. Detection of contextual changes (through application events) that require personalization actions.

3. Application behavioral adaptation, based on the user profile, in order to provide a better response for the user.

The first activity is aimed to collect information regarding user preferences and common activities. The interception is done by aspects that extract parameters entered by the user, for instance the words used in an web search, the preferred order in a listing, or the selected option from a set. With this information it is possible to build the user profile. For instance, in an application that allows the user to search information using keywords, they can be extracted and used to build a semantic web, relating them with other terms. Keywords can be also used to analyze frequency and to find information patterns. Then, the derived information feeds the user profile. This kind of activities also includes:

– Measures of time spent in deferent parts of the application: this can be an indicator of special interest in some service or information offered by the system. The frequency of some kind of input can be also used to detect interest.

– Detection of common user choices. When some option is selected among several ones, in a repetitive way, it is an indicator of interest in that information or service. Frequency and repetition are indicators of user preference.

The adaptation process then consist in the instrumentation of the system in order to intercept those events that trigger internal personalization mechanisms. Eventually, these mechanisms will produce some behavioral changes in the application. For example, given a tourism mobile application, which aids the user showing the list of interesting places to visit, there will be events automatically triggered by the GPS. It is possible to react to those events showing the user new places to visit, basing this suggestion on the information gathered regarding his preferences.

All this behavioral alteration is introduced by means of aspects which can affect the normal control flow of the application. In this way the application is oblivious regarding adaptations, since they are introduced transparently in any application join point.

6 Example

To illustrate these ideas, we present as an example a mobile application that will be personalized using aspects. We will show how the adaptation is made, once the user's profile is built.

6.1 Definition

The application is a kind of tourism guide, for a tourist in a Buenos Aires journey, using a PDA as his assistant. This user is interested in local folklore, food, music and traditional dances. He is familiarized whit Argentina's history and also is a sport fan, specially soccer.

This person has a tour of places to visit and wants to be notified when he is close to some place that may interest him, but do not belongs to the original tour.

The tour crosses the neighbourhood of La Boca, the Plaza de Mayo, and the Obelisco. The tour starts in La Boca, so his PDA will show him information about this neighbourhood.

As he walks the La Boca's streets, he get close to the well known soccer stadium La Bombonera, that is not registered in his tour. Nevertheless, the system recognizes that the user is interested in soccer and notifies him that he is close to the famous stadium.

6.2 Functionality Distribution

In this case, the tourism guide is the base application on which the adaptation of the user's preferences will be made. This application is fully functional independently of the personalization capabilities.

The profile modeling has been already discussed in [4] and [2]. These models can be adapted to fulfill the Profile Model role in Fgure 2, so that we do not analyze this topic, and concentrate in the adaptation topic. The Adaptation Engine decides which adaptations have to be introduced in the application when an event occurs. The engine can use different technics to infer the adaptation such as semantic nets, neuronal nets, agents, etc. These topics have already been discussed in [9], that work shows different ways to filter information considering user's preferences. Since filtering technics are not the objective of this paper, we only will focus on the role that fulfills the aspects, how they relate with the base application and the components that implements the personalization (*ProfileModel* and *Adaptation Engine*)

The aspects that implements the *Profile Builder* component intercepts execution points, as those described in Section 5.2. From the keywords collected from searches and user chosen options, information that defines his preferences is captured. This information that is captured automatically without disturbing the user, is known as implicit construction. The aspect is in charge of intercepting the methods that implements the search and the selections, in order to inspect the values entered by the user. Since this information capture is done using AOP provided constructions (join points, point cuts, and advises), the base application does not need to implement any behavior related to information capture in order to build the profiles.

There also exists what is known as explicit profile construction, where the user express his preferences by filling forms. This information complements and feeds the profile with the information captured automatically by the aspects.

Once the information is captured within the *profile model,* the personalization layer is ready to make the adaptations. This adaptations begin with the detection of some event by the *Event Listener* component which is, in fact, an aspect. This aspect intercepts the application's control flow in order to detect the events that launch the adaptations. In the example, an aspect can intercept the geographic position change notification, notifying the *Adaptation Engine* that the user's geographic position has changed.

The *Adaptation Engine* finds that the position is close to the soccer stadium and since the *Profile Model* holds information that allows to establish that the user is a sport fan, the adaptation engine decides to launch an adaptation of the suggestion kind.

The aspects that implements the *Adaptation Introducer,* intercepts, through pointcuts, all the interface actions, so when a user generated event occurs, the suggestion to visit the stadium is presented to the user. Closing the adaptation process cycle.

7 Conclusions and Future Work

The application of technology that allows the advanced separation of concerns, like *Composition Filters, Subject Oriented Programming* and like this case Aspect Oriented Programming, in general produce higher levels of modularity. The benefits of modularity, well known in computer science, includes flexibility, maintainability, design and implementation clarity.

In this work have presented general foundations of an architecture that allows to isolate in a effective way the application core from such not functional concerns related with the personalization. We have defined the essential aspects and join points that allows to establish the connections between the architecture components. The presented proposals have foundation in previous experiences and are in implementation phase, we trust that the result will give support to the exposed ideas. We have also analyzed the impact of doing the adaptations in mobile gadgets, considering hardware limitations present in mobile computing.

The use of aspects to adapt the behavior of mobile applications is novel, and follows the ideas presented in [11]. Still remains the study of the integration of the architecture presented in this work in a way that incorporates the elements of context awareness as they were explained. The implementation of prototype applications that materialize this ideas, will help to make a concrete evaluation of the benefits reached by applying aspect oriented programming in mobile systems.

References

1. J. Blom. Personalization a taxonomy. In CHI 2000 Workshop on Designing Interactive Systems for 1-to-1 Ecommerce, 2000.
2. W. W. W. Consortium. Composite capabilities/preference profiles, 2001.
3. S. Herrmann and M. Mezini. PIROL: A case study for multidimensional separation of concerns in software engineering environments. In OOPSLA, pages 188–207, 2000.
4. G. Kappell, B. Prll, W. Retschitzegger, and W. Schwinger. Customisation for ubiquitous web applications. In Int. Journal of Web Engineering and Technology (IJWET), Inaugural Volume, Inderscience, volume 2299. Publishers 2003, 2002.
5. G. Kiczales, J. Lamping, A. Mendhekar, C. Maeda, C. Lopes, J.M. Loingtier, and J. Irwin. Aspect-oriented programming. In Mehmet and S. Matsuoka, editors, 11th Europeen Conf. Object-Oriented Programming, volume 1241 of LNCS, pages 220–242. Springer Verlag, 1997.
6. C. Mesquita, S. D. J. Barbosa, and C. J. P. de Lucena. Towards the identification of concerns in personalization mechanisms via scenarios. In AOSD 2002, Workshop on Early Aspects, 2002.
7. R. Pawlak, L. Duchien, G. Florin, F. Legond Aubry, L. Seinturier, and L. Martelli. A uml notation for aspect-oriented software design. In AO modeling with UML workshop at the AOSD 2002 conference. Proceedings, 2002.
8. L. A. R. Rui Alexandre P. P. da Cruz, Francisco J. García Peñalvo. Perfiles de usuario: En la senda de la personalización. Technical report, Departamento de Informática. Universidad de Salamanca, 2003.
9. S. Stewart and J. Davies. User profiling techniques: A critical review. In 19th Annual BCSIRSG Colloquium on IR. Springer Verlag, 1997.
10. M. Wagner, W.T. Balke, R. Hirschfeld, and W. Kellerer. A roadmap to advanced personalization of mobile services. In 10th International Conference on Cooperative Information Systems, 2002.
11. A. Zambrano, S. Gordillo, and I. Jaureguiberry. Aspect based adaptation for ubiquitous software. In International Workshop on Information Retrieval. Mobile HCI, 2003.

Empirical User Studies in the Design of Mobile Distributed Collaborative Applications

Raquel Navarro-Prieto
Fundació Barcelona Media- Universitat Pompeu Fabra, Ocata 1
08003 Barcelona. Spain, raquel.navarro@upf.edu, +34 935421543

Eva Patrícia Gil Rodríguez
Internet Interdisciplinary Institute – IN3, Universitat
Oberta de Catalunya, Parc Mediterrani de la Tecnologia Av. Del
Canal Olímpic s/n, 08860 Castelldefels. Spain, egilrod@uoc.edu,
+34 936735025

1. INTRODUCTION TO THE PROBLEM

The goal of our work is to contribute to bridging the critical gap between the body of literature dedicated to rapid and innovative technology development, and the literature dedicated to theoretical and empirical knowledge in Mobile Distributed Collaborative Work. Specifically, regarding Ubiquitous Computing, in parallel with recent developments in mobile communications, a significant number of case studies have tried to investigate the effect of handheld devices and mobile applications. Unfortunately, most of the previous work in this area has been focused on the creation of a particular system and its supposed advantages. However, this work has been done without proper user evaluation or analysis of user requirements [12, 10, 1]. In addition, in spite of the rapid development of distributed work and learning environments, and the growth of mobile technologies, at present very little attention has been paid to applying the results from basic research on the cognitive processes behind group collaboration in mobile environments. For example, researchers in the new hybrid area of mobile distributed work are paying attention mainly to the development of prototypes that prove the technological feasibility of concept [17] while neglecting to investigate the theoretical basis that should guide developments in this area. For this reason, we tried in our work to bring together basic research about users with research into technological areas. In order to do this, our research

41

R. Navarro-Prieto and J. L. Vidal (eds.), HCI Related Papers of Interacción 2004, 41-54.
© 2006 Springer. Printed in the Netherlands.

group is investigating a number of new challenges that have been introduced by the research advances in Handheld Computing[3] in different application areas. The work presented in this paper is focused on the area of distributed work for conducting clinical trials. As Schmidt, Lauff and Beigl [16] have pointed out, "handheld computing needs to be distinguished from mobile computing as witnessed over the last years, where location–independent usage is the main focus. In contrast, Handheld Computing implies new ways of using computers rather than mobilizing traditional usage". Our goal was to study collaborative work in the particular case in which users are in mobile environments, as opposed to being in fixed environments (e.g. the user is in their office, or at a location that would not change its characteristics during the whole realization of the collaborative task).

Before the arrival of Computer Supported Groupware[4], traditionally most of the work on collaborative teams was done with co-located members. The need for co-location was related with the need to 'see' and share the same information, and the need of awareness about what the rest of the group is doing (e.g. this need could be fulfilled by overhearing and observation). In the last two decades, Researchers in the area of Computer Supported Cooperative Work have done much work on supporting distributed (i.e. non-co-located) groups. Most of the research has been centred on PC environments, and very little attention has been paid to scenarios when one or several of the group members are distributed and mobile. However, research advances and growing interest in Handheld Computing in recent years have introduced a number of new challenges that need to be taken into consideration by the CSCW research community. Therefore the key question that we need to ask is if there really are differences between mobile and non-mobile group work, and if that it the case, what are the major differences.

To answer the first question, we only need to go to previous literature and realise that a number of differences have been reported, as well as problems related with these differences in work environments. For instance, Bellotti & Bly [2] reported a field study of distributed work at a design-consulting firm that wanted to increase the mobile capabilities of its workers. After analysing the data gathered via brainstorming meetings,

---

[3] Schmidt, Lauff and Beigl [16] define "Handheld Computer" as an unobtrusive computing device that is accompanying the user most of the time and provides assistance in different situations and for a wide range of tasks.

[4] For an extended classification and review on Groupware, please refer to Gross and Traunmüller (1996).

interviews, attending project meetings and close observation, they concluded that the team members preferred face-to-face communication. Some specific problems for distributed collaboration due to mobility were locating people, lack of awareness, lack of communication and coordination. The author suggested a number of design ideas to solve these problems ranging from a location awareness device to a virtual site in the web, which record images of the goings-on in the social meeting points. Another example of this type of research in real work settings is the work of Luff and Heath [14]. The authors conducted three observational studies in very different work settings: health consultants, construction sites, and the London Underground metro system. Again several problems were reported in which the "introduction of mobile systems made the users less mobile, less able to monitor the ongoing work and less available to engage in activities with others on site". For instance, some problems arose from the underestimation of role of traditional paper sources. To summarise, we can conclude that there are a number of differences between mobile and non-mobile group work, and that these differences seem to gravitate around the lack of shared context among group members (i.e. they cannot see/hear each other, nor what the other members are working on). Although this lack of shared context is common for all distributed work, the literature reviewed has shown that to have this information is more critical in mobile distributed work. Therefore, we would argue that the design of an application for mobile distributed collaborative work will need to take into account the particular differences with non-mobile distributed work. Special attention should be paid to study the shared context among different group members and the impact of migrating work practices to a mobile context for a task that was previously conducted in a co-located manner. Indeed, as Lanzi and Marti [13] had pointed out the failure of most technological devices and applications is due to the fact that developers don't take into account the psychosocial impact of these devices on users and their organizational culture.

The structure of the paper is as follows: First, we will briefly review some theoretical approaches to design of CSCW applications. Second, we will present an analysis of how the Contextual Inquiry method can be applied to these approaches. The goal of the project presented was the re-design of a mobile application for the management of data in clinical trials. A web-based application is already being used by some of the actors in a fixed environment. In order to familiarise the reader with the main concepts of clinical trial work, some general background will be provided. Special attention will be paid to the description of how we adapted CI methodology in our particular area of study to gather the information that we consider to be critical. Therefore, we will expose our methodological approach to data gathering and data analysis through the definition of the methodology used in this study. The main results of this study will be presented including the user requirements gathered and the information architecture developed. We will finish with the main conclusions that we have drawn from this work.

2. SOME THEORETICAL APPROACHES FROM COMPUTER SUPPORTED COOPERATIVE WORK

As stated before, our research was focused on the design of user interfaces and functionalities of mobile applications that support mobile cooperative work. It's important to emphasize that from our perspective, a group that cooperates is not only a set of people: in a collaborative group, people must have a common task and/or goals, a context, and in order to reach a common understanding, team members must share and exchange information. We agree with [5, page 93] that "basically, computer-supported cooperative work is not just an information management problem. It is, rather, an interdisciplinary application domain in which mechanisms and methodologies of computer science, telecommunications, information management (...) sociology and organizational theory converge." Therefore, our goal is to make distributed communication supported by technology equally efficient as face-to-face communication.

Moreover, successful coordination supposes the highest level of communication between individuals, groups or organizations. As argued by [5, pages 110 – 111] "on the cooperation level, the demand for face-to-face meetings as an integral part of teamwork has particular emphasis. Goals of the team have priority over personal goals. In general, decisions have to be based on group consensus. The result of such decisions is the responsibility of all team members. Regular and frequent interaction is combined with evaluation of the team as a whole. Besides cooperation, the social process has to contain all work modes, from loose cooperation to tight cooperation." This is why in CSCW the study of the technological impact and usability aspects are so important.

Context and organizational culture are two key aspects to study the impact of technological devices in group work. This is the hypothesis of one of classical theoretical approaches to study technological application from User-Centred Design perspective: the Activity Theory [11]. From Activity Theory, it is argued that the problems with the implementation of a technological application are generally due to the fact that its context has not been taken into consideration. Therefore, in order to make sense of group work we will need to study in-depth the contextual information and organisational culture of this particular group.

Lanzi & Marti [13] clearly illustrated the consequences of ignoring context and organizational culture in their example of the implementation of new technologies for air traffic controllers. The problems were mainly due to the fact that the tasks of air traffic controllers have been studied outside their context and did not take into account the importance of informal group relationships. For this reason, we argue that the study of organizational culture and informal processes in a work group is very important in order to understand if some technologies are going to be successful.

Much work in CSCW has prioritised supporting synchronous group processes, because recreation of "off-line" situations in "on-line" applications has been thought to be the best way to design technological applications. The underlying assumption is that "face to face" communication is a natural and immediate way to communicate. On the other hand, technologically mediated communication is understood as having negative effects that we must minimize, in order to recreate as much as possible the "natural situation". As a consequence, many applications have been developed which try to recreate these processes thought to be natural (e.g. a videoconference from a teacher in e-learning).

We argue in this paper that all collective communication processes – whether mediated technologically or not – are symbolically mediated because language is not literal, but rather subjective to interpretation. In this way, we don't regard face-to-face interactions as natural, and interactions mediated by computers as artificial. On the contrary, following the Actor Network Theory, we consider all group communication processes, both face to face and mediated by technology, as processes constructed collectively and submitted to a constant process of interpretation and reinterpretation. We understand communication from a linguistic perspective, and focused mainly on the semantic level. That is to say, we are interested in the meaning of different symbols used in group communication.

Therefore, our theoretical hypothesis is that we should not recreate human communication processes as they take place in the face-to-face situations, but rather understand these processes, to design technologies that enhance these processes though providing the possibility of taking place in mobile contexts.

For all these reasons, our research focus is not only the user's task, but also the different ways in which people interact among themselves, and with technological artefacts, within their organizational and cultural context. Therefore, as a consequence of our theoretical approach, we propose to use a qualitative methodological approach that allows us to gather information about the organisational culture and the interrelations inside the group. We have chosen CI as an approach that combines several methodologies and offers a structured approach to the analysis of the data gathered with real users in their context. In the rest of this paper we will try to validate our theoretical claim though our research in a research project that will need to design a new application for Mobile Distributed Collaborative Work.

3. STUDYING DISTRIBUTED COLLABORATIVE WORK IN CLINICAL TRIALS

In this section, we will illustrate our research on the design of mobile applications for clinical trials in order create applications that are not only easy to use, but also optimised for the work practices use by researchers, monitors and Study Managers of clinical trials.

The main goal of our research was to design a user interface for a mobile device which would gather and manage data and support communication between the different agents involved in clinical trials. To reach this goal, we submerged ourselves in the daily work of all potential users of this application. Before we explain our methodological approach in detail we will briefly explain what a clinical trial is and what the roles of different potential users of this device are.

3.1. What is a clinical trial?

A clinical trial is an experimental study, whose goal is to test a drug or therapeutic artifact in order to guarantee its reliability, before it is brought to the pharmaceutical market. When a drug laboratory studies a new medicine, it's necessary to test it in patients before its commercialization. Clinical trials have a rigorous control not only in a scientific sense, but also in a legal and medical sense. Confidentiality, and correct management and transmission of data, are key aspects to obtain reliable results from a clinical trial.

In a clinical trial we find different kinds of organizations involved to different degrees. We will describe two of these organizations in detail. The most important organizations to our research objectives are those specialized in clinical research, the *Clinical Research Organization* (CROs). These organizations offer their services to drug companies, to manage and execute clinical trials on their behalf. The second organization on which we focus are hospitals. Working closely with CROs, we find doctors who will prescribe medication in the experimental phase, with informed agreement, to patients under treatment. The doctors who prescribe medication in the experimental phase are also the *researchers* who rigorously control the effects of the treatment on the patients. Researchers visit patients who test new medicines periodically and introduce their data in a standardized form developed for this specific clinical trial. These data will be statistically analysed to test the hypothesis of the researchers about the effects of this new drug.

Before the data can be analysed, they have to be revised by people whose task is to monitor the clinical trials, these people are *monitors*. Monitors test the authenticity of the data, comparing it with the clinical record of each patient. Monitors also generate queries to researchers in case of doubt. After the data have been revised by the monitors, the *Study Manager* – who is the person who manages the specific clinical trial within the CRO – validates them. After the validation of all the data the statistical analysis can start.

In this context of cooperative work between actor's involved in a clinical trial, the main instrument that supports all these cooperative processes by different agents is the Clinical Research Form (CRF). The CRF is the main means of communication between monitor and researcher. At present, most CRFs are filled in a paper format. Therefore, another people needs to enter all these data into a digital format in order to be analysed statistically using a statistical software package. In recent years, CRFs implemented as a client web applications for PCs have started to appear, allowing data to be enter electronically in the first place by the researcher. Our objective was, starting with an already existing web application, to design an application that allowed the information gathering process and the communications involved to be perform in mobile contexts. One way to approach this challenge could have been to create an application that resembled the already existing web application, and adapt it to the specific limitations of the PDA's screen and input methods. We could have introduced mobile video conference facilities (allowed by UMTS) to re-create the face to face situations. On doing that, we would have replicated the same work practices and communication patterns, now mediated by a different technology. Instead, we tried to understand how the existing work practices could be enhanced by the mediation of a different technology, in our case mobile technology.

The CRO that was involved in our study is at present using a proprietary web-based application. At the outset we wished to understand which of functionalities already provided in the web-based application would enhance the clinical trial process if this work were to be carried out on a mobile context. In addition, we wanted to identity new functionalities that may support informal processes not yet identified. The second step of our research would be to gather the requirements for each of the tasks and processes to be supported. Finally, the last part of our work was to define the user interface for this application.

In order to reach our goals, we have defined a qualitative methodology based on a CI approach. Specifically, we conducted contextual observations in the users' work environment. Our end users were the monitors and Study Managers.

3.2. How to use ethnographic methodology to study user's requirements of mobile devices in clinical trials

In this section we will describe in detail our methodological approach. In the definition of our methodology we have taken into account the theoretical concepts previously described and we have applied them to the design of a mobile application to gather and manage data in clinical trials. Coming back to our theoretical point of view, we consider technological mediation is not a problem, but a new possibility for group work and group communication. Our goal has been to define different functionalities both on-line and off-line, that could improve cooperative work processes. In this specific case, we refer to a mobile application for gathering and managing data, and communicating among the different agents implied in a clinical trial. We consider that each group creates specific processes of communication, and share different meanings about their tasks, different roles, goals, priorities, etc. For this reason, it's very important to design applications focusing on the real work context of our end users. As a consequence of this theoretical position, we designed for our study an **ethnographic methodological approach**, with which we can study the interactions between organizations, people and technological artefacts.

3.2.1. Methodology for gathering data

The goal of our study was to gather user requirements and design the user interface for a mobile application for monitors, Study Manager and researchers from hospitals involved in a specific clinical trial[5].

---

[5] Researcher's requirements were inferred from the gathering of data from monitors and Study Manager, because the privacy policies of hospitals hindered our ability to make observations.

The different agents of the clinical trials observed in our research had already been using a web-based application to gather and manage data at their work. This web-based application was our starting point in our requirements gathering process.

In our methodological approach we took into account the daily work context of monitors, Study Managers and researchers. We observed how they used the existing web-based application in the context of their work. In order to gather information about the impact of usage of this application, and the possible mobile application, we decided to make participant observations. In addition, we completed our data gathering process with individual interviews, to gather information about meaningful processes of group work and perceptions about the impact of technological applications in their work.

We used semi-structured interviews because they allowed us to gather interviewer's impressions better than closed questions. To gather meaningful information about their daily work, observations were carried out in a non-intrusive way. In other words, the observer immersed himself/herself in the context of people observed during their normal work routine, sharing knowledge of context and sometimes participating, because he/she can ask about actions in any moment. Nevertheless, the observers never break the normal process of user's work. In order to gather data from these observations, we video-taped users doing their tasks, in addition to notes taken in a field diary.

Unfortunately it was not possible to do observations in hospitals. Therefore, we couldn't include observations of researchers in our study. Nevertheless, the users observed are an important subgroup of the potential population of users of our application: monitors and Study Managers of Clinical Research Organizations. When we performed our observations we identified two degrees of technology penetration:

1. Monitors and the Study Manager didn't use any technological applications, because they used a clinical research form on paper.
2. Monitors the and Study Manager used an electronic CRF in a web application.

In summary we used the following methods to gather user requirements following a Contextual Inquiry approach [4]:

1. Participant observation of users in their normal context of work, complemented with semi-structured interviews and gathering of documents of work that served to support communication and management of information.
2. To understand implicit communication in the daily work of monitors, the observer did specific training on clinical trials monitoring.

3. In addition, previous to the interviews and observations, the observer studied the existing web application and took specific training in Clinical Trials.

To do rigorous observations of the interaction of different tasks involved in the coordination of clinical trials, we used the portable usability laboratory of our research team. This lab allowed us record video and voice of the users, as well as navigation screens of the web application at the same time. Therefore, we were able to record all the different work documents and applications running on their PC while performing their work.

The elements gathered with the interviews and observations were:

- structure of group cooperation, and roles,
- processes of group work, how they do these task
- how they relate between themselves to achieve goals
- where, in what conditions, these interactions take place
- formal and informal knowledge of user about tasks of other members of the group.

Lastly, we also observed the interactions with different technological artefacts, and we evaluated in the impact of the technological artefacts used in group work processes.

3.2.2. Data analysis using Contextual Inquiry models

The goal of our analysis was to identify what functionalities could enhance work practices if they are implemented in a mobile application. We also wanted to identify what information would be needed by the user in order to take advantage of those functionalities.

We wanted to take into account the interactions between different organizations (hospitals, different departments of CROs, laboratories), people (monitors, Study Managers, researchers) and technological artefacts (clinical research forms on paper, web applications, electronic documents).

Towards this goal we decided to analyse our data using a work flow model, as it is proposed in Contextual Inquiry [4]. Using the technique of work flow modelling, we can analyse and identify processes, objectives, roles and tasks that are really meaningful to group members. In this way, we can draft informal and implicit processes in addition to formal and standardised procedures. These processes are part of intersubjective knowledge constructed by the group, that are only possible to identify using ethnographic observation. We obtained a holistic vision of the complete set of processes of group work that were really meaningful to users, and we could identify critical points to implement the mobile application.

During the development of the work flow models we created diagrams of their work processes. We also modelled the different interactions between technological artefacts, people and organizations in a graphic and accurate way. By means of this technique we represented interactions and work processes both on clinical trials that use paper CRF's and also on clinical trials that use electronic CRF's. These analyses was made by a team of researchers, using long sheets of paper, that allowed us to reflect the complete set of interactions that we had mentioned previously.

After the workflow of all the processes involved in the users trials were diagrammed, the research team identified the *critical points* where the communication between actors was broken, or where the actors were in a mobile context. In order to study these *critical points* in more detail, we used the analysis technique of Sequence Flow (Figure 3), also from CI. With this technique we represented the sequence of tasks that were part of the critical points identified (for example, the task illustrated in Figure 3 was the monitoring of data with a web application).

These analyses allowed us to identify processes, and in which way the mediation of a mobile application can improve these processes. In addition we obtain three kinds of user requirements:

a. User requirements and needs for the mobile application in PDA for electronic gathering and managing of data, and the coordination with other users.

b. User requirements and needs for mobile applications in a tablet PC for electronic gathering and managing of data.

c. User requirements and needs useful to improve the web application.

For each of the functionalities in PC, PDA and tablet PC, we described what specific user goals will have to be supported, what information can be represented, and a specific representation proposal for this information. For instance for the user goal of "Tracking of visits" we have described that the information needed to be represented will be "Visualization of expected, validated and non-validated visits". In addition, our recommendations for the representations on the interface were: "Visit Schedule with expected visits. Visualization of expected visits with the period of dates and the following colour coding:

- Next visit: only bold if we are in the period of dates, in blue.

- When the period of dates is almost finished, the representation colour must be red.

After we defined the tasks users would perform with the mobile application, our next goal was to define the architectural information structure of user interface. With the analysis of user requirements we have obtained information about:

1. Functionalities of mobile device for gathering and managing data in clinical trials, identifying advantages of mobility and limitations (for example, reduced scope of screen to visualize information).
2. Ways of interpretation and processing of information by users to define the information structure in the user interface.

With this information we developed the conceptual design for the application. During this first step of the conceptualization of the user interface, we created simulations of the interface in slides. We have seen that two important tasks to do in each hospital are the tracking of visits and the contact with researchers. In consequence, when we select a hospital on the application, the monitor can choose between the visit schedule of this hospital and the contact data of researchers. In Figure 1 we can observe the translation from two user's requirements to specific proposals of visualization of information.

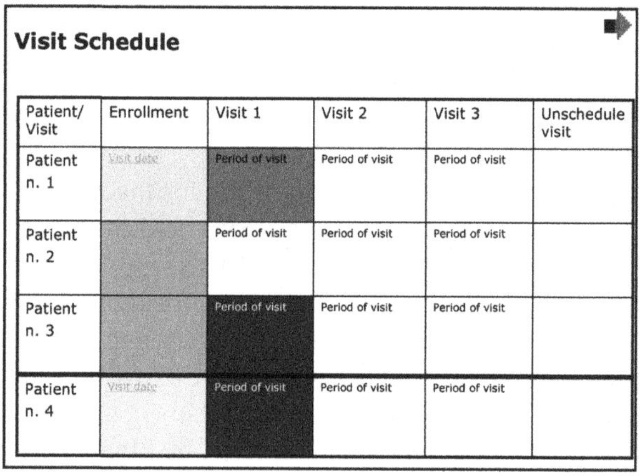

Visit Schedule

Patient/ Visit	Enrollment	Visit 1	Visit 2	Visit 3	Unschedule visit
Patient n. 1	Visit date	Period of visit	Period of visit	Period of visit	
Patient n. 2		Period of visit	Period of visit	Period of visit	
Patient n. 3		Period of visit	Period of visit	Period of visit	
Patient n. 4	Visit date	Period of visit	Period of visit	Period of visit	

Figure 1. Screen visualising the tracking of visits.

4. CONCLUSION

In the first part of our paper we stated that it is important to take into account the particular differences with non-mobile distributed work in the design of an application for mobile distributed collaborative work. We argued that special attention should be paid to study the shared context among different group members and the impact of changing work practices to a mobile context for a task that was previously conducted in a co-located manner. Based on activity theory and a linguistic interpretation of Activity theory and Actor Network Theory approach, we our theoretical claim is that we should not try to recreate the same processes of face-to-face communications through technology, but understand how different technologies will impact communications patterns and work practices. Investigating this impact by modelling user's work practices, we can attempt during the design process to foresee how we can have a positive effect, enhancing the processes though the introduction of mediation of a new technology.

In the second part of this paper, we have illustrated our theoretical approach with an example about how these concepts could be studied using the Contextual Inquiry methodology. The research project presented concerned the design of a mobile application for the management of data in clinical trials. According to our theoretical approach we have applied an ethnographical methodology, and have based our analysis on the CI framework. Our approach has been proven to be successful and has allowed us to identify implicit and informal communication process, and to predict how to enhance these processes. In addition we have gathered information to design the user interface for this mobile application. Our next step would be to empirically evaluate the application that has been design with real users.

ACKNOWLEDGEMENTS

Results shown in this paper are part of a research project called **Gateway**, financed by the program PROFIT 2003 of the Ministry of Science and Technology of Spanish Government. We thank RDES and Medtronic for their collaboration in discussions of user interface design and their help in the usage of their facilities and personnel to perform the interviews and participant observations. Without them our research would have not been possible.

REFERENCES

1. Ancona, G. Dodero, V. Gianuzzi, Proc. HUC99 (Int. Symp. on Handheld and Ubiquitous Computing), *Lecture Notes in Computer Science*, 1707, Springer-Verlag, pp.222-233, 1999.

2. Bellotti, V. and Bly, S. (1996) Walking Away from the Desktop Computer: Distributed Collaboration and Mobility in a Product Design Group. *Proc. Of Computer Supported Collaborative Work'96*. Cambridge. MA. USA.

3. Bertelsen, O. W. & Bodker, S. (2003). Activity Theory. En Carroll, J. M. (Ed.) *HCI Models, Theories and Frameworks. Toward a multidisciplinary science.* Amsterdam: Morgan Kaufmann Publishers.

4. Beyer, H. & Holtzblatt, K. (1998). *Contextual Design.* San Francisco: Morgan Kauffman Publishers.

5. Borghoff, U. & Schlichter, J. (2000). *Computer Supported Cooperative Work.* Berlín: Springer.

6. Blumer, Herbert. (1969). *Symbolic Interactionism: Perspective and Method.* Englewood Cliffs, NJ: Prentice-Hall.

7. Decortis, F., Noirfalise, S. & Saudelli, B. (1998). *Distributed cognition as framework for cooperative work.* COCTOS – WP1.

8. Doménech, M. & Tirado, F. (1998). *Sociología Simétrica. Ensayos sobre Ciencia, Tecnología y Sociedad.* Barcelona: Gedisa.

9. Gutwin, C. & Greenberg, S. (2002). A descriptive framework of workspace awareness for real – time Groupware. En *Computer Supported Cooperative Work*, 11:411-446.

10. Holmquist, L.-E., Falk, J. and Wigstrm J. (1999) Supporting group collaboration with interpersonal awareness devices. *Personal Technologies*, Vol. 3, p. 13-21.

11. Hutchins, E. & Klausen, T. (1992). Distributed cognition in an airline cockpit. En Middleton, D. y Engestrom, Y. (Ed.) *Communication and cognition at work.* Cambridge:

12. Jose, R., and Davies, N. (1999). Scalable and Flexible Location-Based Services for Ubiquitous Information Access. *In Proceedings of the First International Symposium on Handheld and Ubiquitous Computing*, pages 52-66, Karlsruhe, Germany, September 27-29.

13. Lanzi, P. & Marti P. (2002). *Innovate or preserve? When technology questions cooperative processes.* Eleventh European Conference on Cognitive Ergonomics. Catania, Italy. www.dblue.it/pdf/ECCE11_Lanzi_Marti_v3.pdf

14. Luff, P. and Heath, C. (1998). Mobility in Collaboration. *Proc. Of Computer Supported Collaborative Work'98.* Seattle, Washington. USA.

15. Schmidt, A., Lauff, M., and Beigl, M. Handheld CSCW. *Workshop on Handheld CSCW at CSCW'98*, 14 November, Seattle1998.

16. Smith, M. A. (2000). Some social implications of ubiquitous wireless networks. *Mobile Computing and Communications Review*, 4 (2), 25-36.

17. Stein, R., Ferrero, S., Hetfield, M., Quinn, A., and Krichever, M. Development of a commercially successful wearable data collection system. *Proc. IEEE Int. Symp. on Wearable Computers 1998*, 18-24.

18. Perry, M.; O'Hara, K.; Sellen, A.; Brown, B. & Harper, R. (2001). Dealing with Mobility: Understanding Access Anytime, Anywhere. *ACM Transactions on Computer-Human Interaction, Vol. 8, No 4*, p. 323-347.

Remote Support to Plastic User Interfaces: a Semantic View

Sendín, M. and Lorés, J.

University of Lleida (Spain).

GRIHO: HCI research group.

1 Introduction

Nowadays technology allows users to keep on moving with computing power and network resources at hand. Computing devices are shrinking while wireless communications bandwidth keeps increasing. These changes have increasingly enabled access to information; "anytime and anywhere". This makes computing possible in multiple and varied *contexts of use*[1] in which a great amount of variable parameters come together. This provides us tremendous versatility. Consequently, current interactive systems should be prepared to face up this continuous and diverse variability. They should be able to offer the capacity of systematically producing as many User Interfaces (henceforth UIs) as contextual circumstances have been identified. This fact raises a first challenge. Moreover, the adaptive capacities should evolve in runtime, as the real time constraints vary. This would offer, in addition, continuous adaptation to each concrete UI in use, with the aim of solving the contextual changes in a dynamic and automatic way. We identify this problem as a second challenge different from the previous one.

Until now these two issues have been designated a single term: plasticity of UIs[2] , introduced by Thevenin and Coutaz in [26] in 1999 along a framework and research agenda development work. This work was

---

[1] Set of environmental parameters that describe a particular context in which a set of conditions of real time come together, related not only to the restrictions in hardware resources, but also related to the user, and even to the environment.

[2] Capacity of a same generic UI to support variations in multiple contextual circumstances preserving usability and at the same time minimizing the development and maintenance costs [7].

R. Navarro-Prieto and J. L. Vidal (eds.), HCI Related Papers of Interacción 2004, 55-70.

put in practice in these two works: ARTStudio [25] and Probe [3]. It was also revised in 2002 in [4], within the Cameleon project [5].

Nevertheless, according to the distinction between the two challenges mentioned above, we understand plasticity as a dichotomy, that is to say, a separation into two parts. We see these two parts closely associated with the diverse stages of reconfiguration and readjustment the UI comes cross during the whole system lifetime, respectively. They can be considered as the design operation level and the runtime operation level. Both of them were distinguished and defined in [20] as two sub-concepts of plasticity (explicit plasticity and implicit plasticity, respectively) with two different goals clearly identified. They have also been presented as an extension to the Thevenin and Coutaz work in [23].

As it appears in [23], we define the explicit plasticity as the capacity of automatically generating a specific UI valid to a concrete context of use, starting from an abstract specification *generic UI*[3]. In a parallel way, we define implicit plasticity as the capacity of incremental adaptation that the specific UI obtained in the production stage should show in real time, preserving at the same time a predefined set of usability properties as the user goes across new contexts of use. The explicit plasticity tackles important changes in the UI that are caused either by unforeseen situations – a change in the user or the device or by the request of new contents – changes in the user location or in the task to perform. Both cases involve a reconfiguration of the UI to be solved in the server side upon explicit request. This is the reason why we use the term "explicit". Comparably, the implicit plasticity tackles specific modifications in the UI, originated by predictable contextual changes-changes in the brightness level, server connectivity level, bandwidth, small advances made by the user, etc. We state that this kind of changes should be solved with an automatic local readjustment on the client side, without any express request or action. This is why we chose the term "implicit".

In the works mentioned previously, we also propose a client/server-based architectural framework to solve both challenges on the opposite sides of the architecture. The framework proposed to solve the explicit plasticity is located on the server side and is called explicit plasticity engine. The architecture proposed to solve the implicit plasticity is located on the client side (on his/her own device) and is called implicit plasticity engine. The former consists of a systematic development support

---

[3] Unique and flexible abstract specification of the layout and composition of the resulting interface, as well as a description of how the UI evolves in time. It is related to the concept of canonical expression of the UI.

capable of generating or redesigning (reconfiguring) remotely a suitable UI for each case presented. The later consists of an architecture with evolving capacity capable of detecting the environment and of reacting appropriately. It is in charge of applying locally the necessary adjustments to the UI and thereby adapting to the contextual changes on the fly.

This architectural framework tries to reach a certain balance between both sides. Certainly, it contributes to some benefits derived from certain autonomy that allows adaptivity also to be performed on the client side. On the one hand, as the contextual representation is stored in the client side, the resultant system becomes more robust to possible fails in the server or communication system. This makes possible to keep on running till new reconfiguration needs appear. On the other hand, this autonomy contributes to an automatic and transparent reaction in real time. Moreover, the timely communication between client and server provides a mechanism for propagating contextual changes in both ways. This is one of the most important shortcomings detected in the literature. The client notifies to the server the changes produced in the current UI by means of a trustworthy request (i.e. that reliably reflects the real time constraints). On receiving the request, the server has the chance of updating its contextual map and, as a consequence, of generating a UI as adjusted as possible to the current situation. This mechanism allows keeping both sides in continuous feedback and updating.

This paper deals with the explicit plasticity problem associated with the increment in the complexity of the design of plastic UIs, and more concretely of its conceptual modeling. We aim to offer a remote support to the plastic UIs development, taking the development framework upon request presented in [22] as starting point. The major difficulty in this issue is dealing with the multiplicity of parameters that a plastic UI is supposed to withstand when it can operate in many contexts of use. This is especially so for the complexity of the design phase, which dramatically increases by adding many design options to choose from to produce a UI for each possible contextual circumstance. The framework we are referring, which is inspired in the model-based approach, constitutes a correct structured way to capture, store and manipulate multiple elements of the context of use. Its focus of attention consists of solving the anticipation to contextual changes providing a mechanism of propagation, as one of the most important shortcomings detected in the literature. However, it has important drawbacks in which we are focusing now. Thereby, the particular information to each system or domain of application has to be incorporated externally each time, limiting so in a great deal the set of models and parameters to be considered. Thus it is not flexible enough to consider multiple parameters following the universal design principle [9]. Instead, it derives in content adaptability problems [12]. This is a very important shortcoming detected in the literature.

We propose to incorporate a conceptual layer to locate an *ontology*[4] of the domain of discourse. This layer will be in charge of managing universal parameters, providing a medium to derive a *conceptual model*[5] as flexible as possible, following the universal design principle. Providing a semantic approach to this kind of frameworks would also contribute to another important shortcoming from literature.

This paper is composed of three sections more. Firstly we survey the existing methodologies related to the explicit plasticity problem, making an especial mention to the model-based approach. Secondly, it is presented a sketch of our previous development framework, which is object of revision. Finally, we outline a semantic approach to be incorporated in the framework and revise the state of the art on this issue.

2 Solutions to Explicit Plasticity: State of the Art

Obviously, the traditional approach for developing plastic UIs consisting on writing different versions for each possible modality of interaction remains put aside. It is necessary to make flexible this process migrating towards generic methodologies, which motto is "write once and run anyone, anywhere, anytime".

The essential idea of generic methodologies consists of specifying a unique, generic and abstract UI, flexible enough to tackle the multiple sources of variations and use it to produce as many UIs as necessary. This idea, advocated by authors as Eisenstein, Vanderdonkt and Puerta [8], has evolved towards two well-differentiated approaches: the *Model-Based techniques* [15] and the use of a UI appliance-independent language.

---

[4] A medium to specify complex knowledge focused on the interface's domain model for building the necessary data models and to define complex relationships.
[5] Formal, declarative and implementation-neutral description of the UI.

2.1 Model-Based Techniques

2.1.1 Conception and Advantageous Aspects

The main idea of this kind of techniques is, on the one hand, the fact that all of the relevant aspects of the UI are explicitly formalised and represented in declarative models that get together all the different requirements of each context of use (the conceptual model), storing that way the conceptual representation of the interface. On the other hand, this kind of techniques also provides methods and tools that exploit these models for supporting the systematic development of the interface. The assemblage of the interface model with the underlying development tools is what is called Model Based technique (henceforth MB) [15].

Each one of the existing MB techniques uses a different set of declarative models. The selection of the appropriate set of models depends on what is considered as component of a context of use in each case, and so will influence in the configuration of the UI from a position of abstraction. As important as to determine which models are necessary in each case, and to set their internal structure is also to establish the connection (mapping) between the different models, at different levels of abstraction. These connections are so important that determine the interactive behaviour of a UI.

MB techniques provide a lot of benefits. We can remark these ones as the most remarkable:

- Provide a more abstract description of UI than other UI development tools.
- Facilitate the creation of methods to design and implement UIs in a systematic way and provide infrastructure to automate tasks related to UI design.
- Provide a comprehensive support of the whole system lifecycle.
- They are a user-centred design methodology.

There exist a great variety of examples, even diverse commercial products that use this kind of tools. In [18] we can find a complete overview of some of the best-known MB techniques.

2.1.2 Drawbacks and Shortcomings

In general, the techniques proposed until now are substantially static. This means that situations provoked by contextual changes are not enough anticipated. It will be better a more dynamic solution. In short, there exist aspects that must be studied in order to increase their acceptance. In general, we can collect this set of problems and shortcomings:

- Complexity of the models and their notations.
- Multiple and meaningful differences (no consensus) in range, nature and notation of supported models, which make difficult the comparison and reusability of models. It would be beneficial to dispose some standard notation.
- Difficulty to model the relationships between models (mapping).
- The problem of post-editing refinements.
- They mostly support the generation of form-based UIs only (limited set of interactors, and also very simple) [24]
- The integration the different UIs with their underlying application. Nevertheless, the problems we consider more important are these:
- The problem of flexibility in content adaptation and coherence, which remains unsolved [11].
- The fact that they are in general substantially static, leaving without solving the anticipation to contextual changes, as it occurs, for example, in ARTStudio (Adaptation by Reification and Translation) [25]. This is the problem where we are especially focused.
- The lack of semantic information inside the models.

Definitely, the MBUI development environments should improve for addressing the problem of plasticity. We can assert that they are still challenging. In our opinion, the set of models taken into account is quite limited. In general, they only consider tasks, users and platform models, leaving without modelling the contextual aspects. The only exception is Probe [3]. Nevertheless, it is not formalised yet as an environmental model. As a consequence of that, the anticipation to contextual changes rests still without solving. As far as we are concerned, the context model has also to be considered and appropriately related to the rest of models.

At present, the Cameleon project [5] considers, among other things, the context-dependent information in the set of models. It also tackles the construction of a development framework and a runtime-architecture.

2.2 UI Appliance-Independent Languages

Numerous UI appliance-independent languages, which are XML-based have been arising. All of them reinforce the conceptual separation between the logic of the application and the presentation aspect.

UIML (User Interface Markup Language). It is a simple, universal, appliance-independent and very versatile language. As limitations we can point to it does not take into account the research work in the area of MB-techniques. It does not handle any notion of task model or user model [1].

XUL (XML-based User interface Language). Developed as a W3C standard technology, it is based on existing standards. It provides easy customization and enhanced UI capabilities [33].

Xforms. Specification of the new generation of Web forms. It is characterized by the conceptual separation between the design and the concrete presentation. It highlights the need for meaningful models [31].

XIML (eXtensible Interface Markup Language). Arises in the research labs of the RedWhale Software Corporation as a universal UI specification language. It aims to provide a standard mechanism to interchange and interoperate interaction data. Nevertheless, we can remark two important limitations: it mainly focuses on syntactic aspects, leaving without attending the semantic aspects and it is not publicly available [32].

3 Our Initial Explicit Plasticity Engine

3.1 Implied Models

From our point of view, the models that we consider relevant are the following: User Model (UM), Task Model (TM), Domain Model (DM), Dialogue Model (DgM), Presentation Model (PM), Platform Model (PltM) – explicit expression of the target platforms in terms of quantified physical resources, Spatial Model (SM) – the detailed spatial model from the real world, and finally the Contextual Model (CM) to take into account daily aspects. A precise description of each one, as well as their implication in the development of plastic UIs can be seen in [22].

Apart from these models, there are other specifications that also take part in the plastic UIs production process: the *Abstract User Interface* (AUI) and the Concrete User Interface (CUI). We define the AUI or generic UI as an abstract specification of the layout of the resulting interface, as a static structure, as well as a description about how the UI evolves in time. It is high-level and appliance-independent. We define the CUI as a concrete instance of an AUI, low-level and appliance-dependent.

3.2 General Description and Performance

Let us take a look at the components and phases implied in the development framework that we propose:
- It is composed of two sequential phases called Abstract Rendering Process (ARP) and Concrete Rendering Process (CRP) respectively, in which the set of models that intervene vary, as shown in figure 2. The first phase attends to obtaining the AUI. The models that intervene are the following: SM, TM, DM, UM and DgM. The second phase manages the selection of the set of final interactors, which reside in the PM, according to all the contextual information represented in these models: UM, SM, PltM and CM, and governed by the DgM. More specifically, it consists of deciding which concrete component of the interface will represent the functionality described by each abstract component, with the aim of progressively shaping the suitable interface for each case. As a result, this stage obtains the expected CUI, resulting from the restrictions propagation.
- We propose the use of model repositories. This allows each model to populate a common area with the specific concepts from each one. We use a model repository for each rendering process, making it possible to share concepts between the involved models. Equally, we consider it necessary to use two groups of mapping rules, one per phase, to manage the relations between the models in each group.
- Ergonomic heuristics, style guidelines and usability patterns [27] also intervene in the second phase to manage the transformation from Abstract Interaction Objects (AIO) to Concrete Interaction Objects (CIO), according to runtime conditions and preserving usability.
- With regards to the relations between the models, these are carried out by means of the repositories, upon which the mapping rules act to obtain the AUI and the CUI, respectively. Apart from that, the connection between the PM and the AUI reflects a direct relation as the objects in both specifications complement each other.
- Finally, we want to remark that in the SM the static geographical objects will be specified following a relevance level order, as well as particularizing to each user profile, covering that way a semantic gap. This order will facilitate the transformation carried out in the CRP phase, by means of the appropriate heuristics.

When the server receives a request from the client adapted to the current contextual conditions, the explicit plasticity engine triggers. Nevertheless, previous to the process of generation of a new specific UI suitable to the new situation, the following models updating process must be solved.

• The real time restrictions specified in the client's request are collected in the second repository of models–the one that acts on the CRP phase. From there, each one of these restrictions is addressed to the appropriate model. Each model will be either updated (is the case of the CM), or simply notified (upon a new user's location –SM, a new task to realise –TM and DgM, and/or a change in the used device – PltM), without causing any interruption in the system performance. Label U for Updating or N for Notification in figure 1.

• With regards to the UM, depending on the cases it will require either an updating –changes in user's role or state, or a notification –the user has changed and the system takes the control of the new user without interrupting the system performance. Label U/N in figure 1.

• With regards to the DM and PM models they do not suffer any type of feedback. Once obtained the AUI, are selected the widgets from the gallery–PM that better couple to the abstract data types. Equally for the involved domain concepts. Label S of Selection in figure 1.

This model corresponds to a shared model approach that allows informing the models of any change in any concept produced in the UI, providing so a propagation mechanism. The lack of a mechanism to propagate changes is one of the relevant limitations we have detected in the MB tools we have analyzed. In particular, these ideas have been inspired in the approach used in the Teallach system [10]. It can be consulted [22] for a full explanation of our initial approach for this framework, which focuses on certain shortcomings detected in literature.

Figure 2 shows the scheme of our plastic UIs development framework, depicting all the relations among the models.

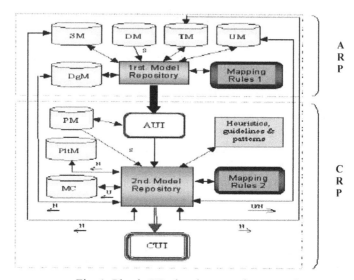

Fig. 1. Plastic UIs development frame work.

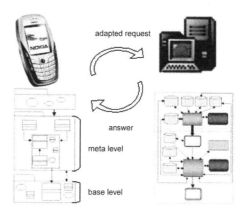

Fig. 2. Overview of the Plasticity Process.

3.3 Overview of the Plasticity Process

The implicit *plasticity engine* is located in the client side. It is supported over a threelayered architecture that facilitates the detection and control of the contextual factors and consequently the UI readjustment. See [21] for more detail. The explicit plasticity engine, which is object of the present paper, is located in the server side. It is not always active, but rather it acts upon client demand, producing a new UI suitable for the current circumstances. The implicit plasticity engine is in charge of launching the requests as much adjusted to the runtime conditions as possible, as well as of maintaining the connection to the servers. The request for the reconfiguration of the UI implies a process of updating of the involved models as required, thereby guaranteeing the propagation of contextual changes and the necessary feedback for the benefit of plasticity. That will establish an iterative and alternative process not established beforehand, which depends on the circumstances. This process will guarantee the updating of the contextual map on both sides.

4. Towards a Revised Explicit Plasticity Engine

4.1. Outlining a Semantic Approach for this Framework

Our framework object of revision can be considered as a correct structured way to capture, store and manipulate multiple elements of the context of use. However, as the set of concepts is particular to each system, the set of models and parameters to consider is also particular to each case. Therefore, it is not flexible enough to consider multiple parameters for universal design principle [9]. Actually, current practicalities of arranging a systematic plastic UIs development framework that considers all of the aspects present some important problems related to the flexibility in contents. It means that it is pretty difficult to progressively take multiple parameters for universal design into account, deriving in content adaptability problems [12].

Our proposal can be summed up this way. Instead of settling the set of models beforehand, it will be better to define an ontology of the domain of discourse in each case. Once the ontology is defined, the set of concepts and attributes can be instantiated for each context of use of a domain to obtain the suitable set of models for each design case considered. In short, the ontology defined will determine not only the models to intervene, but also the information they have to store in order to derive a conceptual model as flexible as possible, following the universal design principle.

Definitively, we propose incorporating a conceptual layer to locate ontologies in order to manage universal parameters, following the for universal design principle. The conceptual layer is therefore intended to enable domain experts to identify common concepts, relationships and attributes involved in any particular way in a universal design without limiting the set of parameters to be considered, instead allowing the incorporation of external information. This layer should be incorporated in the server, which, as a result, will consist of a *semantic web server*[6]. Moreover, the client's request to be sent to the server, as well as the resulting specific UI that this one generates will be specified in an XML - based language. This will also contribute to a standardization effort. This approach constitutes an improvement to the initial proposal in [22].

4.2. Ontology-based Conceptual Modeling: State of the Art

The explicit representation and use of semantic knowledge about a domain to facilitate or guide the access to information has been a primary concern in hypermedia systems from early times. Many ways to structure knowledge have been proposed in the literature on adaptive hypermedia. Most of them are based on a level of contents and a level of semantic structure, which is used as a road map to guide navigation. There is a great variation however as to how the contents are structured, how the conceptual network is organized, and how both levels are connected.

To mention a few examples, in the educational field, Interbook [2] structures courses into hierarchical aggregate units accompanied by a set of interconnected concepts. The relative simplicity of this two-relation model contrasts with the lexical richness of other tools like HyperTutor [17], where the conceptual map takes a wide variety of relations from the educational theory literature. AHA [7] allows a more flexible composition of pages, based on conditional HTML fragments. DCG [29] and TANGOW [6] are distinguished for generating the course structure at runtime. In other systems, the generation of semantic relations is even more dynamic and takes place by means of automatic search mechanisms based on metadata that are associated to information units [30]. This approach is useful when the knowledge space is too large and/or volatile to define and maintain explicitly the desired relationships.

Outwit of the hypermedia field, Eon [14] takes a more general approach than the preceding systems, allowing the author to define his/her own knowledge categories (*topics*), and the relations between them that he/she considers appropriate.

---

[6] A kind of server that provides access to metadata (ontology) describing any kind of resources, which are made available to users in a machine processable format. This kind of server is intended for use primarily by automated systems and is not optimized for human use.

Existing adaptive hypermedia systems miss an explicit presentation model. As a consequence, presentation is partly intermingled with contents, and partly set up automatically by the system according to rigid design choices (e.g. link annotation) that the designer cannot configure. In PEGASUS (Presentation modeling Environment for Generic Adaptive hypermedia Support Systems) [13], the separation of content and presentation is achieved by defining a presentation template for each class of the ontology. Templates are complemented with presentation rules. They consist of a generic and automatic hypermedia presentation systems for adaptive educational hypermedia. These support the definition of made-to-measure domain ontologies for the description and conceptual structuring of subject matter. Whereas in Eon, user interface components are associated with specific units of knowledge, in PEGASUS presentations are defined by categories of knowledge. The approach followed allows the specification of the presentation independently from the elaboration of contents, enhancing presentation consistency and content reuse, and reducing the development cost.

5. Conclusions

The actual practicalities of arranging a systematic plastic UIs development framework that considers all of the aspects that take part in the context of use present some important problems related to the flexibility in contents. This fact makes difficult to progressively take multiple parameters for universal design into account.

This paper tackles this notable problem and proposes the use of ontologies to describe the domain of discourse and then to instantiate the conceptual model of a UI in a MB framework. On the one hand, ontologies introduce a semantic component – one of the most important shortcomings detected in the literature. On the other hand, the MB approach makes the development of plastic UIs substantially easier thus allowing an automatic process of reverse engineering. This fact permits a reduction in maintenance costs and efforts. The use of ontologies also contributes to an effort towards the standardization of specification languages in the face of the evident lack of consensus on the nature of models. It also facilitates multidisciplinarity and reusability and the fact that changes carried out at any level are instantly propagated to subsequent levels.

In short, we assert that ontologies provide a sound medium to derive the conceptual modeling in a flexibly way, contributing so to content adaptability and flexibility. We believe that its use in a MB framework is a decisive step towards the consolidation of the plastic UIs development framework we pursue.

6. References

1. Abrams, M.; Phanouriou, C.; Batongbacal, A; Williams, S.; Shuster, J. (1999). UIML: an ApplianceIndependent XML User Interface Language. Proceedings of 8th WorldWide Web Conf. WWW'8 http://www.8.org/w8papers/5bhipertextmedi/ uiml/uiml.html
2. Brusilovsky, P.; Eklund, J.; Schwarz, E. (1998). Webbased Education for all: a Tool for the Development of Adaptive Courseware. Computer Networks and ISDN Systems, 30-17.
3. Calvary, G.; Coutaz, J.; Thevenin, D. (2001). Supporting Context Changes for Plastic User Interfaces: a Process and a Mechanism. Proceedings of IHMHCI'2001, 349-363.
4. Calvary, G.; Coutaz, J.; Thevenin, D.; Limbourg, Q.; Souchon, N.; Bouillon, L.; Florins, M.; Vanderdonckt, J. (2002). Plasticity of User Interfaces: A Revised Reference Framework. Proceedings of TAMODIA 2002, 127-134.
5. CAMELEON – Context Aware Modelling for Enabling and Leveraging Effective interactiON. (2003). http://giove.cnuce.cnr.it/cameleon.html
6. Carro, R. M.; Pulido, E.; Rodríguez, P. (1999). Dynamic generation of adaptive Internetbased courses. Journal of Network and Computer Applications 22, 249-257.
7. De Bra, P.; Calvi, L. (1998). AHA! An open Adaptive Hypermedia Architecture. The New Review of Hypermedia and Multimedia, 4. Taylor Graham Publishers, 115-139.
8. Eisenstein, J.; Vanderdonckt, J.; Puerta, A. (2000). Adapting to Mobile Context with UserInterface Modeling. Workshop on Mobile Computing Systems and Application. Monterey.
9. Furtado, E.; Vasco, J.; Bezerra, W.; William, D.; da Silva, L.; Limbourg, Q.; Vanderdonckt, J. (2001). An OntologyBased Method for Universal Design of User Interfaces. Proceedings of Workshop on Multiple User Interfaces over the Internet: Engineering and Applications Trends.
10. Griffiths, T.; Barclay, P.; McKirdy, J.; Paton, N.; Gray, P.; Kennedy, J.; Cooper, R.; Goble, C.; West, A.; Smyth, M. (1999). Teallach: A ModelBased User Interface Development Environment for Object Databases. Proceedings of User Interfaces to Data Intensive Systems, 86-96.
11. Lemlouma, T.; Layaïda, N. (2002). Device Independent Principles for Adapted Content Delivery. INRIA.
12. Lemlouma, T.; Layaida, N. (2003). Adapted content delivery for different contexts. Symposium on Applications and the Internet.
13. Macías, J. A.; Castells, P. (2001). Adaptive Hypermedia Presentation Modeling for Domain Ontologies. Proceedings of HCII' 2001, New Orleans.

14. Murray, T. (1998). Authoring Kowledge Based Tutors: Tools for Content, Instructional Strategy, Student Model, and Interface Design. Journal of the Learning Sciences 7, 1 564.

15. Paternò, F. (1999). ModelBased Design and Evaluation of Interactive Applications. Springer Verlag, ISBN 185233155.

16. Pausch, R.; Conway, M.; DeLine, R. (1992). Lessons Learned from SUIT, the simple User Interface Toolkit. ACM Trans. on Office Information Systems, Vol. 10, 4, 320-344 http://www.cs.virginia.edu/~ uigroup / docs / publications / Suit. lessons.paper.ps.

17. Pérez, T. A.; Gutiérrez, J.; Lopistéguy, P. (1995). An Adaptive Hypermedia System. Proceedings of Artificial Intelligence in Education (AIED'95), Charlottesville.

18. Pinheiro, P. (2000). UMLi: Integrating User Interface and Application Design. Proceedings of Workshop on Towards a UML Profile for Interactive Systems Development. TUPIS2000.

19. Pinheiro, P. (2002). The Unified Modeling Language for Interactive Applications. http://www.cs.man.ac.uk/img/umli/links.html

20. Sendín, M. (2004). Dichotomy in the Plasticity Process: Architectural Framework Proposal. Advances in Pervasive Computing. Austrian Computer Society. Doctoral Colloquium in Pervasive Computing. 141-147.

21. Sendín, M.; Lorés, J. (2004). Plastic User Interfaces: Designing for Change. Proceedings of the Making modelbased UI design practical: usable and open methods and tools Workshop (IUICADUI'04).

22. Sendín, M.; Lorés, J. (2004). Hacia un Motor de Plasticidad Explícita Retroalimentado. Proceedings of the V Congreso en Interacción PersonaOrdenador.

23. Sendin, M.; Lores, J. (2004). Plasticity in Mobile Devices: a Dichotomic and Semantic View. Proceedings of Workshop on Engineering Adaptive Web, supported by AH 2004, Eindhoven, 5867, ISSN: 09264515.

24. Schlungbaum, E. (1996). ModelBased User Interface Software Tools. Current state of Declarative Models.

25. Thevenin, D. (2001). Adaptation en Interaction HommeMachine: Le cas de la Plasticité. PHD Thesis, Joseph Fourier University, Grenoble.

26. Thevenin, D.; Coutaz, J. (1999). Plasticity of User Interfaces: Framework and Research Agenda. Proceedings of Interact'99, Edinburgh, 110117.

27. Tidwell, J. (2002). UI Patterns and Techniques. http://timetripper.Com/unipatterns

28. Unified Modeling Language Version 1.1. (1997). Rational Software.

29. Vassileva, J. (1997). Dynamic Course Generation on the WWW. Proceedings of 8th World Conference on Artificial Intelligence in Education (AIED'97), Kobe, 498-505.

30. Wilkinson, R.; Smeaton, A. (1999). Automatic Link Generation. ACM Computing Surveys.

31. Xforms. (1999). The next generation of web forms http://www.w3.org/MarkUp/Forms/#implementations

32. XIML. eXtensible Interface Markup Language, a universal language for user interfaces. (1998). http://www.ximl.org
33. XUL. XMLbased User Interface Language. (1998). http://www.mozilla.org

Hyco Authoring Features

Francisco J. García,

Adriana Berlanga,

Jorge Carabias,

Ana Gil,

Joaquín García

University of Salamanca

1. Introduction

The Hypertext Composer (HyCo) [5] is a user-friendly tool to create hypermedia learning resources which target group is primarily teachers without a computer background. HyCo is a multiplatform tool that uses the index metaphor and a set of galleries to assist authors in the creation of hypermedia learning contents. Moreover, it supports the management of bibliographical references, and the generation of output files of the learning resources in different formats (e.g., HTML, PDF, XML, text, etc.) [4].

However, learning is more than contents; it is a process where learners interact with activities, resources, teachers, and classmates, and it is a process that should consider that learners are not identical. Therefore, we find it meaningful to enhance HyCo in order to provide teachers with an authoring tool to support the design of learning, and particularly the design of adaptive learning experiences. Adaptive Learning Designs (ALD) contain learning strategies that take into account the learning styles and knowledge of the students [2].

Currently, we are transforming HyCo from an authoring tool for learning resources to an authoring tool for ALDs. Figure 1 illustrates its definition process showing the relationships between the required definition tasks and the tools to perform those definitions. Squares with a double line represent tools, and double-dot arrows symbolize their connection with the definition task.

R. Navarro-Prieto and J.L. Vidal (eds.), HCI Related Papers of Interacción 2004, 71-79.

In this paper, we outline some of the authoring tools we are developing to be able to define ALD (i.e., coloured elements in Figure 1). The rest of the paper is structured as follows: section 2 explains briefly the definition of metadata for learning resources in HyCo. Section 3 introduces the learning design concept and explains the authoring of adaptive learning designs. Finally, section 4 presents conclusions and future work.

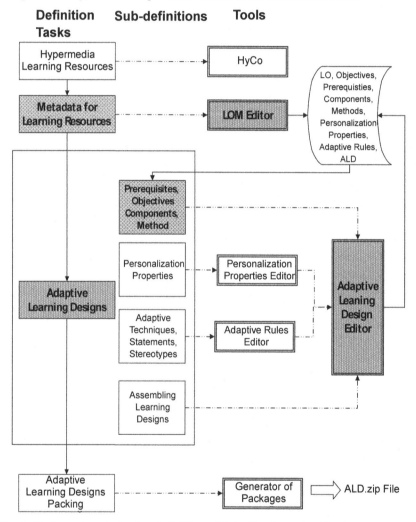

Fig. 1. Tasks and tools for the definition of Adaptive Learning Design

2. Metadata for Learning Resources

A Learning Object (LO) is any digital learning resource annotated with its metadata that can be used to perform or support learning or training activities (for more definitions of LO see [7][8][1][7]). Metadata, in its simplest definition, is data about data. Its inclusion in learning resources labels their characteristics and helps to find, retrieve, search, combine, re-use, and exchange them. However the use of common metadata labels (or annotations) is compulsory to guarantee learning resources interoperability, reusability and accessibility among different systems.

Some international organizations —such as the IMS Global Consortium Inc. (IMS www.imsproject.org), the IEEE Learning Technology Standard Committee (LTSC ltsc.ieee.org), or the Advanced Distributed Learning (ADL www.adlnet.org)— are developing standards and specifications that state a general agreement about the characteristics learning elements should have. For instance, the IMS LOM specification (Learning Resource Metadata) [11], now the IEEE LOM standard [8], depicts a framework of metadata labels to categorize LOs. These categories include, for instance, information about authors, educational and pedagogical characteristics, technical requirements, intellectual rights and conditions of use.

2.1. Learning Objects in HyCo

HyCo has a metadata editor compliant with IMS LOM (see Figure 2). In the editor each category of the specification is separated into tabs. Each tab contains the elements of the category and default values and combo-boxes with possible values for each element. Once a LO has been defined it can be incorporated in learning design elements such as prerequisites, objectives, or components (i.e., learning activities, activity structures).

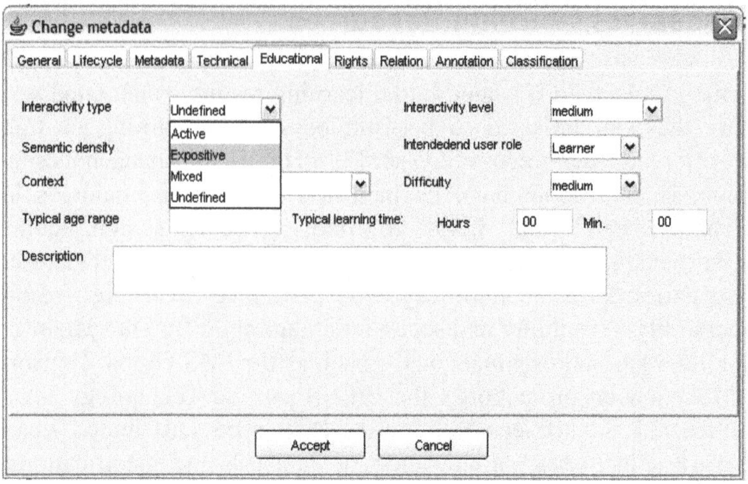

Fig. 2. HyCo LOM Editor

3. Adaptive Learning Designs

Learning design is the application of learning design knowledge when developing units of learning (e.g., lessons, courses, curriculum, etc.) [12]. This kind of knowledge can be identified as prescriptions of the instructional design theories (as in [15]), specific examples of best practices, or patterns and experiences [14].

The aim of Educational Modelling Languages (EML) is to describe learning designs in terms of a semantic notation, in order to support their reuse and interoperability among different courses, platforms and applications. Examples of EMLs are OUNL-EML [13] and the IMS Learning Design specification [10]. Other popular initiative is the ADL Sharable Content Object Reference Model (SCORM) [16] that defines, from the technical point of view, a model to support learning (rather than the process itself) based on existing specifications and standards. For a comparison between OUNL-EML, IMS LD and SCORM see [1].

3.1 IMS Learning Design

Figure 3 shows the conceptual model of IMS LD.

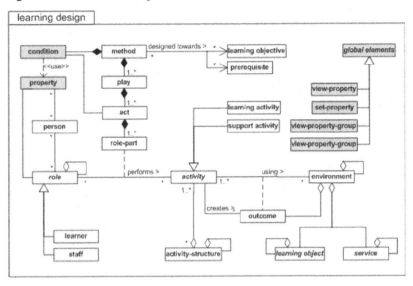

Fig. 3. IMS LD Conceptual Model 10

The objective of this IMS LD, which is based on OUNL-EML, is to allow authors to create many types of educational designs, following a consistent notation, that can be implemented homogeneously in several courses or learning contexts.

The element *learning design* groups the method of teaching, components, objectives, and prerequisites. A method is formed by a play (that defines who execute what activities and when), conditions (if-then-else statements) and notifications. A component can be a role, property group, property, activity structure, activity, environment, or outcome. Resources, which are aggregated to objectives, prerequisites and components, can be a web content, person, service facility, or dossier.

3.2. Adaptive Learning Designs and HyCo

As pointed out before, at present we are extending the functionality of HyCo in order to convert it into an ALD authoring tool.

The objective is to provide teachers and instructional designers with a learning design authoring tool that does not prescribe neither an instructional approach nor personalization variables or conditions. As a result, we are developing an ALD Editor compliant with IMS LD that includes adaptive rules and personalization properties that can be managed by teachers and instructional designers.

The HyCo LD Editor is included in the new menu "Learning Design". Within this menu users can define the following options:

1. Learning objectives. The desired outcomes of the learning design or learning activities. Their definition include a title, a resource (URI or HyCo resource), and metadata.
2. Prerequisites. The requirements for any learning design or learning activity. Their definition include a title, a resource (URI or HyCo resource), and metadata.
3. Components. It includes:
   - Roles. The participants in the learning design. Their definition includes a title, a type (learner or staff), and metadata.
   - Learning activities. The learning activities to be performed in order to reach a learning objective. To depict them is necessary to indicate their properties (title, complete activity options, and metadata), learning objectives (a choosing-list of the existing learning objectives), prerequisites (a choosing-list of the existing prerequisites), description (title, related resource, metadata), and feedback (title, related resource, metadata) (see Figure 4).
   - Activity structures. The groups of learning activities or learning structures that will be performed. To define them is necessary to indicate their properties (title, type of structure, and complete activity options), information (associated resource, metadata), and the elements of the new structure (two combo lists of learning activities and learning structures to define new learning structures).

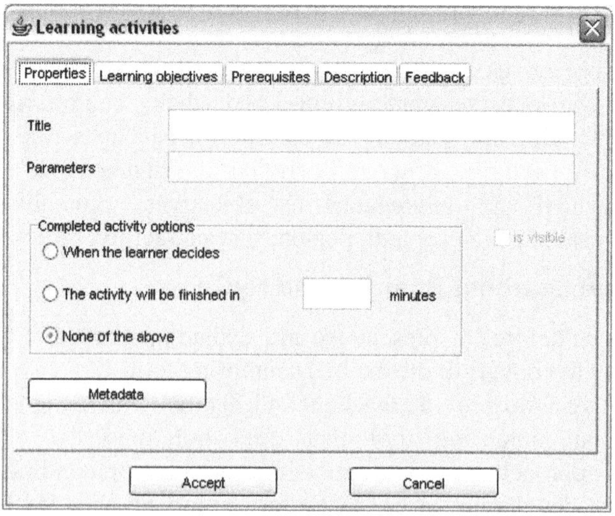

Fig. 4. HyCo ALD Editor

4. Method of instruction. It includes:

– Acts. The learning activities that will be performed by the roles (identified as *role-parts*). They include the definition of role-parts and their corresponding learning activities or learning sequences, properties (title, complete act options, and metadata), and feedback (title, related resource, metadata).

– Plays. The sequences of acts that will be performed. They include properties (title, complete play options, and metadata), a choosing-list of the existing acts, and feedback (title, related resource, metadata).

5. Personalization Properties. The variables (e.g., learning style, knowledge, etc.) that will be considered to adjust the learning design. To define them it is necessary to indicate their title, URI, data-type, restrictions, initial-value, and metadata.

6. Adaptive Rules. The prescriptions that will be taken into account to adjust the learning design. The definition of conditions and actions will be possible by means of an expression-builder tool. It will support users on the definition of adaptive conditions and actions (if-condition-then-action formalism) that can include learning design elements, personalization properties, logical and relational operators, and actions.

7. Assembling Learning Design. The method of instruction considering certain learning objectives and prerequisites. It includes properties (title, version, URI), general learning objectives (a choosing-list of the existing learning objectives), general prerequisites, (a choosing-list of the existing prerequisites), a method of instruction (title, a choosing-list of the existing plays, complete options, and feedback), and adaptive rules (a choosing-list of the existing adaptive rules).

As the HyCo LOM Editor, this new editor uses a tab structure to gather the set of elements that might be described and, when possible, it displays default values and combo-boxes. Moreover, it is connected to the HyCo LOM Editor for the metadata definition of learning design components.

It is important to point out that elements such as learning objectives, prerequisites, components (i.e. learning activities and activity structures), methods, personalization properties and adaptive rules are stored as separate objects. This makes them reusable elements among different learning designs.

4. Conclusions and Future Work

Nowadays, IMS LOM is supported by products such as WebCT (www.webct.com) and Blackboard (www.blackboard.com), which also will incorporate IMS LD [3]. Clearly, adoptions of IMS LD are hanging on accessible authoring tools, engines, players and repositories. We are on the road to develop tools for working with IMS LD. Well-known initiatives are the RELOAD project (www.reload.ac.uk) and the CooperCore engine (coppercore.sourceforge.net) (see 6 for an overview).

In this paper we presented how we are transforming HyCo from a content authoring tool to an adaptive learning design tool. We aim at developing a tool where teachers could define not only hypermedia contents but also instructional designs.

At present we are finishing the HyCo ALD Editor for the definition of objectives, prerequisites, components and methods of instruction. Afterwards, we will incorporate adaptive characteristics to those learning designs by providing users with forms to define personalization properties, adaptive rules by means of an expression-builder tool, assembling options to define ALD, and an automatic packing feature to generate ADL files (compliant with IMS CP [9]). Subsequently, we will test if HyCo is able to reuse other learning designs compliant with IMS LD and vice versa.

5. References

1. Berlanga A, García, F (2005) Learning Technology Specifications: Semantic Objects for Adaptive Learning Environments. Special Issue m-ICTE 2003. Int. J. Learning Technology (in press).
2. Berlanga A, García FJ (2004) Towards Adaptive Learning Designs. In: De Bra P, Nejdl W (eds) Adaptive Hypermedia and Adaptive Web-Based Systems. Springer-Verlag, Berlin, pp 372-375.
3. Etesse, C (2004) Leading the Way on Standards-Based e-Learning. http://www.blackboard.com
4. García Peñalvo FJ, Carabias González J, Gil González AB, García Carrasco J, Berlanga Flores AJ (2004) Facilidades de Interacción en la Herramienta de Autor HyCo para la Creación de Recursos Docentes. In: Lorés J, Navarro R (eds) V Congreso Interacción Persona Ordenador. Interacción 2004, Lleida, pp 113-120.
5. García F, García J (2005) Educational Hypermedia Resources Facilitator. Computers & Education 3:301-325.
6. Griffiths D, Blat J, García R, Vogten H, Kwong K (2005) Learning Desing Tools. In: Koper R, Tattersall C (eds) Learning Design. Springer, The Netherlands, pp 118-135.

7. Hummel H, Manderveld J, Tattersall C, Koper R (2004) Educational modelling language and learning design: new opportunities for instructional reusability and personalised learning. Int. J. Learning Technology 1: 111-126.
8. IEEE-LOM (2002) IEEE 1484.12.1-2002. Standard for Learning Object Metadata. http://ltsc.ieee.org/wg12
9. IMS CP (2003) Content Packaging specification. http://www.imsglobal. org
10. IMS LD (2003) IMS Learning Design specification. http://www.imsglobal. org
11. IMS LOM (2001) IMS Learning Resource Metadata specification. http://www.imsglobal.org
12. Koper R, (2005). An Introduction to Learning Design. In: Koper R, Tattersall C (eds) Learning Design. Springer, The Netherlands, pp 3-20.
13. Koper R, (2001) Modelling Units of Study from a Pedagogical perspective. http://hdl.handle.net/1820/36.
14. Pedagogical Patterns Project (2005) http://www.pedagogicalpatterns.org
15. Reigeluth CM (1999) Instructional Design Theories and Models. A New Paradigm of Instructional Theory. Hillsdale, Erlbaum.
16. SCORM (2004) Sharable Content Object Reference Model v1.3. http://www.adlnet.org
17. Wiley D, (2002) Connecting Learning Objects to Instructional Design Theory: A Definition, a Metaphor, and a Taxonomy. In: Wiley D (ed) The Instructional Use of Learning Objects http://reusability.org

Design and evaluation of a simple eLearning authoring tool

S Sayago, J Martínez, J Blat, R García, D Griffiths, F Casado
Interactive Technologies Group, Universitat Pompeu Fabra

1. Introduction

Traditionally eLearning has been implemented by building monolithic learning applications, which were often too focused on specific learning objectives. This is a complex and expensive process, and consequently current approaches seek to create more reusable and interoperable learning materials. Open eLearning interoperability specifications are the principal means whereby this simplification of structure and potential reduction of costs can be achieved. Several bodies promote open eLearning specifications, some of which have become de facto standards. Some key examples are the IEEE-LTSC (Learning Technology Standards Committee) promotes LOM (Learning Object Model), ADL (Advanced Distributed Learning) promotes SCORM (Sharable Content Object Reference Model), and IMS Global Consortium promotes QTI (Question and Test Interoperability), LD (Learning Design), amongst others.

A number of eLearning authoring tools based on these specifications have been developed. Examples of free and open source tools include Colloquia, Reload, CopperCore (which works with IMS-Learning Design levels A, B and C), Canvas Learning [2], (which works with IMS-QTI). Other non-open source tools worth mentioning are EDUBOX, which interprets and executes eLearning courses described in EML (Educational Modelling Language), which is the basis of IMS Learning Design, and the SCORM extension for Macromedia Dreamweaver.

Our analysis reveals that a fair number of these tools are too focused on the eLearning specifications, and consequently have reduced usability. These tools could be better described as meta-tagging tools, since their interfaces are very close to the specifications. Our analysis also suggests two common usability problems; the terminology (which is very close to the specification, and is not well understood by teachers); and a failure to pay sufficient attention to the actual needs of learning designers. On the other hand, those authoring tools which do not comply with eLearning interoperability specifications tend to be more focused on users needs, and take into account the practice of creating learning contents (for example

R. Navarro-Prieto and J. L. Vidal (eds.), HCI Related Papers of Interacción 2004, 81-88.
© 2006 *Springer. Printed in the Netherlands.*

enabling an IMS-QTI author to preview questionnaires as HTML). These tools, however, work with proprietary formats, which leads to a lack of interoperability.

With QAed we aim to show that there is no need for this dichotomy to exist. QAed aspires to providing both ease to use and support for teachers' needs, while at the same time binding the IMS-QTILite specification. The remainder of this document is divided into four sections. The first describes the QAed application. In the second section we detail how we support both interoperability and usability requirements. The third shows how we mapped the QTILite specification into the interface and provides detail of the design process. Finally, we describe the evaluation process, along with the main conclusions and some research directions.

2. Brief description of QAed

QAed is an eLearning authoring tool for the edition of questions and assessments binding the QTILite specification [10]. QAed is available for download under the GNU / GPL license from: http: //www.tecn. upf.es/gti/leteos. QAed is multiplatform, open source, developed in JAVA, and it is a result of the SCOPE project (*Structuring Content for Online Publishing Environments*).

The QAed design philosophy was to develop a user interface that would render the specification invisible, enabling users to work in terms of assessments and questions without the need for any specialized knowledge. At the same time, the fundamental relationships which characterize the model used in the specification itself were respected, so that those users who know the specification were able to work with QAed at a deeper level.

QTI [11] is an IMS specification that provides a structure for the representation of assessments and questions. QTILite [10] is a subset of QTI which is restricted to the core functionalities of multiple choice, true or false and subjective scale questions. Questions can use any combination of text and images. Even though these questions have limitations, they are widely used, and can be a valuable resource for learning designers.

QAed aims to go beyond a traditional eLearning editor, attempting to support teachers' actual practice. The principal characteristics and functionalities of QAed are the result of a user centered design approach, which we detail later. The application provides output in number of formats (HTML, ZIP, XML), several granularity levels, search mechanisms, assessments preview, etc.

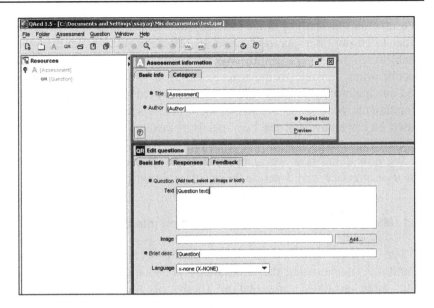

Image 1: QAed main screen

3. Support for interoperability and usability

In order to improve the usability of QAed, one of the first design activities was to carry out a competitive analysis [7] among similar eLearning authoring tools. HotPotatoes [4] and QuestionTool Simple Set [12] are two widely used authoring tools for questions and assessments editing. Both of them provide a fair number of functionalities (assessment preview, search...) and allow learning designers to edit different types of questions (multiple choice, true or false...). They also both support a number of output formats. On the other hand, because these authoring tools only work with their own proprietary formats, neither of them support reusability, since it is not possible to import questions or assessments created using other authoring tools. Canvas Learning is another authoring tool for questions and assessments editing, which does support reusability and interoperability by binding QTI. It does not, however, provide as many functionalities oriented toward teachers' needs as HotPotatoes and QuestionTool Simple Set. Its user interface is too close to the QTI specification, which leads to a reduced usability, as it is difficult to use without detailed know ledge of the specification.

As a result of this analysis, our approach with QAed consisted of attempting to support both interoperability and usability requirements.

We take as our starting point the need to support open specifications in order to ensure interoperability, and we selected QTILite. We then sought usability in two ways. Firstly we made all the details of the QTILite specification invisible to the teacher (using a terminology less technical and much closer to the user). Secondly, we provided support for additional structures beyond those defined in the QTILite specification. These were based on our analysis of teachers' needs, for example their need to classify assessments into categories.

We now detail how we mapped QTILite (elements and structure) into the user interface, and describe the interface design process.

3.1. Mapping the IMS-QTILite specification into the user interface

The QTILite specification defines assessments as sets of questions. Questions (items, using the terminology of the specification) are divided into three sections: presentation (body of the question) responses (including both correct and incorrect answers) and feedback, (for both incorrect and correct answers). For further information on the specification, see [10].

In order to map QTILite into the user interface, we used a multiple window paradigm. Our work with users, which we detail in the following section, showed that questions and assessments can be regarded as different entities, and the use of separate windows for each improved the usability of the interface, as shown in image 1.

The QTILite specification defines required and optional elements for questions and assessments, and this distinction is shown in by using blue labels for required elements (see image 1) in both the question and assessment windows. Indeed, all required elements use the same labels, to support interface consistency. As shown in image 1, the question window is divided into three tabs, corresponding to the structure of QTILite: presentation, responses and feedback. Table 1 shows how we mapped the QTILite terminology in the QAed interface.

QTILite does not include any description of assessments, but during the first stages of the QAed design, we carried out several brainstorm meetings with our users which suggested that information such as author, category and assessment title, would be very useful in assessment editing tasks. We included these functionalities in QAed, as well as the creation date, which is generated automatically.

IMS-QTILite terminology	Type of element	Our terminology
Ident attribute of the item element	Required	Automatic alphanumeric
Title attribute of the item element	Required	"Brief description" label
Lang attribute of the mattext element	Optional	"language" list
Mattext and mattimage elements	Required	"text" and "image" text boxes

Table 1: Mapping the IMS-QTILite terminology

3.2. User interface design

In order to design and evaluate the QAed user interface we followed a classical user centered approach, as defined by Nielsen in [7], which we enhanced by adding two activities at the prototyping stage: role and task modeling, which come from the Usage Centered Design (UCD) methodology [3]. These enabled us to gather specific information about the usage of the application and include it in the design.

The first design activity was a competitive analysis of eLearning authoring tools for questions and assessments editing, which consisted of heuristic and feature evaluations, detailed in the next section. Next, we performed role and task modeling to contextualize the problem in terms of usage. Both models were derived from several brainstorming meetings with our users, as the UCD methodology specifies, and are reflected in Table 2.

The second stage was the design and evaluation of conceptual prototypes, carried out by using participatory and parallel design approaches. As Norman mentions in [9], conceptual prototypes are useful design tools in order to identify serious usability problems, which usually are difficult and expensive to solve during high level design stages. Participatory design [7] consisted of involving users during the design of the conceptual prototypes and gathering their feedback. To explore different solutions each team member worked in parallel to develop his or her own design proposal in parallel, and the solutions were then analyzed collectively. This process, together with a formative evaluation described in the next section, led to the conceptual model for the final design.

Role	Brief description
Questions editor	Temporal role. Tasks: create, delete, modify, preview, search questions
Assessments editor	Temporal role. Tasks: create, delete, modify, preview, search assessments
General user	Assessment and questions editor tasks

Table 2: User role and task models

Next, we designed and evaluated high-level prototypes. As graphic design is the aspect of the interface first which users see, the visual integrity of user interfaces plays an important role in usability [6]. Graphic design practices developed in book design to ensure visual integrity were applied in order to achieve simplicity, visual organization and symmetry.

In JAVA, all graphics components have a default look-and-feel [14], which, however, does not always provide the best approach. For instance, the application background and the Tab default colors were too similar and we decided to change the Tab color to make the difference more clear to the user.

In designing multiplatform interfaces it is important to check that the user interface graphic components display correctly on the target platforms [5]. In our case there were visualization problems of the labels under Linux and Windows. After tests this issue was resolved by enlarging the labels. More generally, we note that many design problems are recurrent, and that a number of solutions have been documented [1]. Consequently during the design stage we used Tidwell's Human Computer Interaction patterns [16]. In response to problems identified by users we used the hierarchical set pattern for the repository tree, and the forms pattern for the form design, amongst others.

3.3. Evaluation

Within the framework of a user centered design approach, the evaluation was both formative (to improve the interface as part of the iterative design process) and summative (to assess the overall quality of the interface). We applied two usability inspection methods [8], heuristic and features evaluation, to analyze similar authoring tools. Heuristic evaluation was used to analyze the applications in general, while feature evaluation was used to analyze the procedures for carrying out specific questions and assessments editing tasks. To evaluate our conceptual prototypes, we carried out an application domain evaluation. This determined which of the prototypes should be developed, on the basis of development cost, etc. We also carried out flexible semi-structured interviews [17] which provided subjective information on a wider variety of details.

After the design, the evaluation actions were summative. Three usability tests were carried out involving users who had not participated during the design. The usability tests consisted of carrying out a set of pre-defined tasks [13], which were related to questions and assessments editing. During the usability tests, the thinking-aloud protocol [7] was used.

4. Conclusions and research directions

QAed improves on similar eLearning authoring tools by supporting both usability and interoperability requirements. In order to ensure compliance with the specification, the user interface retains both the number of elements defined in QTILite, and their relationships. The main usability enhancements are obtained by translating the terminology of the specification into one much closer to the user, and providing functionalities supporting reuse, sharing and viewing of the content (in this case, questions and assessments). We have described the different techniques supporting the user centered design process, and the evaluation closely intertwined in this process.

The potential benefits of interoperability specifications and standards in reducing the cost and complexity of the development process will not be realized without widespread adoption. This will not be achieved unless compliant applications also meet the needs and usability requirements of learning designers. Our experience with QAed has shown that the development of such tools is possible.

In the future we hope to resolve some outstanding design problems in the current version of QAed. We will also carry out further research to provide the basis for a more complex application, which will support, among other features, flexible pedagogical models, additional question types, and collaborative authoring.

References

1. Borchers J (2001). A pattern approach to interaction design. John Wiley & Sons

2. Canvas Learning (2004). http://www.canvaslearning.com

3. Constantine Larry, Lockwood Lucy A D (1999). Software for Use. A practical guide to the Models and Methods of Usage. ACM Press

4. Hot Potatoes (2004). http://web.uvic.ca/hrd/halfbaked/

5. Marcus Aaron et al. (1995). The Cross-GUI handbook for multiplatform user interface design. Addison-Wesley

6. Mullet Kevin, Sano Darell (1995). Designing Visual Interfaces, communication oriented techniques . Prentice Hall

7. Nielsen Jakob (1993). Usability Engineering. Academic Press

8. Nielsen Jakob (1994). Usability Inspection Methods. CHI Tutorials, pp. 413-414

9. Norman Donald A (1998). The psychology of everyday things. Basic Books

10. QTILite (2001). IMS Question & Test Interoperability QTILite Specification. Final Specification Version 1.1 http://www.imsproject.org/

11. QTI (2002). IMS Question & Test Interoperability: ASI Information Model Specification. Final Specification Version 1.2. http://www.imsproject.org/

12. QuestionTool simpleSet (2004). http://www.questiontools.com/free.html

13. Rubin Jeffrey (1994). Handbook of usability testing: how to plan, design, and conduct effective tests. John Wiley & Sons

14. Sun Microsystems (2001). Java look and feel design guidelines. Addison-Wesley

15. Tidwell J (1998). COMMON GROUND: A Pattern Language for Human-Computer Interface Design

16. http://www.mit.edu/~jtidwell/interaction_patterns.html.

17. Wimmer Roger D, Dominick Joseph R (1991). Mass media research: an introduction. Belmont Wadsworth, 3rd edition

Setting Up a Multimodal Dialogue System for Ubiquitous Environments

Ramón López-Cózar, Zoraida Callejas, Miguel Gea, José L. Garrido, Marcelino Cabrera

Dpto. Lenguajes y Sistemas Informáticos, E.T.S. Ingeniería Informática, 18071 Universidad de Granada, Tel.: +34 958 240579, FAX: +34 958 243179,{rlopezc, mgea, jgarrido, mcabrera}@ugr.es, zoraida@correo.ugr.es

ABSTRACT

This paper presents our current activities in the development of a system to assist students and teachers in their activities in educational environments. The system combines features of two different technologies: multimodal dialogue systems and ubiquitous computing. The former aims at developing computer programs that emulate the behaviour and communication of a human being in a specific task. The latter aims at developing intelligent systems adaptable to the user needs by interfaces usable in a intuitive way, making these systems available anytime and anywhere. The paper describes the main features of the system we are developing and discusses implementation issues, including system architecture, user identification and localisation in the ubiquitous environments, automatic speech recognition, natural language processing, dialogue management and response generation. Finally, it presents the conclusions and sets out some possibilities for future work.

Keywords: Dialogue systems, ubiquitous computing, mobile computing, augmented reality.

1. Introduction

In the last years there have been extraordinary advances in digital and mobile communication that have promoted new computational paradigms. One of these paradigms is the so-called *ubiquitous computing*, which is based on the utilisation of multiple, cheap, small computing devices available in the physic environment of the users (e.g. home, office, etc.)

R. Navarro-Prieto and J. L. Vidal (eds.), HCI Related Papers of Interacción 2004, 89-101.
© 2006 Springer. Printed in the Netherlands.

[1]. The term "ubiquitous" means that these devices are so widely spread among commonly used objects that they are hardly noticed by people. Moreover, the computational behaviour of these devices is so closely related with the specific function of the objects, that they are "transparent". Most of these devices have very limited resources in terms of computation power and memory, and are able to communicate among them using wireless connections. This technology integrates computing devices with the real world to enhance it, making these devices imperceptible for the user [2].

The so-called *augmented reality* is a new computational paradigm that aims at reducing the interaction with the computer by using the environmental information as an implicit input. The advantage is that the user can interact with the real world augmented with computer-generated information. The point of interest for the user is not into the computer but into the real world, thus the computer goal is assisting him to enhance his interaction with the real world [3].

The paper is organised as follows. Section 2 sets out a short introduction to the technology of spoken and multimodal dialogue systems, which includes a conceptual description of the architecture and performance of both types of system, as well as a discussion of the lacks of spoken-only and the strengths of multimodal communication. Section 3 presents the multimodal dialogue system for ubiquitous educational environments that we are developing, describing its main features as well as the work done and the tasks to be carried out in terms of system architecture, user identification and localisation, automatic speech recognition, natural language processing, dialogue management and response generation. Finally, section 4 presents the conclusions and describes possibilities for future work.

2. Dialogue Systems

The so-called *dialogue systems* are computer programs that aim to emulate the behaviour and communication of a human being interacting with another person. Several companies and public institutions use these systems to provide automatic services to their customers, such as air travel information and reservation [5], weather forecast information [5], fast food information and ordering [6], train travel information and reservation [7], etc. The setting up of a dialogue system is a complex problem that is typically addressed by dividing it into several simpler problems, each associated with a module of the system that carries out specific tasks.

These systems can be classified into two types (*spoken* and *multimodal*) depending on the number of interaction modalities used to handle the user-system communication.

2.1 Spoken dialogue systems

In spoken dialogue systems the user-system communication is carried out using speech as the only interaction modality. Typically, these systems are used to provide telephone-based information through an interaction that aims to be as similar as possible as the one carried out with a human operator. These systems are based mainly on five technologies: automatic speech recognition (ASR), natural language processing (NLP), dialogue management, natural language generation (NLG) and speech synthesis. The system module that implements the ASR (called speech recogniser) processes the user voice and transforms it into a sequence of words in text format. The module that sets up the NLP (called semantic analyser) processes the word sequence to extract its meaning. The module that implements the dialogue management (called dialogue manager) controls the interaction with the user and carries out the necessary actions to provide the service required by the user, which typically implies querying a database to provide information. Additionally, this module deals with ASR errors and generates expectations about the sentence types the user will likely utter in his next dialogue turns. For example, if the system generates a prompt for which the expected user response is of type "yes/no" (e.g. "Did you say your telephone number is 9 5 8 2 4 3 1 4 5?") the dialogue manager can generate expectations so that the speech recogniser uses the most appropriate language model to recognise an affirmative/negative sentence. The module that implements the NLG deals with the creation of grammatically correct sentences in text format from the internal representation of the information handled by the system. Finally, the system module that implements the speech synthesis (called speech synthesiser) generates the system voice. The synthesis can be carried out using different approaches according with the requirements of the system application. Typically, it is carried out by a text-to-speech conversion of the sentences created by the NLG module, which allows converting into voice any sentence in text format. However, for some small-vocabulary applications, with fixed number of words and sentences, concatenation of pre-recorded words and/or sentences is an accepted technique which increases intelligibility (although some current text-to-speech systems generate voice of excellent quality).

2.2 Multimodal dialogue systems

In the last years there has been an increasing interest on the joint use of speech and other interaction modalities to build dialogue systems, leading to the so-called *multimodal dialogue systems* [8]. Using several modalities, users can receive more information from the dialogue system, and vice versa, thus reducing the interaction errors. In fact, human communication is based on the use of several communication modalities, such as speech, gazes, gestures, facial expressions, etc. Humans use all this information, unconsciously in most occasions, to add, modify or substitute information in the spoken communication, which allows achieving high recognition rates even when there are communication problems in the environment (e.g. noise, other people talking near, etc.). Multimodal systems typically allow that users can choose the most adequate interaction modalities to carry out the communication, allowing the adaptation to the environmental conditions in terms of light, acoustic conditions, etc. This advantage allows, in addition, that some disabled people can communicate with this type of system using some of the interaction modalities available.

Thus, interacting with a multimodal dialogue system, the user is not restricted to use his voice as the only communication means, but can interact using several input devices (e.g. keyboard, mouse, microphone, camera, touch-sensitive screen, etc.). For example, the SmartKom system, developed at the Centre for Artificial Intelligence of Germany, allows the user interaction via speech, hand gestures and facial expressions [9]. The system interacts with the user orally and using graphics projected on a plane surface over which the user moves the hand to point to objects. In addition to using a variety of input modalities, a typical multimodal dialogue system uses a variety of output modalities to provide information to the user, such as speech, text, graphs or images, in order to stimulate several of his senses simultaneously. Characteristic of the output interface of these systems is the so-called *animated agent*, which is a computer-generated character (typically with the appearance of a human being) that moves parts of the face (e.g. lips, eyes, eyebrows, etc.) and other parts of its body in synchronisation with the speech output. For example, the August system [10] provides information using an animated agent and also uses thought balloons to transmit graphically information not provided orally. In addition to provide the user with the requested information, the animated agent of this system has its own personality for socialising with the user in order to make the interaction more friendly and human-like.

3. Multimodal Dialogue System for Ubiquitous Educational Environments

Ubiquitous computing is promoting significant changes in educational environments as it allows to personalise and adapt the didactic tools and teaching models to the student needs and/or preferences. For example, in the Classroom 2000 project [11] a system was developed to store the teaching activity of teachers at the blackboard, and make it accessible for students through web pages. The teachers used an electronic blackboard for their explanations in which they showed slides and additional material for the classes. The blackboard allowed teachers to introduce hand-make annotations on the slides, as they would do on a classical blackboard. All the activity carried out by the teachers was stored (together with time stamps) by an ubiquitous system and was made accessible for the students, who did not need to take notes and thus could concentrate better on the teacher explanations.

As an improvement of this system, we are working on a new system to combine the features of ubiquitous computing and dialogue systems. The system goal is to assist users (students and teachers) in their typical activities within an educational space comprised of several ubiquitous environments (e.g. library, classrooms, teachers' offices, etc.). The system is multimodal and is being set up to provide the users with a comfortable interaction via sound, speech, graphics and text. The multimodal input allows to combine several modalities in one interaction; for example, a user may ask for information about available books on a particular topic either by speaking the topic, selecting it on the computer screen using the mouse (or stylus), or written the topic in a form field. Since the system output is also multimodal, a spoken message may indicate that the requested information has been sent to the screen, where it may appear as a list of books in text format.

We plan the system will be "proactive", i.e. will react to specific events without an explicit intervention of the user. In this way, when a user comes into the library, the system may generate a spoken message (via earphones) to remind him of books he must return soon, as for example "John, you must return soon the books shown on the screen". The output modalities to use will depend on the user preferences and/or needs, and may also depend on the messages to generate; for example, if the number of books to return was small (e.g. less than three), the titles may be provided using speech and text on the computer screen. We also plan the system will have an agenda to allow the user can schedule his activities for each day (e.g. class timetables, meetings with other students, meeting with teachers, etc.). Using this agenda, the system will generate a multimodal message (depending on the features and/or preferences of the user) to warn him about each scheduled activity some minutes before it begins. As the teachers will also be users of the ubiquitous environments, we plan the system will also be able to make operations in their environments depending on their preferences. For example, when they arrive into their offices in the morning, the system could switch on lights, play specific music, etc.

The setting up of this system is a very complex task to be carried out in a three-year project in which we will work on several technologies to integrate the final system. In the remaining of this section we report on the work we have carried out at the moment, and discuss plans for addressing some tasks in the near future.

3.1 System architecture

The system is being implemented using the language XHTML+Voice and a toolkit downloadable from the Internet for the setting up of multimodal applications. This language combines XHTML (for the visual part of the application) and VoiceXML (for the spoken part). The system is a set of .vxml documents with which the user interacts using a web browser that supports speech as well as the classical GUI (mouse/stylus and keyboard). Two of such browsers are installed with the toolkit: Opera and NetFront. The documents are comprised of forms containing fields that are filled in by the user input, either by speaking or using the mouse (or stylus). In response to a system prompt, the user may utter a sentence that can fill in one or more form fields. Alternatively, he can fill in the fields using the keyboard and/or the mouse/stylus.

The final dialogue system will work on a variety of mobile devices (laptop computers, tablet PCs and PDAs) although at the moment it is only implemented in laptop computers. It will communicate through wireless connections (e.g. Wi-Fi, Bluetooth, etc.) [12] with a web server that will contain the user profiles and preferences. In this way, users will be allowed to move freely among the different environments. In the case of particular users, the system will also communicate with control devices in the ubiquitous environments to query or change their state (e.g. to turn on/off lights, music, etc.), which will require using technologies for operating over such devices. For achieving this task, a candidate is the EIB bus (European Installation Bus) [13], which allows controlling and communicating service functions inside a building using just one interconnection line. Another candidate is the HomePNA bus (Home

Phoneline Networking Alliance), which allows using the telephone line to interconnect the devices [14]. At the moment we are using our lab wireless network to connect with an experimental web server. In the following months we will start setting up the control of some devices (e.g. lab lights) from the mobile devices.

3.2 User identification and localisation in the ubiquitous environments

To be identified in the ubiquitous environments of the educational space, the users (students and teachers) will fulfil a profile in a web server to indicate their personal data, mother language and personal preferences, such as preferred and default interaction modalities (e.g. speech or text), type of voice for the system spoken output (e.g. male or female), etc. This information will be used by the dialogue system to adapt the information to provide to each user depending on the features and preferences in his profile. Therefore, in the case of a hearing disabled user, the system will provide information in written text mode and/or graphic format through the devices screen instead of using the spoken modality. Moreover, if a teacher sends a file to his students via e-mail and several versions of the file are available, written in different languages (e.g. Spanish, French and English), each student will receive the file in a language according with the language preference indicated in his personal profile. In the following months we will start setting up these profiles.

We are testing two methods for the localisation of the users in the different ubiquitous environments of the educational space. Since the global positioning systems (GPS) is not appropriate for indoor spaces, on the one hand we are experimenting with Bluetooth emitters, one for each space of the ubiquitous environment due to their small coverage. On the other, we are placing WI-FI access points (at least three) to obtain a complete coverage of all the ubiquitous environment. In this second case, using the signal intensity, we wish to triangulate the position of the mobile device. By these experiments we aim to decide the best positioning method. Our goal is that, using the position information, the interaction with the dialogue system can also be adapted to the features of the current environment in which the user is at a particular moment, for example, the default .vxml page to be shown in the device screen when the user enters into an ubiquitous space.

3.3 Automatic speech recognition

The setting up of the system requires facing a diversity of problems concerned with the ASR in the ubiquitous environments (such as reverberations, echoes, noise sources, interferences, etc.). In terms of acoustic modelling, several approaches and techniques to face these problems can be found in the literature [15, 16]. A possible method is to use acoustic models trained for non-noisy conditions and to employ adaptation and compensation techniques to use these models in the different ubiquitous environments of the educational space. Another possibility is to use specific acoustic models trained for each environment. In our current experiments, the ASR is carried out by the speech recogniser integrated into the development toolkit. The acoustic models are trained by the user during the toolkit installation and cannot be adapted to different environments without explicit retraining. Since such a retraining would be "unnatural" in the ubiquitous environments, it would be the system's responsibility to adapt or select automatically the acoustic models depending on the current ubiquitous environment. Thus, we must study whether it could be possible to use another open-source speech recogniser (e.g. based on HTK_1) and VoiceXML interpreter (e.g. OpenVXI). If it was possible, we could set up an HTK-based recogniser to be called from the OpenVXI interpreter, deciding at run time the acoustic models for the current ubiquitous environment.

Concerning the language modelling, the setting up of the system requires to study the different sentence types the users will likely utter in the different environments, in order to create specific grammars for the different tasks (e.g. borrowing books in the library, interaction with devices in the teachers' offices, etc.). Each grammar will have a probability of being used depending on the environment in which the user is interacting. Thus, if the user is in the library, the speech recogniser will use by default the grammar compiled from the sentences used in that context, typically concerned with bibliographic queries, book borrowing, etc., whereas other grammars could also be active to accept other sentences that might be uttered in all the environments.

In our current setting, the ASR is carried out using the "tap-to-speak" method, i.e. when the user wants to speak, he must click and hold a "microphone" button shown on the screen, and must release the button when he has finished the utterance. The system also uses the "barge-in" technique, i.e. the system spoken output is interrupted as soon as the user clicks on the "tap-to-speak" button.

3.4 Natural language processing

Recognising the uttered words is not enough for a dialogue system, since in order to interact appropriately with the user, it must "understand" the meanings of the sentences uttered in a given context. At the moment we are using JSGF grammars (Java Speech Grammar Format) which are defined in advance and used at form or field levels. Fields are filled in when some words (or word sequences) are accepted by at least one grammar. For example, a JSGF grammar to accept book queries can be as follows:

₁ Hidden Markov Toolkit.

```
#JSGF V1.0;

grammar book_query;

    public  <book_query>  =  [<disfluency>]  [<courtesy>]  [<disfluency>]
[<greeting>] [<disfluency>] [<desire>] [<interrogative>] [<book>] [<about>
<topic>  {this.topic=$topic}]   [  <written>  <author>  {this.author=$author}]
[<courtesy>] ;


    <about> = about | of;
    <author> = McTear | Araki | Pressman | Stallings | Tanenbaum | ... ;
    <availability> = you have | are there | ... ;
    <book> = book | books;
    <courtesy> = please;
    <desire> = [ I ] [ want | would like | need ] [to know] ;
    <disfluency> = [uhm | ee;
    <greeting> = [hello] [ good morning |  good afternoon |  good evening ];
    <interrogative> = which | what ;
    <topic> = Mathematics | Maths | Physics | Electronics | Algebra | Computers |
... ;
    <written> = [written] by;
```

Using this grammar, if the user utters the sentence "uh … I need books about Maths please" the system fills in the form field "topic" with the word "Maths", which is captured by the grammar construction "{this.topic=$topic}" . The non-terminal symbol "<disfluency>" is used to handle spontaneous speech, since users typically utter filled pauses (e.g. "uhm …") at the beginning of the sentences. The grammars must also be adapted to the changes in the library catalogue. To address this requirement we compile the grammars dynamically from the library database. To achieve this purpose, we have implemented a PHP program that carries out two tasks. Firstly, it accesses the database using MySQL functions and obtains the data from the available books (i.e. title, author, topic, etc.). Secondly, it creates the corresponding grammars (for title, author, topic, etc.) with the information gathered in the previous task. This method is useful to obtain the keywords in the sentences uttered by the users; however, the NLP demands for more effective methods to understand the sentences. In this direction, a promising approach is the Latent Semantic Analysis (LSA) [17], which can be used to analyse the meanings of words in a given context. We plan to initiate studies in the following months to integrate this analysis into our system.

3.5 Dialogue management and response generation

After the multimodal input has been obtained from the user, the system must decide the next action to be carried out. This behaviour is implemented following predefined interaction strategies that are designed from an analysis of the tasks the system must perform in each ubiquitous environment. The analysis allows obtaining information about the structure of the tasks, as well as the data the system must obtain from the user to query a database or provide some service [18]. For example, in the library environment, the tasks are mainly concerned with bibliographic queries as well as borrow and return of books. Thus, we must analyse the way in which these tasks are carried out by a real librarian and the real students, in order to create interaction models that allow carry out them as efficiently as possible using the system. In addition to implementing dialogue strategies specific for the diverse environments considered, we must also set up typical dialogue and confirmation strategies that are common for all the environments. In our setting, the system uses mixed-initiative interaction [19]. Thus, the initial prompt of the system for the library environment is "Welcome to the library. How can I help you?". In response to this prompt, the user can utter the sentence "I need books about computers written by Stallings", for example, which fills in two form fields ("topic" and "author"). The system takes the initiative in the dialogue if the utterance cannot be accepted by any active grammar, generating e.g. the prompt "Please enter the topic for the book".

Another very important issue is the system response generation. In a typical multimodal interaction, the system responses can be provided to the user either orally, in text format or multimodally. In the last case, the output is provided by the combination of the two modalities (and even using additional modalities, if available). The oral output (for spoken and multimodal systems) is carried out using any of the available speech synthesis techniques, mostly text-to-speech [20]. In the case of multimodal dialogue systems, the response is generally accompanied by an animated agent (discussed in section 2.2) to provide a more friendly interaction as well as more intelligibility. The system we are implementing provides text responses on the device screen, and uses predefined text patterns to carry out the text-to-speech synthesis (although some parts of the sentences could be pre-recorded). Unlike most multimodal dialogue systems, which are designed just to provide information, some of our system responses will operate over specific environment devices. For example, teachers will be allowed to use spoken commands (or pointing with the mouse/stylus) to turn on/off lights, air conditioning, music, etc., and in response to these commands, the system must operate the corresponding devices to carry out the action requested by the user. As commented above, we are about to start implementing the operation over such devices.

4. Conclusions and future work

In this paper we have presented a brief introduction to two different technologies (ubiquitous computing and dialogue systems) that can be used to assist students and teachers in educational environments. Ubiquitous computing aims at developing intelligent systems adaptable to the user needs by interfaces usable in a intuitive way, making these systems available anytime and anywhere. Dialogue systems aim at providing automatic services by emulating the behaviour of human beings in specific tasks. As an effort to combine the benefits of both technologies, we are developing a multimodal dialogue system characterised by an ubiquitous interaction. Its goal is to facilitate user access to automatic services within educational environments, via comfortable interfaces that can be adapted to their preferences and/or needs. We have commented the main features of the system, have discussed briefly the tasks in which we are working at the moment, and have pointed out some tasks we plan to address in the next months. Future work mainly includes: i) setting up user profiles, ii) training acoustic models for the different ubiquitous environments in the educational space, iii) studying whether it is possible to set up an open-source ASR engine and VoiceXML interpreter to be used in the multimodal toolkit, and iv) studying more efficient methods for the NLP.

Acknowledgements: The research described in this paper has been partially funded by the Spanish Ministry of Education and Science under the project TIN2004-03140 Ubiquitous Collaborative Adaptive Training.

5. References

1. Weiser, M. The computer of the twenty-first century. Scient. American, pp. 94-107, 1991
2. Streitz, N. A. Smart artefacts and the disappearing computer. Proc. Smart Objects Conference, pp. 9-10, 2003
3. Azuma, R. A survey of augmented reality. Presence, vol. 6, no. 4, pp. 355-385, 1997
4. Seneff, S., Polifroni, J. Dialogue management in the Mercury flight reservation system. Proc. ANLP-NAACL 2000 Satellite Workshop, pp. 1-6, 2000
5. Zue, V., Seneff, S., Glass, J., Polifroni, J., Pao, C., Hazen, T., Hetherington, L. Jupiter: A telephone-based conversational interface for weather information. IEEE Trans. on Speech and Audio Proc., 8(1), pp. 85-96, 2000
6. López-Cózar, R., García, P., Díaz, J., Rubio, A. J. A voice activated dialog system for fast-food restaurant applications. Proc. Eurospeech, pp. 1783-1786, 1997
7. Billi, R., Castagneri, G., Danielli, M. Field trial evaluations of two different information inquiry systems. Speech Communication, 23, 1-2, pp. 83-93, 1997
8. Gibbon, D., Mertins, I., Moore, R. K. Handbook of multimodal and spoken dialogue systems. Resources, terminology and product evaluation. Kluwer Academic Publishers, 2000
9. Wahlster, W., Reithinger, W., Bocke, A. SmartKom: multimodal communication with a lifelike character. Proc. Eurospeech, pp. 1524-1546, 2001
10. Gustafson, J., Lindberg, N., Lundeberg, M. The August spoken dialogue system. Proc. Eurospeech, pp. 1151-1154, 1999
11. Abowd, G. D., Atkeson, C., Feinstein, A., Goolamabbas, Y., Hmelo, C., Register, S., Sawhney, N., Tani, M. Classroom 2000: Enhancing classroom interaction and review. Georgia Institute of Technology, Technical Report GIT-GVU-96-21, 1996
12. Anderson, D. FireWire System Architecture. IEEE 1394A. Second Edition. Pearson Education, 2000
13. Sauter, T., Dietrich, D., Kastner, W. (eds) EIB: Installation bus sytem. Wiley Publishers Canada, 2002
14. Saif, U., Gordon, D., Greaves, D. 2001. Internet access to a home area network. IEEE Internet Computing, vol. 5, no. 1, pp. 54-63, 2001
15. Stouten, V., Van Hamme, H., Demuynck, K., Wambacq, P. Robust speech recognition uning model-based feature enhancement. Proc. Eurospeech, pp. 21-24, 2003

16. Saric, Z., Jovicic, S. Adaptive beamforming in room with reverberation. Proc. Eurospeech, pp. 529-532, 2003
17. Laudaver, T. K. 2002. On the computational basics of learning in cognition: Arguments from LSA. The psychology of learning and motivations, 41, pp. 43-48
18. López-Cózar, R., Rubio, A. J., García, P., Segura, J. C. A spoken dialogue system based on a dialogue corpus analysis. Proc. First Language Resources and Evaluation Conference, pp. 55-58, 1998
19. Levin, E., Pieraccini, R., Eckert, K. 2000. A stochastic model of human-machine interaction for learning dialogue strategies. IEEE Transactions on speech and audio processing, 8(1), pp. 11-23
20. Aylett, M., Fackrell, J., Rutten P. My voice, your prosody: sharing a speaker specific prosody model across speakers in unit selection TTS. Proc. Eurospeech, pp. 321-324, 2003

Usability Effort: a new concept to measure the usability of an interactive system based on UCD

Granollers, T. and Lorés, J.

University of Lleida (Spain). GRIHO: HCI research group.

1. Introduction

The term "usability" (which, colloquially, is usually associated with the "ease of use or to learn" of a certain interactive system) is formally defined by ISO 9241-11 as "the extent to which a product can be used by specified users to achieve specified goals with effectiveness, efficiency and satisfaction in a specified context of use" [16]. Besides, ISO/IEC 9126-1 emphasizes the importance of usability: is highlighted as a primary parameter for the software quality [18].

Moreover, developing a highly usable interactive system is neither a clear nor easily achieved task. Development teams have at their disposal methodologies (from the area of Usability Engineering, UE, [9] based on the approximations of User Centred Design, UCD, [17], Participative Design [7] or Contextual Design [4]), such as those described in [5, 8, 21, 25] or [28], which contain processes and techniques that will guide them to implement usable systems.

Furthermore, J. Nielsen, one of the most outstanding authors in this field, assures that the work of usability will never be complete, because there is no such thing as a perfect user interface and any design can always be improved [23]. Even if we managed to have an interface that complied with 100% of the recommendations from a good style-guide we could never achieve the perfect interface. We would surely find new recommendations to add to that guide which helps to improve the user experience.

Nevertheless, once we have a new system we will not resign ourselves to saying this is very, little or not at all usable; we will wish to know a type of measurement that reflects, quantitatively, its usability level.

However, usability itself is a highly subjective, relative attribute, which, as a consequence, is so difficult to measure that to even try to quantify it presents a truly difficult and interesting challenge.

R. Navarro-Prieto and J. L. Vidal (eds.), HCI Related Papers of Interacción 2004, 103-117.
© 2006 *Springer. Printed in the Netherlands.*

In the rest of the article we will see how, at present, the problem of measuring usability is dealt with, in order to present our alternative from a point of view completely different from the existing ones.

2. Present measurement of usability

For several years there have been various alternatives that allow the measurement of the usability attribute of software systems. Basically, these fall into two categories differentiated by the type of procedure used. While some only use questionnaires to discover the level of user satisfaction regarding their experience of system-use; others use specialised software tools which facilitate a more precise, automated measurement.

Questionnaires

It is well known that in the field of usability metrics one of the most successful techniques is the use of questionnaires to find out the use, and particularly the degree of satisfaction, of a specific system through specially designed questions. The most relevant questionnaires in usability field are:

- QUIS (*Questionnaire for User Interface Satisfaction*) [27, 6, 29]: is a subjective evaluation technique focussed on measuring the degree of user satisfaction while they interact with the interface. The questionnaire was designed at the end of the 80s but undergoes constant renovation to adapt it to such changeable present times.
- SUMI (*Software Usability Measurement Inventory*) [30, 3]: is an inventory of usability measurements that forms part of the global project MUSiC [19]. The spirit of this questionnaire is to evaluate the quality of use of a system or prototype.
- WAMMI (*Web site Analysis and MeasureMent Inventory*) [31]: questionnaire that arises as an extension of SUMI from the attempt to orient it towards the measurement of usability on the Web.
- MUMMS (*Measuring the Usability of Multi-Media Systems*) [22]: also has arisen as an extension of SUMI and attempts to evaluate the usability of multimedia products in general.

The main advantage of questionnaires is that they harvest specific answers that bring forward discrete data verifiable through, for example, statistical techniques.

3. Tools

Prominent in the field of software tools developed specifically to measure interactive system usability are:
- PROKUS (*PROgram system zur Kommunikations ergonomischen UnterSuchung rechnerunterstützer Verfahren – Program system to communication ergonomic examination of computer-aided procedures –*) [32]: is a software developed that measures the usability of a system based on ergonomics as the main quality criteria.
- DRUM (Diagnostic Recorder for Usability Measurement) [15]: software tool, developed as an integral part of the MUSiC project [2], that analyses usability through video recordings of evaluation sessions.

Problems with present usability metrics

Despite being quite efficient, the two groups of techniques described in the previous point they demonstrate the following drawbacks:
1. The measurements that both, questionnaires and tools, provide are mainly obtained measuring just the user's satisfaction with the system[12]. But we cannot forget that *satisfaction, as we have seen, is only one of the parameters that define usability.*
2. Questionnaires are excellent for measuring the requested aspects. However, *they do not allow space for aspects that are not reckoned for but which can be important from the user's point of view.*
3. There is a *strong dependence between the results obtained and the sample of users chosen* (quantity, representation and motivation).
4. It has been observed that *when users answer questions related to usability they often confuse usability with utility* [14]. They readily grant the feeling of usability to some capacity of the system that has been useful to them (forgetting if this utility has been easy to find or sufficiently satisfactory) and vice versa.
5. Although it was mentioned in the introduction that the convenience of using methodologies originating from the field of UE to develop really usable systems, *not one of the existing usability metrics considers these methodologies for its evaluation*: the presented metrics can be applied indistinctly from the followed process. Consequently we can not assure that the results obtained developing systems following these

---

[12] SUMI it does take into account other factors such as efficiency, help, learning, control and the device itself.

methodologies will be better than those carried out following the habitual Software Engineering, SE, procedures.

There exists, therefore, a difficult to resolve gap that we will try to correct.

4. Methodological Base for a New Proposal to Measure Usability

The main goal of the work presented in this article revolves around explaining our proposal of a new point of view to measure the usability of an interactive system. The focus is radically different from those of today: it is on the activities carried out during development of a system following a UCD model.

The proposal is specifically based on the process model of Usability Engineering and Accessibility, u+eEPM [11, 12] and its application during the development of a high number of experimental cases.

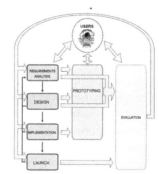

Fig. 1. Model of u+eEPM process

The main characteristics that define u+aEPM are described in [11, 12]. It has its foundations, on one hand, in SE, and on the other hand, in the HCI discipline and UE. Also provides the basis and methodologies that allow to know how a development team should proceed to design usable and accessible interactive systems following the clearly defined UCD process.

The model is organised in a series of phases (each one of the blocks in figure 1) which are repeatedly carried out. Prototyping and evaluation being two key phases for usability and accessibility that are applied from the same instant that each new development is started.

Furthermore, some SE protection mechanisms [1] are used in order of guaranteeing the consistency of the activities, to assure the impact of change and to minimise the risk of errors.

Among these mechanisms, because of its relation with this article, a particularisation of the Software Configuration Management stands out. It is designated Configuration Management Work Sheet, CMWS, [12] in which a two-dimensional table chronologically reflects all the activities carried out during development of the system at the same time allowing these activities to be related to each other.

The structure of this CMWS is the following[13]:
- There is a column for each u+aEPM phase (Requirement Analysis, Design, Implementation, Launch, Prototyping and Evaluation) where the
corresponding activity carried out will be placed.
- The number of rows are different for each project. It supplies fast and visual information about the development sequentialality of the project.

Below we present the proposal that started from the initial idea, the intuitive idea, and, finally, its mathematical resolution with the conclusions obtained.

5. New Metric for Usability: The Usability Effort (UE)

The initial idea is very simple: *we want to find the way to evaluate the grade of usability of whatever interactive system* (a value between 0 and 10, for example).

However, factors such as the subjectivity of the usability itself, the subjectivity of the users or the evaluators, or the difficulty of quantifying numerically this attribute, renewed the focus of the initial idea of *trying to evaluate the dedication or the effort made during the development* of an application in making it usable. This is how the concept of *"Usability Effort"* arose.

UE Definition

We have not found, in our research field, a term like that, so we define the term Usability Effort as the measurement that indicates the resources employed and the activities carried out during the development of an

---

[13] An example can be viewed in [13].

interactive application with the purpose of achieving a certain level of usability.

From now on we will see how to proceed to calculate this measurement.

Obtaining results

We are conscious that for any software development the obtained results are never directly proportional to the effort dedicated during its realisation: in the best case scenario one can obtain an optimum result with minimum effort or the opposite, an enormous effort can be catastrophic. However, *experience habitually shows*, and in whichever area of people's lives, a *greater effort is seen to be rewarded with better results*.

With this reflection we would like to reiterate that even *though the probability of greater usability will be higher for the application with an elevated UE, we will never be completely sure of this statement.*

The intuitive UE

As we have seen, we dispose, on one hand, a UCD methodology for design software systems, and, on the other, a value that we can attempt to calculate from the activities in applying this methodology; specifically, we will calculate the value using the related CMWS.

Nevertheless, before seeing the numerical calculation of the UE we will observe some aspects related to the CMWS of the method that will be useful for understanding the origin of the study and the expected result.

The activities carried out to develop a system draws a zone on the CMWS that intuitively reveals information related to its possible usability.

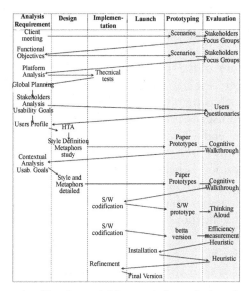

Analysis Requirement	Design	Implemen- tation	Launch	Prototyping	Evaluation
Client meeting				Scenarios	Stakeholders Focus Groups
Functional Objectives				Scenarios	Stakeholders Focus Groups
Platform Analysis		Thecnical tests			
Global Planning					
Stakeholders Analysis					Users Questionaries
Usability Goals					
Users Profile	HTA				
	Style Definition Metaphors study			Paper Prototypes	Cognitive Walkthrough
Contextual Analysis Usab. Goals					
	Style and Metaphors detailed			Paper Prototypes	Cognitive Walkthrough
		S/W codification		S/W prototype	Thinking Aloud
		S/W codification		betta version	Efficiency measurement Heuristic
			Installation		Heuristic
		Refinement			
			Final Version		

Fig. 2. Area determined by the activities carried out during the development of an interactive system.

Specifically, in the example of figure 2, judging by its high and uniformly spread amount of prototyping and evaluation activities, we can know by intuition that the effort made to achieve usability of this system has been considerably high. It also being very regular from the outset makes us think that the system will have a high level of usability or at least the value of the corresponding UE will be high.

We will see in the next figure what would be the extreme UE situations analysing only the area drawn for each development in the CMWS:

1. *Minimum usability effort*: would correspond to an application for which no action of merit had been carried out to improve its usability. The corresponding graph for this situation is figure 3 (a), and unfortunately, is the most frequent situation of today's software. This section includes all those applications whose authors label them "user-friendly" without having evaluated them for even one user.

2. *Maximum usability effort*: This would be opposite case of the previous and, evidently, would be the ideal situation. In figure 3 (b) one can observe the area occupied by activities that respond to the systematic, constant and repetitive application of u+aEPM, both in the prototyping and evaluation and the analysis of requisites and design.

3. *"Cosmetic" usability effort*. At present the topic of the usability of interactive systems is, in a manner of speaking, fashionable. The heads of many software companies know the theory and give "cosmetic make

over" the final result of their products. They evaluate them in the final stage of the project, after which they improve the usability a little; implementing the changes suggested in the evaluation that do not affect the internal structure of the system.

Moreover, heuristic evaluation [26] in the majority of cases this final evaluation is, which certainly is one of the best techniques. But we can not forget that no user is involved in this and, if it is done as a single procedure at the end of the development, *little can we change to improve the usability of the system.*

Certainly this situation is better than the previously mentioned one but it is still this "cosmetic make over" of reality that is driven more by marketing strategies than the real usability benefits. Figure (c) corresponds to this situation.

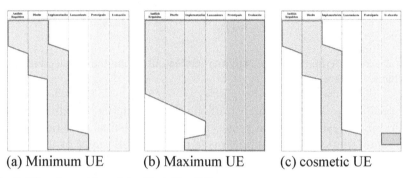

(a) Minimum UE   (b) Maximum UE   (c) cosmetic UE

Fig. 3. Visual graphics of the Usability Effort.

So, it seems evident that the UE of the application of figure 2 is very close to the possible maximum, which is synonymous with a great effort to improve usability and, *presumably, the application will be easily usable.*

Analysis of the mathematical calculation

To calculate mathematically the value of the UE we use the following simplification: we look for a mathematical function to deliberate just the activities of the evaluation column and, from the partial results of these deliberations, we get the UE of the complete system.

The motives of this consideration are:

- Despite it being true that the base of acquisition of usability of a system becomes from the repeated prototyping and evaluation activities carried out during development, it is also true that a prototype is of little use if it is not evaluated.

- Moreover, some evaluation methods do not need prototypes to be carried out, and for those that do need it, they can include a prototype parameter.

Deliberation function of each method of evaluation

Each method or technique of usability evaluation has its own determining factors that differentiate one from another and, consequently, directly condition its corresponding weight function. However, after carrying out a meticulous analysis of these determining factors we have discovered a *unique set of common parameters* that are sufficient to define the particular characteristics of each of them. This unique set of parameters is the following:

- The **u+aEPM phase** in which it is applied. The characteristics of each technique indicate that its application is more appropriate in some phases of the project than in others. This parameter reflects this peculiarity, the value of which will be greater in the more appropriate phases and lesser in the others.
- The **number of users** that take part in the trial. Just as before, the individual characteristics of each technique define the optimum number of users necessary to obtain the best results. Therefore this parameter aims to assess the optimisation of human resources.
- The **number of stakeholders** that share in the evaluation. The stakeholders involved in an interactive system [20] have a vital role in some of the evaluations, an importance that is reflected by this parameter.
- The **number of evaluators** that carry out the trial. As with the users, the result of each method is directly related to the number of evaluators that have taken part. Better results are not obtained by having more evaluators, but each method has its optimum number and this parameter reflects this factor.
- The **prototype used**. Considering that an evaluation activity manages to obtain better or worse results depending on the prototype used, or even that some require no prototype, this parameter reflects the suitability of the prototype used.
- **Completeness** is a percentage parameter that deliberates the quantity of interactive characteristics (related to the usability of the part of the system evaluated) that has been tested. The significance of this parameter is different to the previous as it aims to measure how many of the determined objectives have been checked.

For those cases where a prototype is necessary, this parameter reflects whether all the necessary determined requirements are implemented for evaluation or that they are only partially implemented.

Once the parameters are determined, it is necessary to assign them specific values to characterise the different methods of evaluation in a way that the results will be comparable. With this intention the assignment of values in each method of evaluation has been done from personal experience and according to the following principles.

- *Uniformity and coherence*: to be valid, each parameter should be deliberated following exactly the same criteria.
- *Impartiality*: the value of each "must measure exactly the same" of each method.
- *Identical value range* for all methods (for example between 0 and 100).

Table 1 shows the assignment of values for the different parameters (Function Result column) carried out for the Focus Group [25] method.

Once the parameter values of all the usability evaluation methods have been assigned, we have enough information to calculate the weight for each of the activities of the evaluation column of the WSCM. To deliberate the UE of each evaluation activity we have chosen next function:

$$f_j = \sum_{k=1}^{m_j} \left(\frac{C_k}{k} \cdot \sum_{i=1}^{n} A_{i,k} \right) \tag{1}$$

where, j is the evaluation being deliberated, m_j is each of the sub-evaluations that can compose an evaluation[14], C_k is the completeness parameter for the kth sub-evaluation y $A_{i,k}$ is the parameter i of the k sub-evaluation.

---

[14] Normally $m_j = 1$; so the formula is reduced considerably of evaluations and, evidently, UE is the total Usability Effort.

Table 1. "Focus Group" evaluation parameter assignation values.

Parameter Name	Parameter Value	Function Result
A: phase	R	80
	D	80
	I	80
	L	100
A: num. users	1 to 5	80
	6 to 9	100
	> 9	80
A: num. stakeholders	1 to 3	40
	4 to 6	65
	7 to 10	70
	> 10	70
A: num. Evaluators	1 to 3	40
	4 to 6	65
	7 to 10	70
	> 10	70
C: completeness	%	
A: prototype	Paper	75
	Story Board	50
	Mock-up	75
	Scenario	75
	Video	100
	S/W	100

UE calculation of the developed system

With that formula we will be able to calculate the values of all the reflected evaluations on the WSCM. Now, we just have to add these partial values to obtain the Usability Effort of the application in the following form:

$$UE = \sum_{j=1}^{N} f_j \qquad (2)$$

where, f_j are the deliberation functions of each evaluation j, N is the total number of evaluations, and, evidently, UE is the total Usability Effort.

Meaning

At this point an interesting debate arises. We have a systematic and precise way that allows us to uniformly quantify the effort made towards the highest usability level of a system. This calculation, which as we have seen is obtained from valuing a highly recommended way of proceeding such as the UCD, infers the *first known approximation of valuing the usability of a system from uniting the procedure with the result.*

Conceptually, we agree that the value of the UE of a certain project is no more than an indicative number of a certain effort to acquire a certain objective: in our case, usability.

The concept has been applied to a large number of real developments of very diverse characteristics (all of which developed following u+aEPM) with the intention of obtaining empirical data from experimenting. It allows the extraction of conclusions about the true utility our analysis[15].

Table 2 reflects the UE (with other additional data) corresponding to nine of the most relevant cases studied.

Table 2. Usability Effort and other comparative values calculated in various projects of implemented systems.

	UE	Cost		RATIO (CU1/CU2)
		WITH usability (CU1)	WITHOUT usability (CU2)*	
P1	1.320	5.220 €	660 €	0,253
P2	2.194	20.540 €	17.440 €	0,107
P3	1.460	15.460 €	240 €	0,094
P4	1.800	14.700 €	13.440 €	0,122
P5	3.453	17.980 €	12.380 €	0,192
P6	2.600	34.360 €	33.860 €	0,076
P7	2.600	17.880 €	14.140 €	0,145
P8	2.491	23.640 €	15.860 €	0,105
P9	2.595	26.020 €	17.800 €	0,100

*The cost "without usability" has been estimated by eliminating those activities that would not have been performed with a SE model and adding a percentage to the coding-hours taken from the studies as they appear in [24].

6. Conclusions

This experimental proposal explained in the article and summarized in the previous table has given a collection of conclusions. Next list are the most important:

– The UE is only an indicative value of the performance of a series of activities oriented to the acquisition of usability that, if not compared with the ratio can lead to erroneous conclusions.

For example the projects P6 and P7 have the same UE while the ratio of P6 is half that of P7, which is due to the equivalence of the evaluation activities even though the complexity of both projects is very different.

---

[15] All the cases are detailed in [10].

- The projects with a low ratio correspond to those that have more hours of coding or, as may be, greater complexity. Which is due to the fact that there is no directly proportional relation between the complexity of the project and its inverted UE. Consequently, it is those projects in which the repercussions of the investment made in effort is less.
- The completeness parameter is highly determining; if it is not applied correctly, it may distort many of the results obtained.
- As a result of this study we have been able to determine a minimum number of iterations in the process model with perfectly defined activities that define a minimum UE. Although this does not guarantee the total usability of the system, it permits the affirmation that if this value is not arrived at, the usability of the system remains in the hands of the particular inspiration of the development team. Which is not fruit of the application of a methodological engineering process.
  This minimum UE is a value included in the range [1200, 1600] although the values between [2200, 2500] are those that better harness the experience of the user and contribute to optimise the usability of the system.
- The data in the table reveals that the UE of some projects is very high while its cost without usability is very low. This can make one think that for this type of project it is not worth it to invest even the minimum UE. However, the studies related to Return Of Investment [24] show that the investment in usability is always justified and rewarded.
- On the contrary to what we could expect, taking the UE as a parameter to compare two different projects produces less information than we thought. We would only be able to indicate that the development team had put more or less emphasis on trying to achieve the usability of one system in respect of another.
- The UE value is not equivalent to the money invested in the usability of the system. This is due to the fact that the methodology followed to achieve this value counts the performance of the activities and not the cost of performing them. The important thing is that the activities are carried out well, as their cost can vary a lot depending on parameters such as the aptitude or experience of the evaluator.

7. References

1. Babich, W. (1986). Software Configuration Management. Addison-Wesley.

2. Bevan, N.; Macleod, M. (1994). Usability measurement in context. National Physical Laboratory, Teddington, Middlesex, UK. Behaviour and Information Technology, 13, 132-145.
3. Bevan, N. (1995). Measuring Usability as Quality of Use. Software Quality Journal, 4, 115-150.
4. Beyer, H.; Holtzblatt, K. (1998). Contextual Design. Defining Customer-Centered Systems. Morgan Kaufmann.
5. Brink, T.; Gergle, D.; Wood, S.D. (2002). Design web sites that work: Usability for the Web. Morgan-Kaufmann.
6. Chin, J.P.; Diehl, V.A.; Norman, K. (1987). Development of an instrument measuring user satisfaction of the human-computer interface. Proc. ACM CHI'88, pp. 213-218.
7. Gaffney, G. (1999). Usability Techniques series: Participatory design workshops. Information & Design.
8. Gerrit, C. van der Veer; Lenting, B.F.; Bergevoet, B.A.J. (1996). GTA:Groupware Task Analysis - Modeling Complexity Acta Psychologica. 91, pp. 297-322.
9. Good, M.; Spine, T.M.; Whiteside, J.; George, P. (1986). User-derived impact analysis as a tool for usability engineering. Proceedings of Human Factors in Computing Systems. CHI'86. NY: ACM
10. Granollers, T. (2004). MPIu+a. Una metodología que integra la Ingeniería del Software, la Interacción Persona-Ordenador y la Accesibilidad en el contexto de equipos de desarrollo multidisciplinares. Doctoral PhD.
11. Granollers, T. (2003). User Centred Design Process Model. Integration of Usability Engineering and Software Engineering. Proc. INTERACT 2003 (Doctoral Consortium), Zurich.
12. Granollers, T.; Lorés, J. Perdrix F. (2003). Usability Engineering Process Model. Integration with Software Engineering. Proc.HCI Intl. 2003. (Greece).
13. Granollers, T.; Lorés, J.; Solà, J., Rubió, X. (2003). Developing a Ubiquitous reception-hall using the User-Centred design Usability Engineering Process Model. Proceedings of HCI International 2003. Crete (Greece).
14. Grudin, J. (1991). Interactive systems: Bridging the gaps between developers and users. Computer, vol. 24 n.4, 59-69.
15. Hammontree, M.; Hendrickson, J. J.; Hensley, B. W. (1992). Integrated data capture and analysis tools for research and testing on graphical user interfaces. CHI'92, ACM Press, pág. 431-432.
16. International Standard (1998). ISO 9241-11:1998. Ergonomic requirements for office work with visual display terminals (VDTs)- P11: Guidance on usability.
17. International Standard (1999). ISO 13407. Human-centred design processes for interactive systems.
18. International Standard (2001). ISO/IEC 9126-1. Software engineering — Product quality— Part 1: Quality model.
19. Kirakowski, J.; Porteous, M.; Corbett, M. (1992). How to use the software usability measurement inventory: the user's view of software quality.

Proceedings of UEropean Conference on Software Quality, November 1992, Madrid.

20. Macleod, M. (1994). Usability in Context: Improving Quality of Use. Proceedings of the Intl. Ergonomics Association 4th International Symposium on Human Factors in Organizational Design and Management, Stockholm.

21. Mayhew, D.J. (1999). The Usability Engineering Lifecycle: A practitioner's Handbook for User Interface Design. Morgan Kaufman.

22. MUMMS: Measuring the Usability of Multi-Media Systems, web page at: http://www.ucc.ie/hfrg/questionnaires/mumms/index.html.

23. Nielsen J. (2003). PR on Websites: Increasing Usability. March, 2003 Jakob Nielsen's Alertbox.

24. Nielsen, J.; Gilutz, S. (2003) Usability Return on Investment. Nielsen Norman Group Report.

25. Nielsen, J. (1993). Usability Engineering. Academic Press Professional.

26. Nielsen, J.; Mack, R.L. (1994). Usability Inspection Methods. JWiley & Sons.

27. QUIS: Questionnaire for User Interface Satisfaction. Human Computer Interaction Lab, University of Maryland.

28. Rosson, M.B.; Carroll, J.M. (2002). Usability Engineering: scenario-based developement of HCI. Morgan Kaufmann.

29. Shneiderman, B. (1992). Designing the user interface: Strategies for effective human-computer interaction. 2nd ed, Reading, MA: Addison-Wesley.

30. SUMI: Software Usability Measurement Inventory.

31. WAMMI: Web site Analysis and MeasureMent Inventory.

32. Zülch, G.; Stowasser, S. (2000). Usability Evaluation of User Interfaces with the Computer-aided Evaluation Tool PROKUS. MMI-Interaktiv, Nr. 3, Juni/00,ISSN1439-78

Groupware Task Analysis and Distributed Cognition: Task Modeling In a Case of Multiple Users and Multiple Organizations

Mari Carmen Puerta Melguizo*, Cristina Chisalita[§] &

Gerrit C. van der Veer[§]

Institute of Information and Computing Sciences. University of Utrecht
(The Netherlands).

[§]Section Human-Computer Interaction, Multimedia and Culture.
Department of Information Management and Software Engineering
(IMSE).Vrije Universiteit, Amsterdam (The Netherlands).

Introduction

"Complex interactive systems" are information systems used by different types of users for a variety of tasks and in different situations. Work activities in these cases usually include communication and co-ordination between people and actions of several persons on shared objects and in shared workplaces.

In many cases the (re)design of these type of systems is triggered by an existing task situation. Either the current way of performing tasks is not considered optimal, or the availability of new technology is expected to allow improvement over current methods. A systematic analysis of the current situation reveals problems, conflicts and inconsistencies that occur while performing the tasks. Task analysis may help to formulate design requirements, and at the same time it may later on allow the evaluation of the design. In general, analyzing the current situation means to analyze the "context of use" or, in other words, the world in which the system functions. According to the ISO 9241-11 standards [7] this means to analyze the users, the tasks, the equipment (hardware, software, and materials) and the environment. In the case of complex systems, aspects such as social, historical and cultural context of the human activity are of especial relevance and need to be analyzed as well.

R. Navarro-Prieto and J. L. Vidal (eds.), HCI Related Papers of Interacción 2004, 119 -135.
© 2006 Springer. Printed in the Netherlands.

We are interested in knowing how such complex situations can be best described and analyzed. A possible point of departure is represented by studies focused on the description of simpler situations (e.g. the cooperative work that takes place in settings such as operators' rooms). Such studies suggest that exploring and comparing different frameworks brings important conclusions about the complementary information each framework can bring [2]. Therefore, we decided to use two different frameworks: GroupWare Task Analysis (GTA) and Distributed Cognition (DC) to analyze a case study of a complex situation. In the next sections we will explain briefly both frameworks and show the descriptions we obtained applying both approaches in the analysis of a highly complex system.

GTA: GroupWare Task Analysis

GTA is a broad task-analysis conceptual framework that is based on the integration of several approaches including individual oriented method from Human-Computer Interaction and group oriented methods from Computer Supported Cooperative Work [12, 13, 14, 15]. GTA describes the task world focusing on three different viewpoints:

1. Agents and roles. Specifying the active entities in the task world including users and stakeholders, systems and organizations. The roles and the organization of work (i.e. structure of agents and roles) need to be specified as well. Agents can be characterized on relevant characteristics such us a) psychological characteristics like cognitive styles or spatial ability [12], and b) task related characteristics like expertise or knowledge of information technology.
2. Work. Specifying the decomposition of tasks, the goals, the events that trigger the tasks, and the different strategies used to perform them.
3. Situation. Specifying the objects used in the task world as well as their structure, the history of past relevant events, and the whole social and physical work environment. Objects may be physical or conceptual (non-material: like messages, gestures, passwords, stories, or signatures).

Modeling the task knowledge is not an easy activity. There are several problems that may arise in such situation (e.g. the amount of data can be overwhelming and difficult to organize). In order to overcome these problems the GTA framework describes a task world ontology that specifies the relationships between the concepts on which the task world is modelled (see figure 1). Based on this ontology a supporting tool to model task knowledge was also developed: EUTERPE [1, 15].

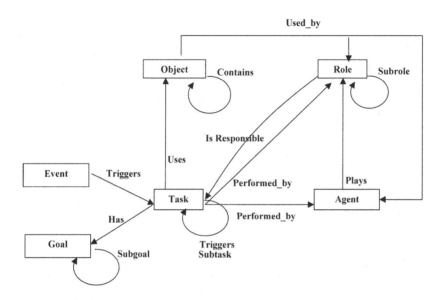

Fig. 1. The task world ontology

DISTRIBUTED COGNITION

Distributed Cognition (DC) is a framework that describes and explains group cognition with the goal of understanding how collaborative work is coordinated. DC takes as unit of analysis the *socio-technical system* (Hutchins [5] calls it the *cognitive system*) and investigates the shared construction of knowledge. The basic assumption is that the socio-technical system consists of multiple individuals as well as the artifacts they work with, and the cognition is distributed between them. According to this approach, cognition is the process of coordinating the distributed internal representation (i.e. in the minds of people collaborating together) and the external representations (i.e. information artifacts). DC studies the way in which the information and the knowledge is transmitted, transferred and transformed through the different representations during system's activities. DC has been applied as a framework to study the cooperative activity in different settings [3, 4, 5, 6, 9, 10].

To analyze the distribution and communication of knowledge, the different interactions that take place within the socio-technical systems are described [8] (see figure 2):

1. Social Distribution: interaction among people.
2. Technological Distribution: interaction among people and artifacts.
3. Interaction among people, artifacts and work environment.

The elements involved within the socio-technical system (individuals and artifacts) hold two types of knowledge [11].

- *Distributed or different knowledge* about the task/activity. Each individual has specific knowledge which represents a part of the knowledge needed in order to perform the task/activity.
- *Shared knowledge* about the task/activity. Each individual shares a part of the knowledge necessary to perform the task. This shared or common knowledge allows the performance of the task to be monitored by different individuals. For example, in the case of individual failure, another member of the system can perform the task and in this way, the system does not need to interrupt its activity.

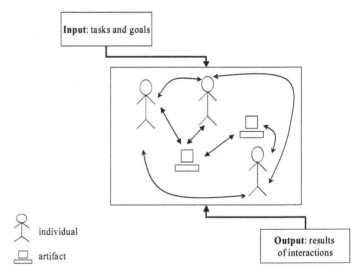

Fig. 2. The socio-technical system

The Task Analysis of a Highly Complex System

The case study that we describe in this paper shows our experience collaborating with a company that produces high-tech machines. The machines are sold to different industries in several countries of Europe, America and Asia. The machines produce very fragile and expensive products that are complex and difficult to use. As a consequence, many errors and problems occur while using the machines. In order to help its customers, the design company offers assistance services provided by different types of engineers. However, users complain frequently, and especially, about the user interface that is difficult to understand and use. Following these complains the company decided to take action and to find new solutions.

We were invited to collaborate with the User Interface Design team of the company. The goals of the design project were: a) to integrate different versions of the same interface (differences were related with the "age" of the systems and the fact that newer versions contain more functions than the first ones), b) to support all types of users who are using the interface and, c) to design and integrate in the interface a consistent "diagnostic toolkit". The toolkit should be able to identify the cause of problems while using the machines and provide a solution. The last aspect is the main focus of this paper.

The first step in the project was to analyze the context of use. We used several techniques to do that: interviews, "focus-group" sessions (in which people from different departments of the manufactory were invited to identify and define the types of users that use the system), documents of the company (including a previous document on task analysis), etc. The task analysis proved to be a very complex process by itself because the tasks and the technology to consider are highly specialized. Because we cannot reveal the identification of the company we will not show a detailed task analysis.

Using GTA: Multiple Users

Following GTA we started to analyze and model by defining the *agents*, the *work* and the *situation*.

Actors, Roles and Tasks

Many different types of users work with the system including end-users (Operators that are the employees of the customer company) and several types of expert's engineers. In total more than 40 different actors were defined (e.g. field application engineers, system packers, etc.). We will not describe all of them but focus on the types of users directly involved in the diagnostic and solution of problems with the systems. We identified the following types of users (see table 1):

- *Operators*: Local operators of the machines or end-users.
- *E1*: First line engineers or local engineers.
- *E2*: Second line engineers.
- *E3*: Third line engineers. This line of engineers consists of several subtypes as a function of their expertise. The users can be characterized according to different variables:

- *Education level*. Operators work directly with the machine and do not require high-level education. The rest of the users are engineers.
- *Expertise*. Operators, E1 and E2 engineers have general knowledge about the system. The level of knowledge increases from Operators to E1 and E2 engineers. E3 engineers have specialized knowledge about the different components of the machines. According to the component in which they are specialized several types of E3 engineers can be defined.
- *Degree of access to specific diagnostic tools, and permission to manipulate things in the system*. As we will see, tools that should be used only by engineers are easily accessible by Operators. Other tools are only accessible in the company that designs the machines.
- *Geographical situation of the users*: inside the Design Company (located in The Netherlands) or at the customer site (see fig. 4). In the Design Company there are E2 and E3 engineers. The users outside the company can be found in different countries of Europe, Asia and USA. Users at customer sites are the Operators and E1 engineers. In Asia and USA there are E2 engineers as well.

The roles we found are:

- *Diagnosing and solving problems*. Whenever a problem with the machine occurs the tasks include detecting the cause of the problem and try to solve it. As we will see, all of the roles considered here will assume this role in different situations.

- *Design, implementation and evaluation of the machine.* E2 and E3 engineers have this role. Different subtypes of E3 engineers are involved in the design of different subsystems. E2 engineers work in the design of the machine as a whole.
- *Installation and maintenance of the machine* in the customer's place by E1.
- *Production* with the machine by local Operators.

Table 1. The users and their associated roles

User	Education	Expertise	Geographical situation	Role
Operator	medium	Whole system	Outside	Production Problem solving
E1:1^{rst} line engineer	university	Whole system	Outside	Maintenance Problem solving
E2:2nd line engineer	University	Whole system	Outside Company	Design Problem solving
E3:3rd line engineer	University	Component	Company	Design Problem solving

Objects in the Current Situation

There are several classes of objects that need to be studied; mainly objects in the user interface and other objects that are located in the Design Company. We will focus in the tools that relate to diagnostic and error-recovery tasks.

The Views in the User Interface

The user's interface contains several views (or windows) with tools to support different tasks. For example, a window offers the possibility to show the values of several variables that can be manipulated to change the status of the machine.

One problem is that the different views are not designed in a consistent way. For example, some windows allow to access to linked information by "clicking" buttons that are in the left side of the screen, others show menus on the top part of the screen, and others require to type commands. As said before, the re-design of the interface aims to make the design of the windows more consistent.

Another related problem is that the Operators should only use the window that is meant for production with the system (so-called Operator's window). The interface however shows and allows access to all of the windows. We think this is not only unnecessary but also dangerous because it allows operators access to tools that, if they are not used properly, can damage the production with the machines.

Tools to Diagnose and Solve Problems

The current tools are all fragmented and some of them are implemented in the User Interface whereas others not.

In the User Interface:

- *Warning and error messages.* The messages normally specify the problem and how to solve it. The problem is that there are not very many of them.
- *Start up software* provides information about the status of each component of the system at the moment of starting up the machine. This information can help to identify the component responsible of the problem. It should only be used by E1 engineers but Operators use it as well (although it is not in the Operator's window). Another problem is that even E1 engineers have difficulties understanding the information provided by this software.
- *Error logging software* writes all of the errors that occur in the different components of the machine while working with it. The main problem is that too much information about each component is provided and the information is not easy to understand. Another problem is that the resulted file is overwritten every 20.000 lines so if the cause of the problem occurs early in the production process, it is very difficult to detect. Although only E2 and E3 engineers should use it, to win time E1 engineers work frequently with it and some customers even pay software engineers to interpret the information correctly.
- *A tool to detect defects in the product* is installed in the interface and can be used by Operators. The problem is that the possible defects are not easy to see directly and the machine does not inform the user about what or where is the defect located. Consequently, the operators have to look actively for any possible defects. The software does not inform about the cause of the defect in the production neither.

In the company:

- *Historical documents*, manuals and emails showing how a specific problem was solved before, but these are incomplete and badly organized.
- *Trace tools* that simulate, reproduce and trace problems are used in the company while working with the prototypes of the machines. They should only be accessed by E3 engineers because they do not offer warning messages and using them inadequately can damage the machines.

Identifying Problems with GTA

Our task analysis showed that the number of breakdowns and problems related with the use of the machines is high and, consequently the machines have stop frequently. Even though there are some tools that help to solve problems, in general they are limited, fragmented, and difficult to use and understand. Furthermore, currently there are not clear ways to identify the causes, nor clear procedures to solve most of the problems. As a result most of the problems are solved by trial and error. For example, designers involved in the implementation of the machine tend to open the machines to look for the cause of the problem. This solution slows down the design process because it takes around 10 hours to make the machines functional again.

One of the most serious problems we found is related to the access of the tools used to solve problems. The access is not always as established in the norms. As a result users are often tempted to apply procedures they are not supposed to perform and are not trained for. On the other hand, sometimes a procedure cannot be performed because the object cannot be accessed in a situation where it would allow a knowledgeable actor to perform the appropriate task.

Emphasizing Tasks and Users

GTA emphasized the analysis of the tasks and the types of users related to them. The information obtained however, did not seem enough to understand the whole situation and identify all of the aspects needed for the redesign of the system. One of the aspects most difficult to represent with GTA was the differences due to geographical distribution and the transfer of information between different types of users. Consequently, to improve our analysis, we decided to use the DC framework to describe the situation emphasizing these aspects.

Using DC: Multiple Complex Organizations

Apart from analyzing the users and the current tool used to solve problems, we needed to analyze the relationships between different types of users, and between users and tools. Furthermore, we found out that in this complex situation different socio-technical systems needed to be considered:

1. *"Local"* socio-technical systems defined when only one company (Customer Company or Design Company) is involved in the solution of a problem with the machines.
2. *"Distributed"* socio-technical systems when interactions between customer's companies and the design company are needed.

The socio-technical system to be considered depends on the complexity of the problem with the machine (input) and the knowledge resources. Briefly, if the problem was too difficult and could not be solved within a "local" socio-technical system (e.g. a Customer Company), the problem was transferred and the original "local" socio-technical system became a "distributed" one (see below section *"Transmission of Knowledge"*). As explained below, an extra difficulty we had to consider in the analysis was the fact that the distribution of knowledge between the socio-technical systems was different in different continents.

Distributed and Shared Knowledge

The knowledge needed to diagnose and solve problems is mostly distributed among types of users and artifacts. In other words, different types of users have different knowledge about how to solve problems. The same can be said about the current tools used to diagnose and solve the problems (see section *"Tools to Diagnose and Solve Problems"*). The distribution of knowledge between users depends on:

- *Educational level*: Operators versus Engineers.
- *Expertise*: the whole system versus components.
- The *access to tools and permission to manipulate the system* is also distributed. For example, trace tools can only be accessed by engineers working in the Design Company.

However, part of the knowledge is shared among users:

- E1 engineers share the knowledge of the Operators about diagnosing a problem. The difference is that E1 engineers have deeper understanding about the situation and have also specific knowledge related to maintenance issues.

• E2 engineers have even a deeper knowledge about the machines and how to identify and solve problems with the machines.

• The different types of E3 engineers have some knowledge about the whole systems but they are highly expert in specific components of the machine.

Transmission of Knowledge

The Norms

When the manufactured products have any defect, the Operators can use the software in the interface to detect defects. In general, when the Operators are unable to solve a problem, they should contact E1 engineers. As explained above, E1 engineers have more general knowledge about the system than the Operators and have permission to access tools in the interface that are designed to solve some of the problems. If E1 engineers cannot solve a problem, they are supposed to contact with E2 or E3 engineers. The choice of calling E2 or E3 engineers depends if E1 engineers localized the component of the system with problems or not (see figure 3).

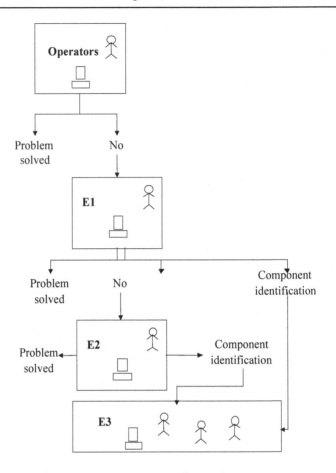

Fig. 3. The transmission of knowledge according to the norms

The Real Practice

The Design Company sets policies on the use of the machine. The policies state the rules to access different tools in the machine and establishes what tasks should be performed for each type of users. The reality however is that customers do not always follow the rules. For example, when the machine stops the Operators should immediately contact E1 engineers. But to save time, they frequently access the "start up software" and try to identify the damaged component. If they are not able to understand the information provided by this software, the Operators end up replacing some components of the machine trying to find the solution by trial and error. The main problems related to access to knowledge are:

- Start-up software: used by Operators when only E1 should use it.
- Error login software: only for E2 and E3 engineers but Operators and E1 engineers use it. Some Customer Companies even pay extra software engineers to understand error logging software.
- Trace tools: should only be used by E3 engineers but E2 engineers use them.

The Format of Knowledge Transmission

The knowledge is mostly transmitted through verbal language in different forms like, telephone calls, emails, reports, error log and sometimes face-to-face interactions etc.

Factors Affecting the Transmission of Knowledge

When considering the companies in different continents we found out relevant differences that affected the transmission of information. The main factors where: differences in the work organization and differences in the way information is transmitted between users and between users and artifacts.

Work Organization

The work organization in different continents affects the transmission of knowledge (see figure 4):

1. In USA Operators and E1 engineers are in the same organization. E2 engineers are located in USA so they do not have to contact E2 from the Design Company.
2. In Asia E1 and E2 are in the same organization and close to the customers companies.
3. In Europe E1 and Operators are in the same organization. E1 and E2 are in the design company.

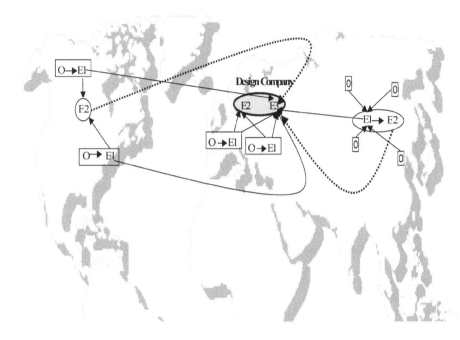

Fig. 4. Transmission of information in different continents

Transmission of Knowledge in Different Socio-Technical Systems

The fact that different roles can belong to different countries was an extra source of problems. To transfer the problem means to communicate with people from other cultures (national as well as professional). In this respect the language proved to be a serious problem. The problems are not only due to the fact that the interface, the manuals and the tools to solve problems are in English. The cross-cultural communication is in English as well and this is a problem especially for Operators and Engineers in Europe and Asia. For example, many complains come from Asia where Operators and Engineers have problems with English, making the use of the systems, including reading the manuals and the communication, more difficult.

The different types of users represent in fact different professional cultures. This situation brings an extra problem specially related to the use of manuals. The manuals for using the machine are written by the E3 engineers who, as any professional culture, have developed a special language that is difficult to be understood by other categories of users.

Conclusions

Modelling task knowledge is not an easy activity, especially when it is necessary to describe and analyze a complex situation. This paper shows how we applied two different frameworks, GTA and DC, to understand and model task knowledge of a very complex interactive system where different types of users, different organizations and cultures needed to be considered. GTA and DC examine the situation from different points of views emphasizing different aspects of the task situation and the information obtained is complementary and necessary when analyzing extremely complex systems.

As a conceptual framework for task analysis, GTA helped us to analyze the situation focusing in the identification of multiple users and the associated roles. The ontology specified by GTA, and the use of EUTERPE to model the task knowledge, proved to be a great help in order to understand clearly the relationships between types of users and roles. Even though the GTA framework was a valuable basis for a first approach to the task situation, the information obtained did not seem enough to understand the whole situation and identify all of the aspects needed for the redesign of the system. Notions such as transmission of knowledge, cultural differences, both regional and professional, needed to be taken into account.

Usually DC has been used to describe rather "simple" settings such as cockpit or software teams [e.g. 3, 6]. In this paper we extend the use of DC to a much larger setting that comprises multiple organizations located in different geographical regions. DC allowed us to understand that, when considering the way information is transmitted and transferred, we were studying a case of multiple organizations. Furthermore, DC offered a clearer framework to analyze what knowledge was shared among users and artifacts, and what aspects were distributed.

Concluding, especially in the case of complex task situations, several points of view need to be considered in order to analyze, describe, and model the task world.

References

1. Chisalita, C., Puerta Melguizo, M.C. & van der Veer, G.C. (2002). Designing Complex systems in Industrial Reality: A study of the DUTCH approach. In I. Aedo, P. Díaz, & Fernández, C. (Eds.). *Interacción 2002: III Congreso Interaccion Persona-Ordenador.* ISBN: 84-607-4501-5.

2. Decortis, F., Noirfalise, S. & Saudelli, B. (2000). Activity theory, cognitive ergonomics and distributed cognition: three views of a transport company. *International Journal of Human-Computer Studies,* vol. 53, issue 1, pp. 5-35.

3. Flor, N.V. & Hutchins, E. (1992). Analyzing Distributed Cognition in Software Teams: A Case Study of Collaborative Programming During Adaptve Software maintenance. In Koenemann-Belliveau, Moher & Robertson (Eds.) Empirical Studies of Programmers: Fourth Workshop, Norwood, NJ: Ablex.

4. Hutchins, E. (1990). The technology of the Team Navigation. In Galegher, Kraut & Edigo (Eds.) Intellectual Teamwork, NJ:LEA.

5. Hutchins, E. (1995). Cognition in the Wild. Massachusetts. MIT Press.

6. Hutchins, E. (1995). How a cockpit remembers its speed. *Cognitive Science,* 2, pp. 14-39.

7. ISO 9241-11 (1998). Ergonomic Requirements for Office Work With visual display terminals (VDT)s – Part 11 guidance on usability.

8. Preece, J., Rogers, Y. & Sharp, H. (2002). Interaction Design, beyond human computer interaction. Wiley & Sons, Inc.

9. Rogers, Y. (1992). Ghosts in the Network: Distributed Troubleshooting in a Shared Working Environment. In Turner & Kraut (Eds.) *Proceedings of the Conference on Computer Supported Cooperative Work,* pp. 346-355, ACM: NY.

10. Rogers, Y (1993). Coordinating computer-mediating work. *Computer Supported Cooperative Work,* 1, pp. 295-315.

11. Rogers, Y. & Ellis, J. (1994). Distributed cognition: An alternative framework for analyzing and explaining collaborative working. *Journal of Information Technology, 9,* 119-128.

12. Van der Veer, G.C. (1990) *Human-Computer Interaction: Learning, Individual Differences, and Design Recommendations,* Ph.D. Dissertation Vrije Universiteit, Amsterdam.

13. Van der Veer, G.C., Van Welie, M. & Chisalita, C. (2002). Introduction to groupware task analysis. In: C. Pribeanu & J. Vanderdonckt (Eds.). *Task Models and diagrams for user interface design.* TAMODIA'2002. INFOREC Printing House, 32-39.

14. Van der Veer, G.C. & Van Welie, M. (2000). Task based GroupWare design: Putting theory into practice. In: *Proceedings of DIS 2000,* New York, United States.

15. Van Welie, M. (2000). Task-Based User Interface Design. SIKS Dissertation Series 2001-6. Vrije Universiteit, Amsterdam. Nl.

Integration of Organisational Patterns into a Group-Centred Methodology

José Luis Isla Montes[1], Francisco Luis Gutiérrez Vela[2], José Luis Garrido Bullejos[2], M. Visitación Hurtado Torres[2], Miguel J. Hornos Barranco[2]

[1] Dpt. de Lenguajes y Sistemas Informáticos, E.S. Ingeniería, University of Cádiz, Spain joseluis.isla@uca.es

[2]Dpt. Lenguajes y Sistemas Informáticos, E.T.S. Ingeniería Informática, University of Granada, Spain {fgutierr,jgarrido,mhurtado,mhornos}@ugr.es

1 Introduction

The usage of user modelling techniques during development phases allows us to obtain tasks which are user's responsibility, and therefore to guide and ease the analysis and design of the software elements to support these tasks. However, more complex systems (e.g. collaborative learning, decision support systems, virtual enterprises, etc.) demand group centred strategies. In these systems the use of new technologies allow users and groups to engage in common tasks. Consequently, it is necessary to develop techniques, methods and platforms to carry out communication, coordination and collaboration between groups.

When a group of people are involved in common tasks, each member (or team) has a concrete responsibility and a set of relationships and dependencies between members. This kind of system has an internal organisational structure controlled by dependences between people and task performed by them. This structure may change through time for several reasons (responsibilities are modified, dependencies are created or overridden, new goals, etc.), so therefore the system is evolving continuously. Additional requirements in relation to interactions between participants (by using computer-based systems as a medium) must therefore be taken into account [1].

R. Navarro-Prieto and J. L. Vidal (eds.), HCI Related Papers of Interacción 2004, 137-146.

Classical Software Engineering methodologies tend to model information systems with a clear separation between, on one hand, users and the activities that they perform using the system and, on the other hand, the social context in which the users are involved. Although in most cases this is a good approach, complex systems (such as collaborative systems) demand an integrated study of both aspects. The separation fails when we need to model aspects such as user responsibilities on the social context or the relationships and dependencies occurring among group members.

We propose to model a complex system as a social structure [2], which evolves dynamically through time, where each member is responsible for carrying out user's tasks for common (organisational) goals. The inclusion of a social structure (organisational structure and a set of social dependencies between users) allows us to analyse more precisely the responsibilities to be assigned to each member during the life of the system.

Different contributions related to modelling social structures have been proposed, most of them have been used for the representation of MAS (Multi-Agent Systems) [3]. In general, these models are focused on the static architecture of the system, and consider agents as structural elements within a complex organisation. Nonetheless, it is also very important for the specification of social organisations in information systems to reflect the dynamic nature of the organisation as well as its architecture.

This work has similarities with others presented by Kolp et al. [4] using the i* methodology proposed by Yu [5]. The motivation of these other works is the inclusion of classical organisational patterns to guide requirement analysis based on the organisational structure of the system. The greatest shortcoming of this approximation is that the representation of the system is only based on one level of abstraction, mixing organisational elements (groups, roles, etc.) with functional elements (activities, objectives, resources used, etc.). Moreover, it fails to represent the dynamism of an organisation.

In the following section we present a conceptual model to define an organisational structure and its relationships. Next, we introduce the use of AMENITIES methodology to model organisations. Afterwards, in section 3, we show how AMENITIES improves the description of organisational patterns based on common organisational structures. Later, in section 4, we describe the Joint Venture organizational pattern, including an application example, by means of a uniform template. Finally, we present the conclusions and future research.

2 Conceptual Model of Organisation

Human-Computer Interaction methods for user modelling can be enriched with descriptions of the users' social organisation. In order to model properly an organisation it is necessary to consider static and dynamic aspects. For example, if we focus on identifying the structure of an organisation, their dependencies, the number of people involved in each task or what users' categories have been established, we are concentrating on structural (static) aspects of the system. However, if we focus, for example, on how members become part of the organisation or change their responsibilities over time, laws imposed by social aspects, reaction to certain events, etc., we are reflecting the dynamic properties of the organisation.

Figure 1 shows a conceptual model (UML class diagram) describing an general organisation. This figure reflects the most important elements that appear in any organisation and it is similar to those which have been traditionally used in collaborative systems modelling [6,7].

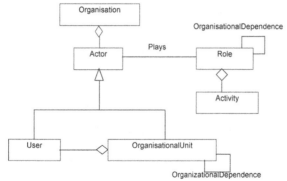

Figure 1 A conceptual model to define an organisation

Figure 1 shows an organisation mainly composed of actors. The *actor* concept includes individual users of the system, organisations and suborganisations (group, team, department, ...).

We introduce two kinds of suborganisations: *static suborganisations*, which describe the general structure of the organisation, and *dynamic suborganisations*, which model groups of users created for a specific task.

At any time, an actor plays a *role* in the system. Playing a role implies the possibility or capability to perform *activities* associated with such a role.

Finally, several relationships between roles (called organisational dependences) can appear. With these assignments we model associations of different natures: an actor can change from one role to another, the inclusion of one suborganisation in another, etc. These relationships model associations describing constraints on the organisational system structure.

In order to model all these aspects of a system we use AMENITIES [8,9] (A MEthodology for aNalysis and desIgn of cooperaTIve systEms). A methodology developed in our research group, based on behaviour and task models used for the analysis, design and development of cooperative systems.

AMENITIES provides different views of the system. One of them, the organisational view, allows us to describe the relevant concepts we have just mentioned. The organisational view uses an extension of UML, called COMO-UML, which uses state diagrams to represent the actors' organisation according to the different roles they could carry out in the system, and their evolution through the constraints imposed by the organisation.

Next we will show how we can model and reuse common organisational structures (organisational patterns) within the AMENITIES methodology.

3 Modelling Organisational Patterns in AMENITIES

From their introduction in the mid 90s in Software Engineering [10,11], patterns have become a valuable instrument for the description and reuse of the empiric knowledge used throughout the different phases which make up the software life cycle. Nonetheless, most effort has focused on the use of patterns during the software design phase.

We consider that the decisions taken during the early stages of requirement analysis and conceptual modelling of the system have a decisive influence on the final product and the remaining stages of its life cycle. The use of patterns (called analysis or conceptual patterns [12]) in these initial stages has a crucial importance. Their application improves decision-making and the specification is faster, more comprehensible and easier to maintain. Consequently, the modelling of the organisation structure and the users' behaviour can benefit from the systematic use of specific conceptual patterns within a development methodology.

Some studies carried out on modelling of organisations [13,14] have proposed general user structures which often govern these complex systems. For example, organisation styles such as *structure-in-5, joint venture, vertical integration, pyramid*, etc. These structures are suitable to model the whole organisation focusing on the distribution of their members (organisational units or individuals) in order to perform common tasks. Nevertheless other social structures (of finer granularity) can often appear within organisations (sub-organisations). The *broker, mediator, embassy*, etc. structures are some examples of these categories.

Our goal is to encapsulate these organisational structures in the form of organisational patterns with the aim of reusing them in different situations and facilitating the specification and comprehension of the organisational context of a system. In order to model these patterns we will use the COMO-UML notation [8]. Its main elements to model patterns are shown in Table 1.

Table 1 COMO-UML notation: Elements used to model Organisational Patterns

Symbol	Semantic
role R Multiplicity	*Role.-* R is a role that a certain number of actors, limited by *multiplicity*, can play at a given moment in an organisation. It is a state belonging to a state machine which represents the dynamism of an organisation.
role Initial ●———→ role Final	*Role Additive Transition.-* An actor who is playing an "initial" role may also carry out the "final" role. If this transition is labelled with a constraint (law or capability), this must be fulfilled.
role Initial ———→ role Final	*Role Change Transition.-* An actor who is playing an "initial" role abandons it to play a "final" role. If this transition is labelled with a constraint (law or capability), this must be fulfilled.
	Decision Box.- This element determines, through restrictions labelling its outgoing transitions, the different possibilities with respect to the roles to be played. When various possibilities exist, the system or the actor is responsible for choosing one of the possible alternatives.
role R	*Notable Role.-* It shows up an essential role for the pattern, ignoring part of the diagram. The transitions and intermediate states that culminate in the role are not presented.
Parameter1 ... ParameterN <<Pattern>> PatternName	*External view.-* It allows us to represent an instance of "PatternName" within a model. Its parameters specify which roles (or other elements) of the pattern will be bound to specific elements of its instances.

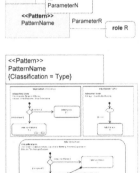

Binding.- The actors who carry out the *R* role in a certain system play the *ParameterR* role in the context of the organisational structure of the pattern *PatternName*.

Pattern definition.- The models that represent the pattern are defined inside a UML-package indicating the pattern name and the classification according to a previously established taxonomy.

4 A Case Study: The Joint Venture Pattern

The Joint Venture Pattern represents the strategic alliance which is established between two or more partners, usually companies specialised in specific tasks, and reflects the engagement of these organisations to achieve a common goal, obtaining collective advantages (partial investment, reduced maintenance costs, greater profitability, shared resources, etc.).

Next, we use a structured template in order to show the important aspects of a pattern and facilitate their use, comparison and learning. In the *Solution* section we can observe how it is possible to model this pattern using AMENITIES. Moreover, the *Example* section shows an illustration of its application.

- **Name:**
Joint Venture
- **Problem:**
It describes an organisation in which each actor (partner) is specialised in a task for a common goal. Each partner shares its resources and capabilities to achieve large-scale goals. There is an administrative unit which manages the strategy of the alliance and coordinates the partners.
- **Context:**
  - The common goal can be broken down into several subobjectives.
  - Each partner is responsible for some of these subobjectives.
  - There is an actor who is the manager (administrator) of the coalition (the outside view).
  - There is an actor who is responsible for coordination and communication between the partners (the inside view).

- **Participants:**
  - *Partner* (role)
    - He performs the necessary tasks to achieve any of the assigned subobjectives (*ObtainSubobjective* task).
    - He shares his resources with other partners (*ShareResource* task).
  - *Administrator* (role)
    - He is responsible for the external relationships of the coalition (*RepresentAlliance* task).
  - Administrator::Director (role)
    - He chooses the best strategy for the coalition (*TakeStrategicDecision* task).
  - Administrator::Coordinator (role)
    - He is responsible for scheduling meetings for alliance partners (*SummonPartners* task).
    - He performs coordination meetings among partners (*CoordinationMeeting* task).
    - He decides coordination tasks (*PartnersCoordination* task).
  - Partner::Manager (role)
    - He is the member who must be present in those meetings where the coalition is requested (*CoordinationMeeting* task).

- **Solution:**

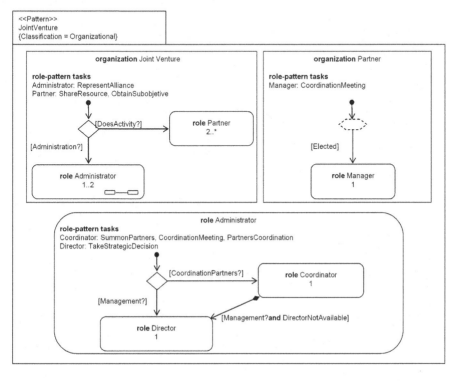

- **Explanation:**

When an actor has the necessary capability to carry out a task (e.g. manufacturing one of the pieces of an aeroplane), he will play the *Partner* role. It is important to observe the role multiplicity, indicating that it must have at least two partners in the coalition.

The *role-pattern task* section specifies the essential tasks that each actor should perform in the context of the pattern. A role may also perform other kinds of activities, but the essential tasks must be reflected here. The *Partner* role must carry out at least the *ShareResource* task (the partners must be able to share resources with each other) and the *ObtainSubobjective* task (each partner must accomplish a specific part of the organisation's final goal, for example, to manufacture some of the final product elements). Moreover, as is shown in the *Partner* organisation diagram, an actor who carries out the *Manager* role is an actor who has been elected by others actors of the organisation. The *Manager* is responsible for holding meetings with the *Coordinator* when it is necessary (*CoordinationMeeting* task). This is a common task for *Coordinator* and *Manager* roles.

When an actor achieves administration capability in the Join Venture, then he/she can act as *Administrator* (note that only one or two actors can take part in this role). In this situation, an actor must perform at least the *RepresentAlliance* task, assuming responsibility for the external relations of the alliance. If this actor can also achieve the capability of coordinating partners, then he plays the *Coordinator* role (only one actor takes part in this role) and therefore, he will have to meet the managers of the partner organisations when necessary (*SummonPartners* and *CoordinationMeeting* tasks) as well as performing coordination among partners (*PartnersCoordination* task).

In this organisation, an actor who has capabilities to manage the strategy of the alliance is responsible for the *Director* role, whose main function is to take strategic decisions for the alliance (*TakeStrategicDecision* task).

In the above diagram we also describe, using an additive transition, the situation in which the actor plays the *Coordinator* role as well as the *Director* role. This situation happens when the *Coordinator* has management capability and the *Director* is not available (i.e. the *Coordinator* acts as a substitute of the *Director*).

- **Example:**

The organization of a cooperative classroom in which the students are divided into groups for the development of each component of a software application.

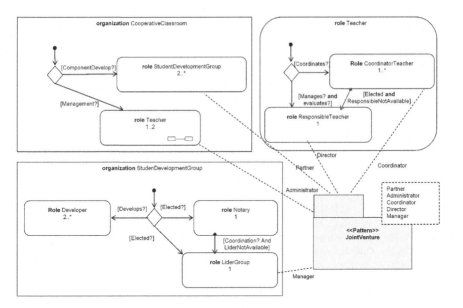

- **Related Patterns:**

Production Line pattern describes a sequential organisation of roles where the sub-objectives have an ordered achievement.

5 Conclusions and Future Work

We have presented the reuse of organisational patterns to model the social structure of a system with the AMENITIES methodology, in order to facilitate the creation, documentation and understanding of the models. Moreover, we have shown how this methodology is suitable to represent static as well as dynamic aspects of a social organisational structure.

The work presented in this paper is included into a broader work whose main goal is the specification and use of patterns within the AMENITIES methodology, which is specifically intended for the development of collaborative systems. In order to achieve this goal, we are extending the required notation to define patterns at a conceptual level (conceptual or analysis patterns) and identifying communication and coordination protocols, information management, etc.

This work can be also extending by creating a catalogue of organisational patterns, which could be used as a good starting point to model an information system.

References

1. Garrido, J.L., Gea, M., Rodríguez, M.L.: Requirements Engineering in Cooperative Systems. Requirements Engineering for Sociotechnical Systems., IDEA GROUP, Inc.USA (2005)
2. Bubenko J.A.: Next Generation Information Systems: an Organisational Perpective. Intl. Workshop on Development of Intelligenent Information Systems, Niagara-on-the-Lake, Canada, April 21-23 (1991)
3. Ferber J. and Gutknecht O.: A Meta-Model for the Analysis and Design of Organisation in MAS. Proc of Int. Conf. In Multi-Agent Systems, IEEE Computer Society (1998)
4. Kolp M., Giorgini P., Myloupoulos J.: Information systems development through Social Structures. In proceedings of the 14th international Conference on Software Engineering and Knowledge Engineering, Ishia, Italy, July 15-19, (2002)
5. Yu. E.: Modeling Strategic Relationships for Process Reengineering, PhD thesis, University of Toronto, Department of Computer Science, Canada (1995)
6. Guareis. C.R, Ferreira. F, van Sinderen. M: A conceptual model for the development of CSCW systems. ACM Transactions on Computer-Human Interaction, Vol. 7, No. 2, Junio 2000
7. Van Welie. M, van der Veer. G.C: An Ontology for Task World Models. In Design, Specification and Verification of Interactive System'98. Springer Computer Science (1998)
8. Garrido, J.L., Gea, M.: Modelling Dynamic Group Behaviours. In: Johnson, C. (ed.): Interactive System - Design Specification and Verification. LNCS 2220, Springer, 2001
9. Garrido, J.L., Gea, M., Gutierrez, F.L., Padilla, N.: Designing Cooperative Systems for Human Collaboration. In Dieng, R.; Giboin, A. (eds.), Designing Cooperative Systems: The Use Of Theories and Models, IOS press, Netherlands (2000)
10. Gamma, E., Helm, R. Johnson, R.; Vlissides, J.: Design Patterns: Elements of Reusable Object-Oriented Software. Reading, MA: Addison Wesley Professional Computing Series (1995)
11. Buschmann, F., Meunier, R., Rohnert, H., Sommerlad, P., Stal, M.: Pattern-Oriented Software Architecture: A System of Patterns. Chichester, UK: John Wiley and Sons Ltd (1996)
12. Fowler, M.: Analysis Patterns: Reusable Object Models. Booch, G., Jacobson, I. and Rumbaugh, J. (eds.), Object Technology Series, Reading, MA: Addison-Wesley Publishing Company (1997)
13. Fuxman, A., Giorgini, P., Kolp, M. and Mylopoulos, J.: "Information systems as social structures". In Proceedings of the 2nd International Conference on Formal Ontologies for Information Systems, FOIS'01, Ogunquit, USA, October (2001)
14. Mintzberg, H.: Structure in fives: designing effective organisations. Englewood Cliffs, N.J., Prentice-Hall (1992)

A spoken interface based on the contextual modelling of smart homes

Pablo A. Haya and Germán Montoro

Escuela Politécnica Superior
Universidad Autónoma de Madrid
28049 Madrid, Spain
{Pablo.Haya, German.Montoro}@uam.es

1 Introduction

Ubiquitous computing, also-called pervasive computing, is an emerging technology that offers new opportunities and challenges [14]. We are especially interested in those that have an impact in home environments. In particular, we are focusing on how context information can enhance user interaction within a smart home environment.

We propose that the context gathered from the environment should be collected in a common model shared by every context-aware application [1]. This model should include the available resources and the relations among them. In this direction, we have implemented a middleware between the model of the smart home and the physical world in such a way that changes in the model are immediately reflected into the real world, and vice versa.

There are several groups researching in how to model the context as a web of relations among concepts, such as the Cobra project [4], Henricksen et al [8] and the Aire project [15]. Our proposal is specifically focused on home environments.

A laboratory has been converted into a real home environment to test our prototypes in a similar way as the Adaptive House [11], the Aware Home [9] and The Intelligent Room [10] projects.

Following sections describe a context information model for smart home environments. Every environment component is represented by a model's instance that contains information about its status and its relationships. This information is used by the home applications to react to the changes in the context. In particular, linguistic information is added to the representation of instances in order to support a contextual spoken dialogue interface.

R. Navarro-Prieto and J.L. Vidal (eds.), HCI Related Papers of Interacción 2004, 147-154.

2 Modelling the environment

We have devised a hierarchical classification of the relevant concepts for home environments. This section presents the ontology that entails these concepts. The following sections will explain how this ontology is employed by a spoken dialogue interface.

In the proposed ontology each concept is represented by a class name and a set of properties. Each property has a value that can be a literal or another concept. When the value of a property is a concept, a relation between the two concepts is established. This relation is considered as having an explicit "direction", that is, in case it holds, the inverse relation must be explicitly asserted.

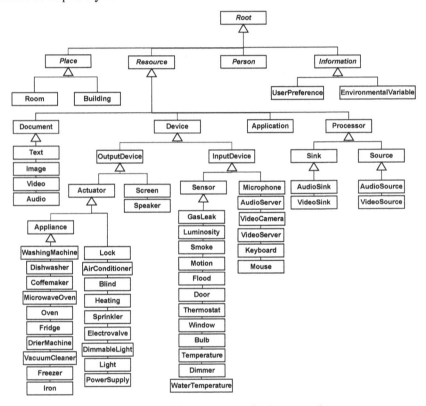

Fig. 1. Global view of the taxonomy for home environments

We have adopted Dey's definition of context to develop our model for a home intelligent environment [6]. Figure 1 shows the complete hierarchical classification of concepts that we propose for home environments. The model starts with four main concepts: *Person, Place,*

Resource and *Information*. A *Resource* is every component that can be used by a *Person* (or other *Resource*) located in some *Place*. *Information* can be a *User Preference* or an *Environmental Variable*, such as the current sound level or the luminosity. The description of a Resource always includes the following set of relations: *handles*, *is-handled-by*, *is-composed-by*, *allowed-user* and *is-located-in*. The *handles* relation establishes that a resource is being used by other resource. Reciprocally, the relation *is-handled-by* defines which *Person* or *Resource* is controlling a given *Resource*. The *composed-by* property allows to describe a *Resource* as composed of other resources. The *allowed-user* property defines the access policy. Finally, the *is-located-in* property represents where the resource is located.

The *Resource* concept is refined by the following four concepts: *Device*, *Document*, *Application*, and *Processor*. A *Device* represents a physical object (i.e. a microphone, a light bulb, a speaker). Each *Device* always includes the status property that, at least, indicates if the device is turned on or off. We have split the device category into *Output* and *Input device* depending on whether they produce or consume information. *Output devices* include video and audio consumers such as screens and speakers and mechanical actuators such as door locks, blinds, lights and home appliances. On the other side, *Input devices* comprise mice, keyboards, video and audio sources, such as microphone and video cameras, and physical sensors. Device classes showed at figure 1 represent simple devices. It is possible to define composite devices by means of the *is-composed-by* relation. Thus, a TV set is composed by an instance of Screen class and two or more instances of Speaker class. Finally, *Documents* and *Applications*, do not correspond to tangible objects. The first class represents digital files that store some information, while the second class represents computational services. Therefore, devices, documents and applications represent existing resources. On the other side, a Processor denotes a capability, something that can be performed by a resource. This allows, for example, distinguishing between the sensing capability and the sensor itself.

3 Working with the model

The ontological representation of the environment, including its instances, is written in an XML document. At startup, the system reads the document and automatically builds:

– A blackboard [7], which works as an interaction layer between the physical world and the spoken dialogue interface.
– A spoken dialogue interface that, by means of the blackboard, works as an interaction layer between the users and the environment.

This blackboard holds a representation of multiple characteristics of the environment. These characteristics correspond with instances of the previous ontology. Each instance is called an entity. Applications and interfaces can ask the blackboard to obtain information about the state of any entity or to change it. Entities can be added and removed to the blackboard in run-time, and the new information can be reused by the rest of applications. Applications and interfaces do not interact directly with the physical world or between them, but they only have access to the blackboard layer.

This blackboard layer isolates the applications from the real world. Physical world entity details are hidden to clients [13], making easier and more standard to develop context aware modules and interfaces.

Entities are associated to a concept. All the entities related to the same concept inheritance some general properties. This means that if we define a new entity its properties will come attached to it.

Some of the properties associated to the entities represent linguistic information. This information is formed by a verb part (the actions that can be taken with the entity), an object part (the name it can be given), a modifier part (the kind of object entity), a location part (where it is in the environment) and other parts. A set of these parts establishes one possible way a user may employ to interact with the entity. One entity has associated a collection of sets of parts, corresponding to all the possible ways to interact with the entity. A single part can be composed of one or more words, allowing the use of synonyms. Additionally, entities inheritance the name of its associated template grammar and the action method that has to be called after its linguistic information is completed. Action methods are specific for each type of entity and execute all the possible actions that may be requested by a user (for instance to turn on, turn off, dim up and dim down the light in an entity of type *dimmable_light*).

The linguistic information is transformed in specific grammars and dialogue nodes that support the spoken interaction process. Users manage and interact with the environment by means of the spoken dialogue interface and the interface employs the information represented in the blackboard to support the dialogue capabilities.

4 Dialogue representation

As it was said above, the spoken dialogue interface is composed of a set of grammars and a dialogue structure.

Grammars support the recognition process by specifying the possible sentences that can be uttered by the users, limiting the number of inputs expected by the recognizer [5]. This way, users will only be allowed to carry on dialogues related to the current configuration of the environment, not considering other possible utterances. The system creates a grammar for each concept. Grammars are based on the grammar template associated to the concept. In the interface creation process entities only have to fill in the corresponding grammar template with their collection of set parts.

The dialogue structure is based on a linguistic tree. Before creating the dialogue interface the tree only has an empty root node. Every set of linguistic parts is transformed in a tree path, with a node for each part. Nodes hang from parent nodes that represent previous parts of the same set. Nodes store the word corresponding to that part and the name of the entity where they belonged. Parts with more than one word (synonyms) will be transformed in different nodes and following parts of the same set will hang from every one of these synonym nodes.

Words are analyzed by a morphological parser [3] in order to get their number and gender. Repeated words are analyzed only the first time and this information is stored for later use at the generation process.

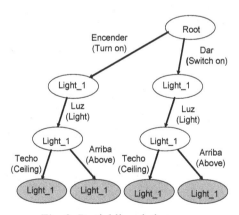

Fig. 2. Partial linguistic tree

As an example, let us suppose that the entity light_1 has the following set of parts: {"encender dar", "luz", "", "techo arriba","}, in English {"turn_on switch_on", "light", "", "ceiling above",""}, where the first column corresponds to the verb part, the second one to the object part, the third column to the modifier part, the fourth one to the location part and the last column to the additional information part. "Turn on" and "switch on" are synonyms, the same as "ceiling" and "above". Therefore this corresponds with four possible ways to interact with the entity light_1. Starting from an empty tree, the system would create the linguistic tree showed in figure 2.

Shadowed nodes correspond to action nodes. When the system reaches one of these nodes the system executes the action method associated to the entity where it belongs (in this case it would turn on the light_1).

Another set of parts may have a word part at the same level as a previous set. In this case the system will not create a new node for that part, but it will reuse that node and will append, if necessary, the name of the entity where it belonged. Let us suppose, for instance, that the entity light_1 has the following two sets of parts: {"apagar", "luz", "", "techo arriba", ""} and {"apagar", "fluorescente", "", "", ""}, in English {"turn off", "light", "", "ceiling above", ""} and {"turn off", "fluorescent", "", "", ""}, which correspond with three possible ways of interacting with the entity light_1. In this case, the word part "turn off" is at the same level in both sets of parts so that only one "turn off" node is created and "light" and "fluorescent" both hang from it. If now, we have a new entity called radio_1, with this linguistic set of parts: {"apagar", "radio", "", "", ""}, in English {"turn off", "radio", "", "", ""}, the system only has to append the name of the entity radio_1 to the "turn off" node. Next it adds a "radio" node as its child, at the same level as "light" and "fluorescent". Starting from an empty tree, the system would create the linguistic tree showed in figure 3.

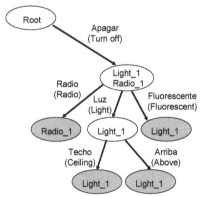

Fig. 3. Linguistic tree for light_1 and radio_1 entities

This automatic process is followed by all the collections of sets of parts of all the entities presented in the smart environment. Once the grammars and the linguistic tree are completed the system is provided with a spoken dialogue interface that supports all the possible ways of interaction for the current smart environment.

5 Conclusions and future work

Current home environments projects require a deployment of a heterogeneous set of technologies. The proliferation of communication networks and protocols complicates the seamless integration of environment devices. As a result, projects are usually developed from scratch, and much time is spent on integration tasks. We propose a standard context layer that defines a common vocabulary for agents who need to share a common context in an intelligent home environment.

Based on this layer and the dynamic composition of smart environments we have developed a spoken dialogue interface that adapts to heterogeneous smart environments. The interface and its behavior vary depending on the environment and its current state. Further information about the spoken dialogue interface can be found at [12].

The use of multimodal approaches can benefit the interface. A new face recognition module is going to be added to the system, in order to identify the people who are in the environment. This information can be used by several modules of the system, including the spoken dialogue interface, to improve their functionality. Following with this idea, the synchronization of speech and hand gestures can help to improve the interaction [2]. For this, a new gesture recognition module should be built. Other possible modal interaction can be produced by showing the information on a screen, instead of uttering a request. The user may answer either by speaking or by clicking on the selected choice.

Acknowledgements

This work has been sponsored by the Spanish Ministry of Science and Education, project number TIN2004-03140.

References

1. Alamán A, Cabello R, Gómez-Arriba F, Haya P, Martínez A, Martínez J, Montoro G (2003). Using context information to generate dynamic user interfaces. In Proceedings of HCI International 2003
2. Bourguet M, Ando A (1998). Synchronization of speech and hand gestures during multimodal human-computer interaction. In Proceedings of CHI'98 (Los Angeles, GA, April 18-23), 241-242
3. Carmona J, Atserias J, Cervell S, Márquez L, Martí MA, Padró L, Placer R, Rodríguez H, Taulé M, Turmo J (1998). An Environment for Morphosyntactic Processing of Unrestricted Spanish Text. Proceedings of LREC'98, Granada, Spain
4. Chen H, Finin T, Joshi A (2004). Semantic Web in the Context Broker Architecture. In Proceedings of PerCom 2004
5. Dahlbäck N, Jönsson A (1992). An empirically based computationally tractable dialogue model. Proceedings of COGSCI'92
6. Dey A (2001). Understanding and using context. Personal and Ubiquitous Computing. 5:1
7. Engelmore R, Mogan T (1988). Blackboard Systems. Addison-Wesley
8. Henricksen K, Indulska J, Rakotonirainy J (2002). Modeling Context Information in Pervasive Computing Systems. In Proceedings of Pervasive 2002, pp 167-180
9. Kidd CK, Orr R, Abowd GD, Atkenson CG, Essa, IA, MacIntyre B, Mynatt E, Starner TE, Newstetter W (1999). The Aware Home: A Living Laboratory for Ubiquitous Computing Research. In Proceedings of the Second International Workshop on Cooperative Buildings
10. Le Gal C, Martin J, Lux A, Crowley JL (2001). SmartOffice: Design of an Intelligent Environment. IEEE Intelligent Systems, 16:4, pp 60-66
11. Mozer M (1998). The neural network house: An environment that adapts to its inhabitants. In Proceedings of the AAAI Spring Symposium on Intelligent Environments
12. Montoro G, Haya PA, Alamán X (2004). Context adaptive interaction with an automatically created spoken interface for intelligent environments. In Proceedings of INTELLCOMM'04
13. Salber D, Abowd GD (1998). The design and use of a generic context server. In Proceedings of Perceptual User Interfaces (PUI'98)
14. Satyanarayanan M (2001). Pervasive Computing: Vision and Challenges. IEEE Personal Communications, 8:4, pp 10-17
15. Peters S, Shrobe H (2003). Using Semantic Network for Knowledge Representation in an Intelligent Environment. In Proceedings of PerCom'03

Model-Based User Interface Reengineering

José A. Macías[1], Ángel R. Puerta[2] and Pablo Castells[1]

[1] E.P.S. Universidad Autónoma de Madrid. Ctra. de Colmenar, Km. 15, 28049 Madrid. Spain. {j.macias, pablo.castells}@uam.es.
[2] Redwhale Software. 277 Town and country Village. Palo Alto, CA 94303. USA. puerta@redwhale.com

1 Introduction

Reverse engineering can be thought of as an application of inverse engineering processes [3]. It has been applied to adapt legacy systems and user interfaces to new platforms and technologies in order to improve their global maintenance [10]. One of the main problems concerning reverse engineering is, in general terms, the lack of high-level information needed to automate the process. Existing techniques are mostly based on extracting domain information about the application's inputs and outputs. These techniques are labor-intensive rather than automatic and as a result, they are unproductive and error-prone.

In the field of user interface engineering, MBUI (Model-Based User Interfaces) methodologies exhibit features that could be very useful for a re-verse engineering approach. MBUI development is based on building up user interfaces by means of high-level, mostly ad-hoc, languages. Such languages codify different conceptual levels of a user interface as opposed to ordinary programming languages that are general-purpose and less expressive.

One of the most interesting challenges in MBUI is how to take advantage of high-level specifications (interface models) to carry out reverse engineering processes for automatic authoring and maintenance of interfaces [15]. In theory, we could extract an interface model from an existing interface, and then generate automatically different versions of that interface for other platforms directly from the model. In order to carry out such automated tasks, suitable modeling languages and architectures need to be defined.

Most of the early MBUI approaches define languages and authoring tools for automatic user interface generation. Nevertheless, little attention has been paid to reverse engineering issues that allow for automatic debug,

R. Navarro-Prieto and J. L. Vidal (eds.), HCI Related Papers of Interacción 2004, 155-162.

maintenance and verification of the generated interfaces by using the underlying specification languages.

This work aims at filling these related gaps by proposing two works that include several specification languages and toolkits intended to implement a reverse engineering approach for user interface processes. On one hand, XIML [12] is a language that enables the specification of the relevant elements of a user interface. The language has been used to support the generation of interfaces for multiple platforms from a single model. On the other hand, DESK [9] is a system that uses domain knowledge to identify changes made to an interface by an end user and to apply those changes in a rational manner to future generations of the original interface or of similar interfaces. DESK uses the PEGASUS [8] specification based on domain ontologies in order to represent explicitly presentation and domain knowledge.

2 User Interface Modeling

One of the key aspects of user interface modeling is that of separating the interface into various conceptual levels or submodels. Each submodel depicts and encapsulates a different part of the user interface abstraction. Some of most common conceptual models widely studied and used are Domain Model, Task Model, Dialog Model User Model and Platform Model [12].

Although all above models are used to carry through a modelbased approach, the domain, presentation and task models are considered more expressive in nature. These three models provide useful information in order to rebuild the inverse path coming from the final generated user interface towards the underlying models.

2.1 Domain Modeling

The role of the domain model has become significant among different MBUI approaches. ADEPT [5] uses a minimal domain model that consists of a list of entity types. ADEPT represents abstract high-level relationships between the domain and the rest of the models. Mecano [4] and MOBI-D [12] use a domain model to generate both layout and dynamic behavior of the interface. These tools enable the creation of domain models by means of frame languages that define class hierarchies. Each class can contain a different number of properties called facets.

2.2 Presentation Modeling

Presentation models are used in a number of user interface generation tools. MASTERMIND [2] includes a comprehensive presentation model that enables the interface to adapt to different platforms. That presentation model is based on older related systems such as HUMANOID [14]. HUMANOID includes a complete interface model with application, presentation and dialog components. Human designers build presentation models and HUMANOID chooses at generation time among the various templates available to display the interface.

2.3 Task Modeling

One of the most noteworthy works in interface task modeling is ConCur-TaskTrees [13]. This approach provides a high-level task hierarchical specification in order to design corporative and interactive applications. MOBI-D also provides a hierarchical model intended to represent the user's tasks. In MOBI-D, each task is divided into sub-tasks, which in turn can include properties and procedural information.

3 Reverse Engineering Modeling

As we hinted before, an interface specification is the key to reverse path construction. Additionally, enough semantic information has to be provided in order to recover maximal information about the interface in the reverse path. To this end, it is important to find a specification that better fits these semantic requirements and allows for relationships between existing interface components and models [9]. Most of the systems mentioned in the previous section allow for this kind of specifications. However most of those systems are focused on specific modeling issues (e.g. tasks, presentation, etc.) that are hard to map starting from the final generated interface. It is therefore necessary to set a more explicit separation among the interface's components [8] but, on the other hand, it is important to avoid missing information of the underlying models and relationships at the final generation step.

3.1 Multi-Platform Modeling with XIML

One relevant issue in user interface design is to adapt the generated interface to different platforms. More precisely, it is worth having procedures that avoid developing a new interface for each version of a multiplatform user interface. To this end, XIML (eXtensible Interface Markup Language) [12] aims at supporting user interface design and multiplatform generation. The XIML specification provides enough expressiveness to represent five different conceptual dimensions of a user interface (task, domain, user, presentation and dialog) as well as the relationships among them. Three of those dimensions are mean to be abstract (task, domain and user) and the other two are concrete (presentation and dialog). As depicted in Fig. 1a, multi-platform user interface design is based on a common representation of abstract dimensions and a specific representation of the concrete dimensions for each kind of platform or device.

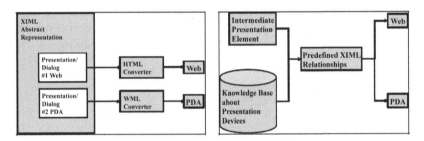

Fig. 1. From left to right: Multi-platform specification using XIML (a) and Correspondences in XIML (b)

XIML also facilitates the creation of specific presentation and dialog components for each platform. As shown in Fig. 1b, XIML allows for an intermediate presentation element that can be automatically specialized to each kind of platform by using a knowledge base (also codified in XIML) about device properties (Web, PDA, etc.). As a practical application, XIML has been used in multi-platform development for geographic information systems [4].

3.2 High-Level Modeling with PEGASUS

Another proposed solution for the reverse engineering of user interfaces is the use of domain ontologies that better codifies high-level semantic aspects of the interface itself. Those semantics will be used later to identify relationships between interface components and, in turn, determine the reverse path efficiently. For this purpose, PEGASUS uses a custom knowledge representation—by way of domain ontologies—to generate dynamic web interfaces automatically.

At run-time, the user interacts with the target web application. Such interaction is the equivalent of navigating through a semantic network of domain objects. Whenever the user selects an object on the web page, PEGASUS responds by generating a new HTML page that corresponds to that object. The system resolves the user's requests by selecting the suitable object and then executing the rules and templates properly. Therefore, the links on the web pages represent domain objects rather than URL based web page calls.

4 Deploying Reverse Engineering Processes

Once an interface specification is obtained, it is necessary to define mechanisms that reconstruct the application models from the generated user interface.

4.1 Reverse Engineering with XIML

The reverse engineering process with XMIL can be divided into two methodologies that match the two kinds of dimensions related in Sect. 1.3: concrete and abstract. The concrete methodology is intended to create both presentation and dialog models from HTML. The abstract methodology is aimed at building a complete XIML representation (task, domain, user, presentation and dialog) from an HTML specification.

Concrete reverse engineering. In the concrete case, the reverse engineering is based on rules. These rules are aimed at converting HTML to XIML by means of a previous developed authoring tool. Such tool also makes the inverse path transforming XIML into HTML. This methodology (including platform adaptation) has been successfully put into practice by means of an authoring tool, called Vaquista [1] that transforms an HTML web interface into a XIML representation.

Abstract reverse engineering. As we commented before, one the most important challenge in this work is to map abstract interface elements to concrete ones [19]. Therefore it is worth noting that the inverse correspondence is even harder to carry out. Up to now, we can only add-on an interactive process with the modeler to carry through an abstract reverse engineering from HTML to XIML.

4.2 Reverse Engineering with DESK

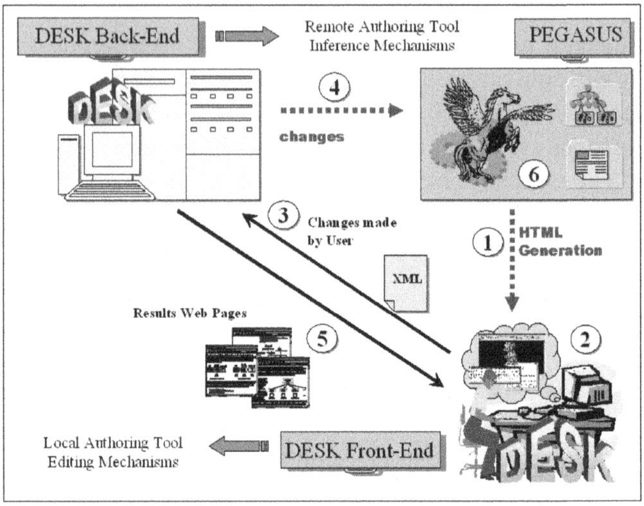

Fig. 2. Reverse Engineering with DESK

DESK is based on a Client-Server architecture that comprises two different applications (see Fig. 2). The client side is a front-end WYSIWYG authoring tool that interacts with the final user in editing a web page (as an ordinary web editing tool). By contrast, the server side is a back-end application that infers and carries out the changes the user makes on the web interface. As shown in Fig. 2, the whole process is as follows: (1) First, the user authors a web interface generated by PEGASUS. (2) The DESK front-end tracks and records information about the user's actions and builds up a monitoring model codified in XML. (3) Such changes are sent to the back-end application. The back-end side processes in turn the monitoring model and applies different inference heuristics by using domain knowledge. (4) As a result of the inference process, the underlying models of PEGASUS (domain, presentation) are modified taking into account each change the user achieved on the web page. (5) A report about the process is sent back to the user. (6) Finally, next time a similar web page (interface) is generated, the changes will appear. DESK development is based on the End User Development approach [7]. This leads us to create an authoring tool by bringing off a tradeoff between expressivity and complexity, that is to say, reducing the complexity of use and increasing the expressivity of the environment as much as possible [9].

5 Conclusions

In this paper, we have presented two approaches to the reverse engineering of user interfaces. These works are focused on specification languages that have been put into practice by means of authoring tools and applications used in different contexts of use.

On one hand, XIML is based on specifying the interface by means of five different dimensions (task, domain, user, presentation and dialog). These dimensions are intended to generate multi-platform interfaces. The main strength of this work is to create relationships between abstract and concrete domains from the specification language, as well as to generate web interface for multiple platforms coming from an XIML representation.

On the other hand, PEGASUS represents information structured in presentation and domain knowledge separately. Therefore, DESK can infer changes introduced by users on a web interface generated by PEGASUS. DESK achieves a reverse path back from the final page generated by PEGASUS, so that DESK can identify the domain and the presentation objects involved and eventually change their state. This implies to carry out changes in the future web page generation procedure by changing the underlying models used to generate the interfaces.

These two approaches facilitate a reverse process for user interface reengineering. In DESK the system is based on End-User Development and Programming by Example [6] principles. In XIML, the methodology is based on a comprehensive interface modeling language.

6 Acknowledgements

This work is being supported by the Spanish Ministry of Science and Technology (MCyT), project number TIC2002-1948.

7 References

1. Bouillon L, Vanderdonckt J (2002). Retargeting Web Pages To Other Computing Platforms. Proceedings of the IEEE 9th Working Conference on Re-verse Engineering (WCRE'2002), IEEE Computer Society Press, pp. 339-348.
2. Castells P, Szekely P, Salcher E (1997). Declarative Models of Presentation. Proceedings of the International Conference on Intelligent User Interfaces (IUI'97). January 6-9, Orlando, Florida, USA, pp. 137-144.

3. Chikofsky E J, Cross J H (1990). Reverse Engineering and Design Recovery: A Taxonomy. IEEE Software, January, pp. 13-17.

4. Eisenstein J, Vanderdonckt J, Puerta A (2001). Applying Model-Based Techniques To The Development Of UIs For Mobile Computers. Proceedings of the 6th International Conference on Intelligent User Interfaces (IUI'01). ACM Press, pp. 69-76.

5. Johnson P, Wilson S, Johnson H. (1994). Scenarios, Task Análisis, and the ADEPT Design Environment. Scenario-Based Design. J. Carrol (ed.). Addison-Wesley.

6. Lieberman H (ed.) (2001). Your Wish is my Command. Programming By Example. Morgan Kaufmann Publishers. Academic Press, USA.

7. Klann M., Fit F (2003). End-User Development. D1.1 Roadmap. Proceedings of the End User Development Workshop at CHI'2003 Conference. Ft. Lauderdale, Florida, USA. April 5-10.

8. Macías J A, Castells P (2001). Adaptive Hypermedia Presentation Modeling for Domain Ontologies. Volume 2 of the Proceedings of HCI International (HCII'01), 9th International Conference on Human-Computer Interaction. New Orleans, Louisiana, USA; August 5-10. Lawrence Erlbaum Associates, Publishers. London. pp. 710-714.

9. Macías J A, Castells P (2003). Dynamic Web Page Authoring by Example Using Ontology-Based Domain Knowledge. Proceedings of the International Conference on Intelligent User Interfaces (IUI'03). Miami, Florida, USA. January 12-15, pp. 133-140.

10. Moore M M, Rugaber S (1993). Issues in user-interface migration. In Proceedings of the Third Software Engineering Research Forum.

11. Puerta A R (1996). The MECANO Project: Comprehensive and Integrated Support for Model-Based Interface Development. Proceedings of the Computer-Aided Design of User Interfaces (CADUI'96), pp. 19-35.

12. Puerta A, Eisenstein J (2002). A common representation for interaction data. In Proceedings of IUI 2002: International Conference in Intelligent User Interfaces. ACM Press.

13. Paternò F (2001). Model-Based Design and Evaluation of Interactive Applications. Springer Verlag.

14. Szekely P, Luo P, Neches R (1998). Beyond Interface Builders: Model-Based Interface Tools. Maybury'98. Section VI: Model-Based Interfaces, pp. 499-506.

15. Truker K, Stirewalt R E K (1999) Model based user-Interface reengineering. Proceedings of the 6th Working Conference on Reverse Engineering (WCRE'99). Atlanta, Georgia, October.

Local Support to Plastic User Interfaces: an Orthogonal Approach

Sendín, M. and Lorés, J.

University of Lleida (Spain). GRIHO: HCI research group.

1 Introduction

Nowadays technology allows users to keep on moving with computing power and network resources at hand. Computing devices are shrinking while wireless communications bandwidth keeps increasing. These changes have increasingly enabled access to information; "anytime and anywhere". This makes computing possible in multiple and varied contexts of use[16] in which a great amount of variable parameters come together. This provides us tremendous versatility. Consequently, current interactive systems should be prepared to face up this continuous and diverse variability. They should be able to offer the capacity of systematically producing as many User Interfaces (henceforth UIs) as contextual circumstances have been identified. This fact raises a first challenge. Moreover, the adaptive capacities should evolve in runtime, as the real time constraints vary. This would offer, in addition, continuous adaptation to each concrete UI in use, with the aim of solving the contextual changes in a dynamic and automatic way. We identify this problem as a second challenge different from the previous one.

Until now these two issues have been designated a single term: plasticity of UIs[17] , introduced by Thevenin and Coutaz in [19] in 1999 along a framework and research agenda development work. This work was put in practice in these two works: ARTStudio [18] and Probe [5]. It was also revised in 2002 in [6], within the Cameleon project [7].

---

[16] Set of environmental parameters that describe a particular context in which a set of conditions of real time come together, related not only to the restrictions in hardware resources, but also related to the user, and even to the environment

[17] Capacity of a same generic UI to support variations in multiple contextual circumstances preserving usability and at the same time minimizing the development and maintenance costs [7].

R. Navarro-Prieto and J. L. Vidal (eds.), HCI Related Papers of Interacción 2004, 163-178.

Nevertheless, according to the distinction between the two challenges mentioned above, we understand plasticity as a dichotomy, that is to say, a separation into two parts. We see these two parts closely associated with the diverse stages of reconfiguration and readjustment the UI comes cross during the whole system lifetime, respectively. They can be considered as the design operation level and the runtime operation level. Both of them were distinguished and defined in [14] as two subconcepts of plasticity (explicit plasticity and implicit plasticity, respectively) with two different goals clearly identified. They have also been presented as an extension to the Thevenin and Coutaz work in [16].

As it appears in [16], we define the explicit plasticity as the capacity of automatically generating a specific UI valid to a concrete context of use, starting from an abstract specification generic UI[18]. In a parallel way, we define implicit plasticity as the capacity of incremental adaptation that the specific UI obtained in the production stage should show in real time, preserving at the same time a predefined set of usability properties as the user goes across new contexts of use. The explicit plasticity tackles important changes in the UI that are caused either by unforeseen situations or by the request of new contents. Both cases involve a reconfiguration of the UI to be solved in the server side upon explicit request. This is the reason why we use the term "explicit". Comparably, the implicit plasticity tackles specific modifications in the UI, originated by predictable contextual changes – e.g. changes in the brightness level. We state that this kind of changes should be solved with an automatic local readjustment on the client side, without any express request or action. This is why we chose the term "implicit".

In the works mentioned previously, we also propose a client/serverbased architectural framework to solve both challenges on the opposite sides of the architecture. The framework proposed to solve the explicit plasticity is located on the server side and is called explicit plasticity engine. The architecture proposed to solve the implicit plasticity is located on the client side and is called implicit plasticity engine. The former consists of a systematic development support capable of generating or redesigning remotely a suitable UI for each case presented. See [15] for more detail. The later consists of an architecture with evolving capacity capable of detecting the environment and of reacting appropriately. It is in charge of applying locally the necessary adjustments to the UI and thereby adapting to the contextual changes on the fly.

---

[18] Unique and flexible abstract specification of the layout and composition of the resulting interface, as well as a description of how the UI evolves in time. It is related to the concept of canonical expression of the UI.

This architectural framework tries to reach a certain balance between both sides. Certainly, it contributes to some benefits derived from certain autonomy that allows adaptivity also to be performed on the client side. As a result, the client only contacts with the server in the necessary cases. On the one hand, as the contextual representation is stored in the client side, the resultant system becomes more robust to possible fails in the server or communication system. This makes possible to keep on running till new reconfiguration needs appear. On the other hand, this autonomy contributes to an automatic and transparent reaction in real time. Moreover, the timely communication between client and server provides a mechanism for propagating contextual changes in both ways. This is one of the most important shortcomings detected in the literature. The client notifies to the server the changes produced in the current UI by means of a trustworthy request. On receiving the request, the server has the chance of updating its contextual map and, as a consequence, of generating a UI as adjusted as possible to the current situation. This mechanism allows keeping both sides in continuous feedback and updating.

This paper deals with the implicit plasticity problem associated with a spontaneous adaptation to contextual changes. We aim to offer a local solution capable of accommodating a continuous variability. This one is to be implanted in the client device. The major difficulty for offering a local support to plastic UIs is dealing with the multiplicity of contextual factors that a plastic interactive system is supposed to control. Moreover, the needs for dynamic and real time adaptation become more and more demanding. Nevertheless, the factors related not only to resources constraints bandwidth, server availability, device physical restrictions, etc., but also others related to the user, and even to the environment, are volatile and require sophisticated adaptive capabilities that today are still challenging. Henceforth, they will be referred to as real time constraints.

In order to apply the necessary adjustments to the UI in a transparent and dynamic way, the system has to be able to selfrecognize and selfmodify in runtime. We have adopted the Aspect Oriented Programming (AOP) paradigm [11], in combination with reflection techniques [12], offering an application of such a relevant technology in the Human Computer Interaction field. This proposal implies an improvement regard a previous architecture based only on reflection techniques [15]. The aim of the present contribution is to solve the tangling code and scattering code problems that the previous solution had. This will contribute to reusability and flexibility, allowing each contextual factor to evolve independently.

This paper is composed of three more sections. In section two the implicit plasticity concept is featured giving an overview. In section three the AOP paradigm is presented. In section four we present the adaptive architecture we propose. This section is complemented studying the aspectual decomposition to be applied in a concrete case study and presenting the implementation tools chosen.

2 Systems with Implicit Plasticity

2.1 Featuring the Domain

We define a system with implicit plasticity as a system capable of detecting contextual information – where it is also considered the user and the hardware resources as part of the context, taking advantage of it to adapt its own appearance to different contexts of use. In this sense this concept comprises both the adaptivity purpose as well as the contextawareness one. In our opinion, the concept of implicit plasticity can be considered equal to the context awareness – which is a decade old, since the moment in which the properties related to the user as well as the restrictions in hardware resources are incorporated as properties that characterize the context. The goal is that all of them are taken into consideration in the adaptation process. In this way, our conception about context corresponds to the Schilit one in [17], who divides it in three categories: computing context, user context and physical context. In [1, 7] a detailed survey of all of these terms is offered.

The combination of varied contextual properties lets us attain a more precise understanding of the current situation. However, apart from the treatment of the location and the user modeling, any other context parameter has been so widely studied [8]. Moreover, it has not been employed too much effort in exploring techniques that combine the user modeling with the context modeling, as is exposed in the next section.

To develop an implicit plasticity engine and being able to adapt the system behavior, it is necessary to know the environment that surrounds it, in order to characterize the context. Next, it must be established the method to model and to integrate such context in the system performance. The aspect of how to effectively use that information is still a challenging problem for developers of this type of system.

2.2 Overview

It is worthy to remark that, despite the apparent correlation and proximity between the adaptation provided by the user modeling and the notion of contextawareness, the explicit combination of both techniques is a relatively unexploited research area, as it is analyzed in [4]. In fact, to date there are few clear examples of developed applications that explicitly combine sensorbased contextaware techniques in conjunction with traditional user modeling techniques.

As user modelingbased applications that implicitly use context data as a part of their user models we can mention, for example, user's interests in [2], and user's tasks in [20]. Similarly, there are few examples of contextaware applications that incorporate the notion of user model to support their adaptive behavior. We can mention a significant example: the GUIDE system [9], which uses a user model in order to represent visitor's interests and preferences. Nevertheless, there exists a great amount of contextaware applications that work without a user model. We can mention the applications within the field called memory prosthesis, which in the early nineties became an important application domain in the research field of contextaware computing, introducing the notion of augmenting human memory. Examples in this field can be consulted in [4].

3 Aspect Oriented Programming

The increasing complexity of software products as well as the need for finishing developments in shorter and shorter periods of time is promoting the Software Engineering community to design and adopt new technologies that provide a more orthogonal separation of concerns. Particularly, the Aspect Oriented Programming (AOP) is gaining relevance, in comparison with other separation of concerns techniques. It is a paradigm extensively developed and used offering a new and promising option to separation of concerns technologies.

To strengthen the separation of concerns, the AOP focuses on those interest points or concerns of the application characterized by two factors:

- On the one hand its influence and treatment crosscuts the system basic functionality, scattering along diverse modules that not necessarily are related each other (code scattering). We are referring to the wellknown crosscutting concerns. Typical crosscutting concerns are the persistence, synchronization, exception handling, the logging operations, authentication, etc.

The code scattering problem generates code redundancy problems.

- On the other hand, these parameters are not orthogonal, but they appear interweaved, getting the main purpose of that code fragment tangled, and causing so a decrease in the code's clarity (code tangling). The multiplicity of parameters to be taken into account in such a complex kind of applications, which inherently are related each other makes this problem unavoidable.

The solution to this double issue will consist of extracting and encapsulating this type of problematic concepts, providing them modularization. Hence, we obtain not only separation, but also the possibility of condensing in a single program unit the whole treatment of the concept. Now then, this modularization requires a composition process (weaving) subsequent to compose the final operational system. It is the weaving phase, to be carried out by an especial compiler called weaver. The modularization unit is a program entity called generally aspect. It consists of an analogous structure to a class, which encapsulates all of its mechanisms. The program whose behavior is affected by aspects is called base program.

The AOP [11] is the technology resulting from the effort in modularizing and decoupling crosscutting concerns, avoiding at the same time redundancy and code tangling. It was proposed by Kiczales et al., (Xerox PARC) in 1990, in an attempt to surpass the increasing complexity of software systems. It was designated with the term of AOP in 1996. This novel discipline causes more and more interest and relevance in the research community dedicated to the Software Engineering.

Ubiquitous Computing, Mobile Computing and ContextAwareness are fields where meet certain circumstances such as treatment of crosscutting concerns that entangle between them and with the application code, presenting even diverse decomposition dimensions. This is due to the multiplicity of factors that should be handled, with the aim of offering the maximum adaptation, and which rebound in a considerable increase of the complexity. The AOP is especially applicable to this type of systems to obtain the desired orthogonality in the separation of concerns that we do not achieve working only with reflection.

AOP offers numerous key advantages as reusability and extension, which facilitate code's evolution, and separation of concerns, which helps to keep the code clean. All these advantages make AOP a powerful programming paradigm.

4 Our Proposal

4.1 Previous Approach and Improvements

On the client side our aim consists of developing an engine capable of adapting a specific UI in real time according to a set of factors related to the context of use (the real time constraints) and to a predefined set of usability properties. All of them should be represented (reification process[19], depicted as the arrow 3 in figure 1) and treated separately from the core functionality of the system, as nonfunctional properties that affect the UI. The aim is to maintain a selfrepresentation (explicit modeling) from the part of the system that we are interested in accessing, controlling and manipulating (the UI, together with the contextual factors that characterize it). The aim is to apply the necessary adjustments to the system's behavior, in a transparent and dynamic way. This is precisely what makes up the essence of a reflective architecture[20] [12]. Therefore we use a reflective techniques to implement the implicit plasticity engine we propose, due to its capacity of selfrecognition and selfmodification in runtime. This makes possible to extend and adapt the system behavior.

Following this approach, the components related to the functionality of the application are represented in the base level of the reflective architecture (logic layer in the figure 1), and they are manipulated by the metalevel (adaptive layer in figure 1). Furthermore, the selfrepresentation of the system is located in the metalevel, making directly explicit and accessible certain properties that usually are not so – those related to the UI and to contextual factors. As these properties are normally common to diverse systems it is interesting to build and consider them as reusable and extensible components. Lastly, the metalevel is also responsible for controlling changes in the different contextual factors. A third level (contextaware layer in figure 1) will be in charge of detecting the environment and notifying the changes to the metaobjects.

---

[19] Process consisting of making concrete and materializing by means of objects the set of nonfunctional properties. This means making hidden aspects explicit and accessible, so amenable to inspection and adaptation.

[20] Architecture that provides a system capacity to reason about and act upon itself, adjusting so its behavior according to certain conditions. Under an objectoriented reflective architecture view a system is considered to be made up of two parts: the application core and the reflective part to be separated in thus called base level and metalevel, respectively, making possible the system to selfrecognize itself and to selfupdating at runtime

Hence, following the principle of abstraction, in the base level the system works without any conception of interface. This one is relegated to the metalevel where is being continually remodeled during runtime, putting introspection[21] and reflection[22] capacities to work. As a result, the changes will be reflected in the system (base level) at an opportune time.

These properties, which are inherent to a reflective architecture, are depicted as arrows 2 and 1 respectively in figure 1.

Undoubtedly, the separation between the functional (base level) and the nonfunctional parts (metalevel) proposed by means of reflection prevents the nonfunctional properties from interfering with the basic functionality of the application, bringing flexibility in the development of the application core. However, the treatment of the nonfunctional properties is still being carried out as a whole, causing the same problems of code scattering and code tangling, although now located in the metalevel. To solve that and contribute to a major flexibility, reusability and orthogonality we propose to model the real time constraints, which constitute crosscutting concepts inherently related each other, as aspects to influence in the metalevel, using the Aspect Oriented Programming (AOP). This idea, resumed in Figure 1, expresses the improvement proposed compared to the previous architecture.

---

[21] Capacity of a system to examine its own state in a fixed moment, making possible to control key events.

[22] Susceptibility to changes in the system, caused by a change in his selfrepresentation. This property guarantees that each change made to the selfrepresentation is immediately mirrored in the underlying system's actual state and behavior.

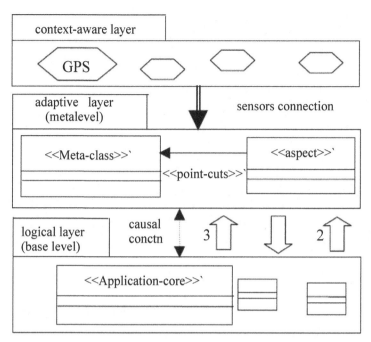

Fig.1.Architecture for the implicit plasticity engine.   The notation based in UML used in Figure 1 has been taken from [13].

4.2 Aspectual Decomposition in the Adaptive Layer: a Case Study

We are currently taking part in an InterReg project whose commitment is the development of a teleaid system for highmountain rescue to be implanted in the Pyrinees area. In order to illustrate an application of the implicit plasticity engine we have chosen this context. The core functionality consists of providing the maximum aid to the lifesaving mountaineer in the assistance tasks (location, aid and rescue) in dangerzones, where both the atmospheric conditions and the relief can be extreme. The system's main goal is to continuously provide useful information to the user, independently of the circumstances related to some fluctuating and critical factors (the so called real time constraints), which need severe control. Therefore, the implicit plasticity engine to be incorporated in the system is in charge of providing incremental adaptation to these factors, automatically modifying the system's behavior or appearance according to the circumstances. Furthermore, the implicit plasticity engine is also expected to preserve a predefined set of usability properties. All these requirements, which could be called quality attributes, will contribute to a major productivity, reliability, effectiveness, efficiency, and definitively, to the user's satisfaction, being, actually, what characterizes an implicit plasticity engine.

The most critical factor, which is also crucial for the performance of the system, is the network connectivity level, due to the poor availability, bandwidth and reliability of mobile connections. Another changing factor also determinant is the user's geographical location. It is obvious that the contents to be shown by the system should be related to location. Finally, we could also consider the altitude as another critical factor, due to the high health risk involved in exposure to high altitudes, as well as the risk derived from the speed of ascent. Let us see how the expected behavior of the system in each case would be.

With regard to the network connectivity level, the system has to be able to detect and adjust automatically its own behavior as far as the network conditions change. This means that the system has to offer offline tasks when the connection fails. An example would be the possibility of looking up useful multimedia information related to the symptoms of high mountain illnesses, illustrations of rescue operations, etc, which would be locally saved in the device. However, when the connection recovers we could look up, for example, the weather forecast. Another possibility much more ambitious, to consider if the equipment was powerful enough and the bandwidth conditions were optimum, would be to make the videoconference functionality available to aid a small surgical operation in a more professional way (telemedicine application). In this case the format of the information to be transmitted would also be subordinated to the screen resolution of the device.

As regards the user's location, the possibility of looking up a zone map reflecting the distance between the current location of the lifesaver and the approximate location of the injured person, as well as other details about the surroundings would be very useful. This kind of map could be evolving as the user moves forward.

With regard to the altitude and ascent speed it would be interesting, as a preventive measure, the automatic generation of statistics, in background mode, in order to control and detect healthy risk situations. In that case, the system could trigger an alert mechanism – audio emissions, for instanceto warn to the user and then show him some graphical data.

Which would be the predefined set of usability properties? Assuming that the computing device to be used is a last generation smart phone, the usability properties to be preserved would be the ones catalogued as mobile usability [3]. A selection of these principles can be summarized as follows:

- Trim the page to page navigation down to a minimum.
- Reduce the scrolling, in favor of simple, short lists of choices.
- Simplify the hierarchy for navigation in the screen layout.
- Reduce the number of keystrokes.

All of these usability properties can be measured, and therefore controlled and readjusted when needed, establishing appropriate join points, as well as efficient and robust poincuts to interfere with them.

Apart from the usability properties, some user's preferences directly related to the UI configuration could also be incorporated. Depending on the user's profile, the user can be specially worried about environmental factors (the altitude, the level of oxygen in the air, the temperature, or even the distance to the accident site), about some healthy aspects (e.g. his pulse rate), or perhaps he is interested in the technological restrictions (network availability and bandwidth). In any case, it would be interesting to maintain graphical and adaptive widgets, according to the user's needs. Furthermore, these needs can evolve in time. Considering all these issues, the user's preferences would also take part in the runtime adaptation, incorporating in this way the user model.

Both the personalization factors and those derived from the fluctuating properties exposed above constitute crosscutting concerns, as its influence and treatment applies across the system functionality, scattering throughout modules and generating redundancy problems. Furthermore, as these factors are not orthogonal, they would interfere with each other inevitably tangling the whole code and, hence, causing code's clarity problems too. As all of them affect either the UI configuration or the system performance, they have to act on the metalevel. Our solution to avoid the inherent problems to crosscutting concerns consists of incorporating them as aspects from the AOP paradigm in the adaptive layer, as it is reflected in the simplified scheme from figure 2.

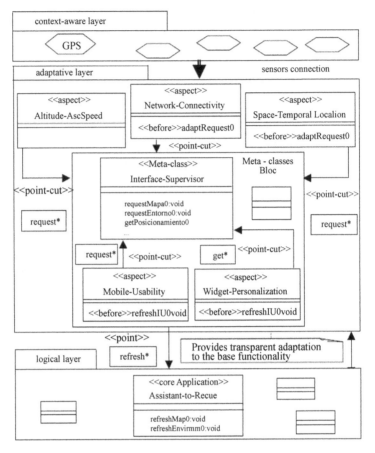

Fig. 2. Aspectual decomposition for our case study.

Particularly, according to the considerations discussed above, the aspects to be considered would be the following ones:

- Network-Connectivity; adapts system's behavior to network conditions
- Altitude-AscSpeed; aids to healthy risk situations.
- SpaceTemporal Location; adapts searches and services to location.
- Mobile-Usability; watches over the mobile usability principles.
- Widget-Personalization; affects UI configuration and appearance.

In the base level (logical layer) the *Assistan-to-Rescue* represents the basic functionality, modeled as a class. This class is affected by the meta-lasses (meta-classes bloc), which are also affected by aspects. In the metalevel (adaptive layer) we would have the main *meta-class*[23]: *Interface-Supervisor,* affected by all the aspects. This metaclass is in charge of appropriately readjusting the UI at runtime. Some of these aspects could affect not only the *Interface-Supervisor* meta-object but also the *Assistant-to-Rescue* object in the base level, setting the suitable pointcuts[24].

The labels request*, get* and refresh* indicate the join points[25], that is, the code points that need an adaptation action to be applied. So the corresponding pointcuts involve all the methods that begin with these words. All the actions described above would be the operations or methods to be executed when the associated join point is captured. In other words, each invocation to each one of these methods would be intercepted and automatically the code of the associated operation executed (e.g. trigger a warning alert mechanism upon a healthy risk situation), thus, showing an automatic system's reaction. This would be the performance of the reflective aspectual layer. The join points could be extended to any other type, not necessarily signature-based ones. Moreover, the context-aware layer contains the necessary sensors to carry out the context detection.

This scheme is aimed to make more explicit the structure from each layer of the architecture for the implicit plasticity engine on the client side.

Finally, we can point out that in the future we could incorporate the control of new fluctuating factors (real time constraints) integrating new aspects, without having any repercussion on the part of the system already developed. Precisely, the reusability is one of the most relevant advantages of AOSD (Aspect Oriented Software Development) [10].

4.3 Implementation Tools

To carry out the adaptive layer structure presented before we will adopt J2SE 5.0 in combination with the AspectJ, as the most popular, extended and consolidated aspect oriented extension for Java, as is proven in [21]. This platform guarantees the integration between both plasticity engines presented, as well as the dissemination of the implicit plasticity engine to the most wide range of mobile devices. Precisely, the J2SE 5.0 version

---

[23] They encapsulate and represent system information, making it explicitly accessible and modifiable. To manipulate them it is defined an interface called MetaObject Protocol (MOP), where specify changes to reflect in the base level
[24] Programming construct to capture the required join points.
[25] Identifiable point in the execution of a system.

brings a new metadata facility as the most significant addition to the core Java language to date, allowing a powerful and at the same time easy combination of metadata and AOP, mutually benefitial. It improves the use of a reflective API making possible reflective access. Specifically, it can be accomplished using the so called metadatabased pointcuts[26].

To port this engine to mobile devices we have the J2ME language. Actually, as AspectJ generates pure Java byte code, applications will be able to be deployed in any device supporting any version of the JVM.

5 Conclusions

Though the benefits of incorporating a plasticity component into a multi-appliance interactive system may be immense, the actual practicalities present some important difficulties. A successful solution to the problem will mark a milestone in mobile computing.

This paper tackles this notable problem and presents an architecture to support the implicit plasticity engine, in which reflection and AOP techniques are combined. On the one hand, the reflection arises as a mechanism to solve the contextawareness, allowing designing for change. On the other hand, the AOP helps to integrate the contextual factors in the system performance. Furthermore, AOP offers a mechanism to decouple the crosscutting concerns optimally, obtaining so the desired orthogonality.

Definitely, we assert that the structure proposed here for the adaptive layer satisfies a double purpose. Firstly, it fulfils with the initial expectances offering an adaptive behavior and UI. Secondly, it is adjusted to the canons of flexibility, reusability and smartness that today should be demanded to any software product. Therefore it constitutes a valid option to manage the intrinsic concepts to systems with implicit plasticity.

6 References

[1] Abowd, G.D.; Mynatt, E. (2000). Charting Past, Present and Future Research in Ubiquitous Computing ACM Transactions on Computer-Human Interaction, Special issue on HCI in the new Millenium, Vol 7(1), 29-58
[2] Ardissono, L.; Goy, A. (2000). Dynamic Generation of Adaptive Catalogs. Proceedings of Adaptive Hypermedia and Web-base Systems.

---

[26] The join point model augmented with metadata. Facilitates simpler pointcuts.

[3] Buchanan, G.; Farrant, S.; Jones, M.; Thimbleby, H.; Marsden, G.; Pazzani,M. (2001). Improving Mobile Internet Usability. Proceedings of the International Conference on World Wide Web, 673-680, ACM Press.

[4] Byun, H.E.; Cheverst, K. (2001). Exploiting User Models and Context Awareness to Suport Personal Daily Activities. Proceedings of Workshop on User Modelling for ContextAware Applications.

[5] Calvary, G.; Coutaz, J.; Thevenin, D. (2001). Supporting Context Changes for Plastic User Interfaces: a Process and a Mechanism. Proceedings of IHM-HCI'2001, 349-363.

[6] Calvary, G.; et al. (2002). Plasticity of User Interfaces: A Revised Reference Framework. Proceedings of TAMODIA 2002, 127-134.

[7] CAMELEON – Context Aware Modelling for Enabling and Leveraging Effective interaction. (2003). http://giove.cnuce.cnr.it/cameleon.html

[8] Chen, G.; Kotz, D. (2000). A survey of contextaware mobile computing research. Technical Report TR2000381. Computer Science Department, Dartmouth College, Hanover, New Hampshire.

[9] Cheverst, K.; Davies, N.; Mitchell, K.; Smith, P. (2000). Providing Tailored (ContextAware) Information to City Visitors. Proceedings of Conference on Adaptive Hypermedia and Adaptive Webbased Systems, Trento.

[10] Jacobson, I.; PanWei, Ng. AspectOriented Software Development with Use Cases. AddisonWesley Object Technology Series

[11] Kiczales, G.; Lamping, J.; Mendhekar, A.; Maeda, C.; Lopes, C.; Loingtier, J.M.; Irwin, J. (1997). Aspectoriented Programming. M. Aksit and S. Matsuoka, ed., 11th ECOOP'97, Vol. 1241 of LNCS 220-242.

[12] Maes, P. (1987). Concepts and Experiments in Computional Reflection. Proceedings of the 2nd OOPSLA'87 147-156.

[13] Pawlak, R.; Duchien, L.; Florin, Gl.; LegondAubry, F.; Seinturier, L.; Martelli, L. (2002). A UML Notation for AspectOriented Software Design. Proceedings of AO Modelling with UML Workshop at the AOSD 2002.

[14] Sendín, M. (2004). Dichotomy in the Plasticity Process: Architectural Framework Proposal. Advances in Pervasive Computing. Austrian Computer Society. Doctoral Colloquium in Pervasive Computing. 141-147.

[15] Sendín, M.; Lorés, J. (2004). Plastic User Interfaces: Designing for Change. Proceedings of the Making modelbased UI design practical: usable and open methods and tools Workshop (IUICADUI'04).

[16] Sendin, M.; Lores, J. (2004). Plasticity in Mobile Devices: a Dichotomic and Semantic View. Proceedings of Workshop on Engineering Adaptive Web, supported by AH 2004, Eindhoven, 5867, ISSN: 09264515.

[17] Schilit, B.; Adams, N.; Want, R. (1994). Contextaware Computing Applications. Proceedings of IEEE Workshop on Mobile Computing Systems and Applications, 8590. IEEE Computer Society Press.

[18] Thevenin, D. (2001). Adaptation en Interaction HommeMachine: Le cas de la Plasticité. PHD Thesis, Joseph Fourier University, Grenoble.

[19] Thevenin, D.; Coutaz, J. (1999). Plasticity of User Interfaces: Framework and Research Agenda. Proceedings of Interact'99, Edinburgh, 110-117.

[20] Vassileva, J. (1997). Ensuring a Taskbased Individualized Interface for Hypermedia Information Retrieval through Use Modeling. Maybury M.T. (ed.) Intelligent Multimedia Information Retrieval, MIT Press, London.

[21] Xerox PARC. (2002). AspectJ home page. Web.

Using A Dialogue Space for Achieving Lightweight Participatory Design of Collaborative Tools

Henrry Rodríguez, Kerstin Severinson Eklundh, Nils-Erik Gustafsson

Interaction and Presentation Laboratory, Royal Institute of Technology, Stockholm, Sweden +468 790 91 57
Raffinaderiet AB Iversonsgatan 6 S-114 30 Stockholm, Sverige +468 730 634 629
henrry@nada.kth.se, kse@nada.kth.se, nils-erik@raffinaderiet.se

Introduction

The process of designing a new system, aiming to support a specific task, might be full of unexpected results. The original goals can easily swerve, and in this process the task is also redefined. Furthermore, the artifact (in this case the system) adapts itself to the requirements that the new task imposes and creates new possibilities that, in turn, may modify the task. Carroll [1] defined this process as the task-artifact cycle.

In this paper, we present our experiences from the design of a collaborative tool, the Domain Help System (DHS), which bears witness of the task-artifact cycle through iterations of user participation. We focus in particular on the evolution of the tool in relation to the contexts in which it was used, and on how the commenting feature of the system contributed to its design "from the inside".

The study has given valuable experiences for the development of collaboration tools, integrating users into the design process in a straightforward way by supporting a dialogue between users and designers.

The approach is to create an easy to access, public, persistent dialogue space embedded in the application to be developed. Users and designers share this dialogue space. The dialogue space is used to make comments on the system not only by the designers but also by the users. Furthermore, users can voluntarily and unobtrusively make comments on the system. It seems that an immediate acknowledgement that the comment will be read by the designers and that a response to those comments are given in the persistent dialogue space have stimulated users participation in the design of the system.

R. Navarro-Prieto and J. L. Vidal (eds.), HCI Related Papers of Interacción 2004, 179-194.
© *2006 Springer. Printed in the Netherlands.*

Also such dialogue space on the WWW is a suitable tool for supporting distributed teams of designers especially in the development of Web-based tools.

The DHS Project: ideas and rationale

The Domain Help System (DHS) [27] project started in 1996, and originally aimed to put forward a new approach for the design of help systems. In contrast to traditional help systems that relate only to the tool in which they are embedded, this system should also support the collaborative development of the domain knowledge relevant for a task or a set of tasks.

The content of traditional help systems is static, in the sense that users cannot add to or modify their information. For example, after solving a problem, users cannot record how it was solved, which might be useful as the user might later forget the steps s/he performed to reach the solution. Neither can the solution be shared with others, e.g. colleagues, who may need to solve the same or a similar problem in the future. One way not to forget a solution is to make annotations about it, but traditional help systems typically lack this feature. To tackle these deficiencies of traditional help systems, we intended to design a help system open to users. Furthermore, the system would not only be problem-oriented, but also support the development of domain knowledge relevant for a task.

The original idea was to let users include and share new items of domain knowledge, and thus collaboratively "feed" the system to build up an "iceberg model of information" [4]. This meant that initially only a minimum of information would be presented, geared towards the information needs of an experienced user, and that gradually more information would be available upon request.

After an initial discussion stage in the design group, the approach to the information structure was simplified. The basic units of domain knowledge were to be represented by Web documents [28] or sections. Comments are a simple way to represent related items of information, so it was decided to use this representation in the system. If expressing an opinion, comments give users the chance to participate in a discussion, and this may be the basis for a dialogue within the system. These features were consequently

---

[27] The DHS is not what usually we know as a help system. For practical reasons and practice the name of the system has not been changed.

[28] The term Web document refers to any document that can be presented on the World Wide Web, usually in HTML format.

chosen as basic elements of the DHS system. The present design of the system has evolved through several studies of use in natural contexts, where users have participated in discussions about the design of the system as well as about the task at hand.

Basic characteristics of the DHS system

A crucial concept in the DHS system is the domain, i.e., a shared information space defined by a specific context or application. Technically, a domain corresponds to a site on the WWW where a collection of Web documents is gathered and to which users can attach comments. The participants share the information contained in the documents, and jointly create an evolving set of comments on each document.

To participate, users send their documents in electronic format to the so-called editor of the domain, who makes an HTML version of them, if needed, and includes them in the domain. Using the DHS, users can retrieve the Web documents and their comments, or add new comments, but they cannot delete or modify any of the original information stored in the domain[29].

An instructional document (so far entitled "About this prototype", ATP) is also included in the domain. This document describes how to use the DHS system, and gives some troubleshooting advice. In the case studies, users were told that they could make any kind of comments (error report,

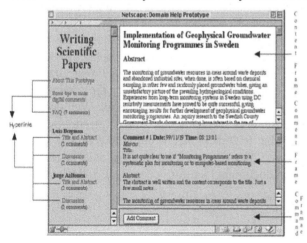

The layout of the DHS in a Web browser

---

[29] In a further development of the DHS system to support collaborative writing, a system has been created which also allows for changes to the document by participants [10].

suggestion, complaint, etc.) on the system or their experiences of it in the commenting space of the ATP document, which would then be read by someone from the design group. In this way we encouraged users to participate in the design of the system, notably while they were interacting with it.

A central concern in the design of the DHS has been how to use the screen space to allow for direct and visual access to both documents and comments.

When the user enters a domain in DHS, the Web browser window is divided into four scrollable frames as follows (see figure 1):

1. The index frame (left frame) displays a table of contents of the domain. This list is generated automatically by the system, and includes links to all the Web documents in the domain. Also, for each link it is indicated how many comments the Web document has received so far. By selecting a link, the corresponding Web document and its comments are presented to the users. The DHS reserves the first place in this list to the ATP document's link.

2. The Web document frame (top-right frame) displays the currently selected document. The document in this frame is what we will call the active Web document. When the user enters the system, by default, the first active Web document is the ATP document.

3. The comment frame (middle-right frame) displays the set of comments made so far on the active Web document. If a Web document has no comments, a message saying so is presented to the user. The comments are chronologically ordered, so that the most recent comment is shown when a Web document is selected. Comments are marked with an id number (sequential), the time of creation, and author.

4. The command frame (bottom-right frame) displays a button for making a comment, "Add Comment". When selected, it pops up the Add comment window (ACW) in which users can write their name (or nickname) and their comment. Once submitted, the comment is appended to the list of previous comments on the active Web document and it is immediately visible in the comment frame (providing instant acknowledgement that the feedback has been received and is now published). An email with the comment is automatically sent to the author of the active Web document (see further below), and the ACW is closed.

Contexts in which the DHS has been used: effects on design

As part of the design process, the DHS prototype has been introduced to groups that were to solve a real collaborative task. The characteristics of the use of the tool in these contexts led to design changes that reflected the different purposes and circumstances of collaboration. In this evolution, users' participation through the ATP dialogue was an essential element. Moreover, the features that the system acquired through its use in these different contexts were gradually changing the goals that we had at the very beginning of the project. Finally, we were not developing a help system but a more general, collaborative tool offering a variety of possibilities.

The first context of use was a pilot study made in our research department. Sixteen participants produced 77 comments that contained almost 4.000 words and a 20-minute interview was held with 13 of the participants. The study lasted for three months. The study used an early prototype of the DHS, and explored the potential of the system for the purpose of revising the department's Web presentations. This context shaped the course of the project in the direction of a general development of a Web-based tool for sharing knowledge, and opened the way for two subsequent case studies. In these studies, data were collected both through interviews and Web-based surveys, and by storing the comments users submitted using the system.

The design group members, consisting of three people, were distributed in different locations. They met occasionally face-to-face during this process, and otherwise communicated via email.

The case studies were made in an educational setting, where students submitted one document each to the domain, and were instructed to comment on each other's documents. Both studies were longitudinal (1997-2001), as data were collected through repeated instances of the courses, and made partly in parallel with each other. In the first study, made within a Computer course, students (68) had been instructed to write about an experience of collaboration with technology and discuss each other's texts using the DHS. Comments therefore referred to information in previous comments as well as in the surrounding document. The students produced 327 comments containing almost 31.000 words. The other study was performed in the context of an academic writing course for graduate students (48). Here, comments were typically made to help participants improve the grammar and style of the document, and thus the individual comments were seldom linked into a dialogue. The students produced 693 comments with almost 81.000 words. This distinction between a "discussion context" and an "annotation context" for the use of the system also had effects on the subsequent design. We will call these studies the D-study and the A-study, respectively[30].

Permanent view of the document to be commented on

The ACW in the version used in the pilot study presented only an input area. A significant change to it was to make this window bigger and divided into two frames, where the left frame contains the active Web document.

If the comment that the user intended to make was related to the content of the active Web document, then the user might need to refer to it while making the comment. In fact, the teacher of the writing course in the A-study expressed how important it was to have a permanent view of the text to be commented on.

Need to quote from the original text

In many of the comments, the users made direct reference to the text of the Web document. Very often, this reference was achieved by cut-and-paste from the Web document frame[31].

It emerged that cut-and-paste of the content of the original Web document was done more frequently when the DHS was used in the annotation context. The students regularly used quotes to refer to the parts of the document that they wanted to comment on, as the comments usually concerned the style and grammar of the text. To support this action we included a button that, when activated, automatically pastes the text of the active Web document into the text area where the comment is about to be written. In this way those users who want to quote the original text are supported by the system. In example[32] 1 (taken from the A-study), Karla has copied part of the text that she is revising into her comment.

---

[30] The case studies are described in detail in [8].
[31] Evidence of this was that a carriage return was left by this action, distorting the marginals of the text.
[32] The examples we will present in this paper are shown in the same format (comment number, date, author, comment text) that were presented in the DHS. The names of the authors have been changed.

1. *Comment #1 99/10/06 16:32:18 Karla:*
   [...]. Later, you write: "The use of refiners for manufacturing mechanical pulps demand a high energy input." Why not make this more clearly a disadvantage? [...]

The use of the commenting dialogue in the design of the DHS

Experiences from the case studies show a variable use of the commenting space, as we have seen above, where the interactive aspect of the dialogue of comments is more or less pronounced. Generally, a new comment in DHS may refer either to the corresponding document or to a previous comment, or both. In addition, certain comments were made on a meta-level, so that their content would refer to the ongoing discussion itself, or to features and experiences of the DHS system. The last-mentioned comments were primarily made in the ATP section of the domains.

These dialogues evolving around the ATP document had a crucial role in the development of the DHS. This space for comments was used in very different ways, reflecting the users' varying background and interest in system design. The following comment made by a user in the pilot study illustrates how a comment contributed to the change of the tool.

2. *Comment # 6 97/04/03 15:16*
   Peter:
   Wouldn't "next" be more suitable than "more"? Nice tool!

After this comment, the design group had an asynchronous discussion (using the commenting feature of the DHS) about a possible change of the word "More" to "Next" in the navigation bar of the commenting space. The word "More" had been used until then, because we were still thinking in terms of the concept of an "iceberg model of information". It was assumed that the navigation hyperlink would take the user to the next level, that is, to more general information, but in this application, it was rather taking us to the next comment on the same level. We might have arrived at this decision in one of our face-to-face meetings, but the important point is that it was a user who made us aware of the situation.

In the following sections, we describe how the presence of the commenting dialogue helped induce changes in the design of DHS. We first describe cases that actually led to the introduction of new features as suggested by users. Then, we describe a case of user input that did not lead to any change in the system, a decision motivated by the overall purpose of the DHS as a document-centred collaboration tool.

New comment awareness

One of the main problems of the first version of DHS was the lack of awareness about new comments. The only way for users to know if a comment had been added to the system was by visiting the domain. In fact, they might have to browse the entire domain to find a new comment. In many cases this search might be fruitless, if the user was expecting to find a new comment and none was found. Even worse, users could accidentally skip a Web document to which indeed a new comment had been added. As a result, users might decrease the frequency of visiting the domain and perhaps forget about it. It was quite possible, therefore, that a response to a comment might take a long time, and might, hence, be less relevant when it arrived.

Example 3 (not taken from the ATP) shows such a situation in which the response to a comment was made almost 27 days later.

To alleviate this problem, an awareness function was introduced so that an email message is sent automatically to the author(s) of the Web document when a comment is made on it. The text of the comment is attached to the email and its subject is labelled in such a way that the receiver would recognize that the message is sent by the DHS system and also to which document it belongs. This makes the author aware of what a particular member has been doing, and especially aware of the feedback on the documents. This approach of awareness is known as shared feedback [2], i.e. presenting feedback on individual users' activities within the shared space (p. 112). However, in this case, receiving a lot of email could be overwhelming. It has been discussed to implement the concept of coupled/uncoupled awareness [3] in a future version of DHS to mitigate this problem.

3. *Comment # 1 97/03/18 22:18*
    Diana:
    I think it is best to remove all the "forthcoming" references. It is much nicer to include them when they get published!

    Comment # 2 97/04/14 09:46
    Oliver: [author of the document]
    I agree with Diana. It seems to me as if the text is an old version. ...

To locate comments in the domain

Sending the comments via email solves only part of the awareness problem. Although the email message indicates to which document the comment has been attached in its subject field, users might prefer to read a comment in its proper context, that is, in the DHS domain itself as all the comments are presented together in one scrollable frame. For this purpose, they would often move from their email program to DHS, where there was accordingly also a need to find new comments quickly. To facilitate for users to locate new comments, it was decided to attach a comment counter tag beside the links in the index-frame to indicate how many comments had been made on the document when the current session started, for example: Introduction (3 comments).

4. *Comment # 24 97/04/15 17:02*
    Sussy:
    There should be a way to check quickly if there are any new comments. ....

Users might recall that the number of comments on one of the Web documents had changed. This feature also helps explorative browsing of the domain. At a glance, users would know whether a Web document in the domain had got comments and how many comments there were so far.

Example 4 shows a user comment in which this solution is suggested.

Error repairs by mutual participation

The Web can sometimes be an unstable user environment, due to the lack of compatibility between different platforms, Web browser versions, and users' own set-up preferences of their computers. To simulate all the possible environments in which users might work would require a lot of effort and be time consuming. Therefore, a positive aspect of the dialogue space in DHS was that it could help identify and repair such Web-related problems, and simultaneously make other users aware of them by providing them with the possibility of "overhearing" the dialogue.

5. *Comment # 37 97/05/05 23:41*
    Mark:
    Using a simple 640x480 pixel PC at home, I find that the comment window has resize handles, but still cannot be resized. (It can, however, be maximized...) It also, unfortunately, appears slightly too small, as the vertical scroll bar is beyond reach and the Clear & Send buttons show up slightly masked by the window frame.

Example 5 shows a technical problem that the developer did not experience in his own environment. It would have been very difficult to detect these kind of errors if other users would not have reported them.

Using the dialogue space it is also very likely that errors that are not seen by the designer might be found and communicated by another person. Example 6 illustrates this situation. Mark discovered an error that is reported via the DHS. About an hour later the error was repaired.

6. *Comment # 7 97/04/03 15:35*
    Mark:
    I just noticed that the mail links to Karla and yours truly are missing: "The requested URL
    /~Charles/mail was not found on this server."
    I would also like to be able to resize the comment window, but perhaps there is a reason for it to
    be fixed that I have forgotten? (Hopefully this, rather than the window itself, can be fixed? ;)

    Comment #8 97/04/03 16:47
    Charles:
    Mark, Your Ref # 7 was a mistake of mine in the HTML tag. Now it works. Thanks. About resize
    the comment window there is no way as this is an HTML parameter and is FIXED. I can modify it
    but not dynamically.

The fact that the users could read comments reporting an error or suggestion inside the system, and that these comments were public, seems to have encouraged them to make comments on the system. Additionally, they could see the response the designers provided to other comments. This presumably assured them that they were heard by somebody, that behind the system there was a person who took responsibility for the system and tried to remedy their problems or fulfil their requirements. All this appears to have increased the users' trust in the system and at the same time their participation in the design. This is consistent with earlier work involving the successful deployment of an integrated email function ("Email Help") into a software tool and the use of an Internet discussion group to facilitate user feedback [5, 6]. It was found in that study that the following were important aspects for successful elicitation of user feedback:

• The user must know how to provide feedback

• The user must feel that the feedback has an impact (at the very least is acknowledged)

• The user must feel that providing feedback does not distract from the work at hand

In the case of the DHS the first and second of these aspects mentioned were facilitated by the fact that ordinary system functions were used for giving feedback on the design. All the users in the interviews and in the surveys reported that making a comment (from the interface point of view) was very easy. Yet, from a practical point of view as all the comments in the system are shown to all the participants, they can see how others have made their comments. The DHS provides users with the sense that their comments are received as they can see them in the system once submitted. The responses that are given to the participants also show others that the feedback has been received. Note that in example 7 the participant wrote "friends behind this" in her comment that means that she expects someone to reply to her request.

7. *Comment #4 98/02/14 14:11*
   Susanna:
   ...can someone of you "good" friends behind this [the DHS], move my previous message to the right topic? ...

A case of unchanged design: the problem of threading

Threading refers to arranging the sequence of contributions to a computer-mediated discussion according to their subject, by using the "reply-to" relationship as ordering principle. In newsgroup readers, for example, users can select to read a particular thread, and the threading of discussions is emphasized by graphical means such as indentation.

In the commenting dialogue of DHS, comments are chronologically ordered, and no subject line is used when creating a new comment. In fact, a threading functionality was requested several times by users of the pilot study, as illustrated in example 8.

8. *Comment #23 98/02/20 14:21*
   Jimmy:
   I think threading of comments will be important as their number grows.

Although this suggestion recurred several times, we decided that threading was not suitable for our goal. Threading requires an initiating post with a subject or topic that users consider a representative one. In our case, the subject of the discussion was given by the Web-document of the particular domain. By creating another subject, the discussion deviates from the original purpose. Another reason was that we were not expecting a large number of comments for each Web-document. Indeed, the average of the number of comments (for all the Web documents that got commented in the domain but the ATP document) were: for the pilot study 2.6, for the D- study 4.3, and for the A-study 2.6. On the other hand, the average number of comments for the ATP document, that was present in all the domains, was 16.2. Here the discussion was not centred on the document, but on various properties of the DHS system itself.

Whittaker, Terveen, Hill & Cherny [11] in a quantitative study on Usenet newsgroups discussions, found that messages on average referred to two previous messages, which indicates a lower amount of interactivity than might be expected (p. 262). This could mean that for a commenting space with a moderate number of comments, say ten, threading would not be necessary. In the DHS case studies, users were using the id number to make reference to a previous comment (see above comment #8 in example 6). We also observed that if a response to a comment was adjacent to it, the author usually did not bother to make an explicit reference to it, which increased the sense of a written dialogue.

An important factor was that during a discussion, participants most of the time made an explicit and direct reference to the content of the document in question. For example, "what you wrote", "the situation you describe", "the people in the examples", "I found your text to be interesting". That means that the conversation was indeed about the active Web document, i.e., the document was the centre of the ongoing discussion. In other Web-based forum tools, such as newsgroups, the original text that started the discussion is not easily reached by users, and the discussion often gets far away from the original topic suggested in the first text (so-called topic decay in computer-mediated communication has been discussed by 7). The tendency to lose the initial focus gets more pronounced as time passes. In the DHS, we found that the central topic of the discussion, in this case, the content of the document, was always recalled in the comments. Even if the new comment was made a long time after the very first comment was made; the new comment would, somehow, touch on the document that originated the discussion. This is presumably related to the fact that users can always view and read the original text while using DHS, and the discussions are not threaded. Generally, the document has a more important role in our system than the starting message of a newsgroup discussion.

The ATP discussion space as a tool for system design

A virtual jotter for designers

The need to make an annotation (of an idea, for example) can occur at any moment in a design process. Members of the DHS design group used the discussion space as a repository of ideas, facilitated by the ubiquitous nature of the Web. In spite of its simplicity, the Web-based commenting space of DHS allowed for annotations in different forms (e.g., text, pictures, sound clips) when users or designers needed to illustrate their ideas.

We observed that when an individual idea was reported in the system by one of the designers, it was, generally, communicated in a clear and explicit manner. It seems that this was done because the designer wanted the rest of the group (not only the designers but also the users) to understand the idea. If not, others would ask questions until the issue was clarified.

We believe that this space was used as a "virtual jotter" for designers because it allowed information sharing in an accessible form, and that it helped designers avoid forgetting their ideas. Most importantly, all the information gathered was in one place for the future design process. In Example 9 John jots down the idea and does not address another person in is comment.

9. *Comment #11 98/07/14 11:53*
John:
One click to resize the frames: The idea is to get a better overview of the section or of the comments, depends on the users what s/he wants

Observe that he bothers to elaborate his idea in a way different from a personal note, where a few words would have been enough as a reminder. The reason given (in personal communication with John) was because the comment was going to be read by other designers as well as the users. The public aspect of the written comments might increase understanding among designers and users. We have not yet investigated the reaction of the users to this kind of annotations, and therefore this problem merits further investigation

A medium for participatory design

Table 1. Project member versus users' participation

	Design group (3 people)		User group (13 people)		Total
	N°	%	N°	%	
Comments	33	69	15	31	48
Words produced	1923	63	1106	37	3029
Error report	6	43	8	57	14
Suggestion for the design	8	44	10	56	18
Statement/opinion	9	64	5	36	14
Encourage the work	4	67	2	33	6
Question design related	4	80	1	20	5
Solution/answer	10	83	2	17	12

We have collected and categorized the comments made on the ATP document in the pilot study. In addition we have counted the number of words in the comments as a measure of the intensity of communication. The results were distributed in two groups according to who made the comment: a user or someone from the design group. In this way, we attempt to assess the participation of the users in the design process of the DHS.

In total, the ATP document in our pilot study received 48 comments, containing 3029 words. One comment could be classified in several categories. The design group made 33 comments (69%) that amounted to 1923 words. In other words, 31% of the comments and 37% of the words in the comments were produced by users who were not formally involved with the development of the project.

The comments made by the users contained error reports, requirements, or reported their impression of the system (see table 1). Note that in the categories "Error reports" and "Suggestion for the design" the users' contributions exceed the one made by the design group members. To some extent, this may be related to the face-to-face meetings that the design group had. However, we may note that users suggested 10 different ideas for the design of the DHS and reported 8 different errors.

Supporting communication among designers

In example 6 above, a request to modify the interface is part of the comment #7. The response about the possibility to perform this request is also given in comment #8 of the same example. It is important to notice that the discussion among designers in the example was carried out in a distributed-asynchronous mode. Face-to-face meetings in a working environment might often be difficult to set up. The comment presented in example 2 (about the word "More" or "Next") was a trigger for a discussion within the design group. Each of the designers sent their opinion with regard to that comment and a decision was taken, again without a face-to-face meeting

The commenting interface supported the use of HTML tags. By using this option in their comments, designers could present high-resolution and high-fidelity prototypes in their communication about new system functionality.

Conclusions

In this paper, we have shown how the DHS system evolved through the influence of the expanding contexts of use. The original system idea was gradually modified both by its use in new areas of collaboration, and by the ongoing dialogue in which both users and designers participated. These experiences show that the quality of user-designer communication is a crucial aspect of successful design. However, it has also emerged that there are areas where some goals for the system must be given priority in relation to apparently well-founded demands in a particular context. Users might demand features that they are familiar with and be reluctant to try a new solution. Designers should keep in mind that users might capriciously define requirements that can dwindle down the novelty of the system. As a result, the new system would be just "one more" system illustrating well-known principles. In the case of DHS, our goals gradually focused on a general and simple design, supporting communication around Web documents as a part of small or medium group collaboration. Threading would, we argue, have concentrated the discussion just on the ongoing dialogue, neglecting the original document as a natural focus.

Users' participation in the design process of the DHS was in fact very active. This might be because they sensed that their comments in the shared space were being read, and responded to. The public response from the designer might also have contributed to increasing the users' trust in the design group. Including a common dialogue space within a system that is being developed is a simple way to increase users' participation in the design process. In fact, collecting other data from users during the use of a system may be too demanding or difficult for reasons of integrity. Giving the possibility to users to report about their impression of the system in an easy, unobtrusive, voluntary way, and ensuring that what is said will be taken into account, will increase users' participation in the design process as well as promote the development of common ground among designers.

References

1. Carroll J. M., Kellogg W. & Rosson M. (1991), The task-artifact cycle. In Designing Interaction: Psychology at the Human-Computer Interface Eds. Carroll J. M. Cambridge Series on Human-Computer Interaction pp.74-102, Cambridge, UK Cambridge University Press.

2. Dourish, P. & Bellotti, V. (1992), Awareness and Coordination in Shared Work Spaces: the Power of Simple Shared Workspaces. Proceedings of ACM CSCW'92 Conference on Computer-Supported Cooperative Work p. 107-114.

3. Fuchs, L., Pankoke-Babatz, U., and Prinz, W. (1995), Supporting cooperative awareness with local event mechanisms: The groupdesk system. In Marmolin H., Sundblad Y., and Schmidt K., editors, Proceedings of the 4th European Conference On Computer Supported Cooperative Work, pages 247-262. Kluwer Academic Publishers, Dordrecht.

4. Gustafsson, N., Severinson-Eklundh, K. & Rodríguez H. (1998), Domänhjälp, Technical report TRITA-NA-D9803, CID-30, NADA, The Royal Institute of Technology of Stockholm.

5. Gustafsson, N-E. (1997), Intranetworking with users – fast & facile feedback, Proceedings of the 16th International Symposium on Human Factors in Telecommunications, Oslo, 1997.

6. Gustafsson, N-E. (1995), Improving the Man-Machine Interface in Network Element Management, Proceedings of Effective Network Management Systems, London.

7. Herring, S. (1999) Interactional coherence in CMC. Journal of Computer-mediated Communication, 4(4).

8. Rodríguez, H. (2001), Using the WWW as infrastructure for collaborative production of documents. Licentiate thesis. TRITA-NA-0117, The Royal Institute of Technology of Stockholm.

9. Rodríguez, H. (1999), "The Domain Help System". Technical report TRITA-NA-P9912, CID-56, NADA, The Royal Institute of Technology of Stockholm.

10. Rodríguez, H., Hee-Cheol K., Severinson-Eklundh K. (1999), Using the Web as infrastructure for collaborative writing and document design, Poster, In Conference supplement for the sixth European conference on computer supported cooperative work, 7-8.

11. Whittaker, S., Terveen L., Hill W. & Cherny, L. (1998), The dynamics of mass interaction, Proceedings of ACM CSCW'98 Conference on Computer-Supported Cooperative Work, 257-264.

Visualizing Shared Highlighting Annotations

M. Villarroel, P. de la Fuente, A. Pedrero and J. Adiego

University of Zaragoza, DIIS, Zaragoza, Spain

University of Valladolid, ESII, Valladolid, SpainUPSA,

EscuelaUniversitaria de Informática, Salamanca,

Spainmavs@acm.org, {pfuente, jadiego}@infor.uva.es, apedrero@upsa.es

Introduction

The importance of being able to create and manipulate annotations when reading a digital document has been stated in various studies [5] [9]. Having access to these functionalities improves the task of reading digital documents though it is not as easy as doing it on paper documents [12]. One of the easiest styles to make annotations is highlighting and it is commonly implemented in many applications for digital document processing.

Annotations can be shared and they can be used as an effective medium for information exchange in collaborative contexts [3] [4] [11] [16]. Highlighting annotations can be shared and, for example, they can be used to identify relevant text areas into a document [17]. Going forward, it would be interesting to compare the highlighting of two or more users in a visual mode. Although it seems to be not a difficult task, the visualization of this style of annotations presents some perception problems. This paper describes some of the problems we have faced when implementing functionalities for visualizing shared highlighting annotations.

Antecedents

Digital documents annotation is the topic of many studies. For example, Golovchinsky et al. [5] used annotations as input for query anticipation functionalities. Cadiz et al. [4] studied annotations as a medium to exchange information in a collaborative environment. Phelp et al. [13] presented an annotation application that is independent of the particular

R. Navarro-Prieto and J. L. Vidal (eds.), HCI Related Papers of Interacción 2004, 195-204.

format of the digital document. Nichols et al. [11] and Bouthors et al. [3] used annotations as input for recommender systems.

In [14] the Web Annotator system is discussed. It is a system for digital web document annotation. In [2] the problem of orphan annotations and some solutions are discussed. In [10] an RDF infrastructure for shared annotations in web environments is presented: Annotea.

It is evident that the digital annotation field has attracted the interest of many researchers. However, it should be noted that just a few of these studies are focused on the more elemental aspects of the problem, such as elements presentation, use of colour, etc.

In [18] the necessity of maintaining the consistency of the design of the user interface for digital-book applications is recommended as well as in [7] and [9]. The same suggestions are given in [20] but in this case in the context of digital annotations. In [11] a few guidelines for the design of user interfaces for annotation-based collaborative applications are pointed out.

Previous work

We have developed an application to create and manipulate annotations on HTML documents; the documents are localized in a digital library. Documents are not modified and annotations are stored independently of them. The application has two main functions: a) to provide annotation facilities on the documents [16] and b) to process these annotations in order to improve the performance of the digital library query system [17]. The users share their highlighting annotations and, assuming that they point out interesting fragments of a document, the application tries to identify relevant terms, using these annotations as input for the process. Details of the identification of relevant terms and how they are used to improve the query system performance are presented in [17].

Visualizing higlighting annotations

As the application described in the previous section was being developed, it was evident that it could be interesting to visually compare annotations made by different users. Our first attempt consisted in assigning different colours to annotations of different users. Fig. 1 shows the highlighting annotations made by three different users. The colours assigned to each user are already shown. We want to compare these sets of annotations.

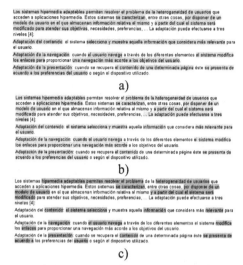

a)

b)

c)

Fig. 1. Highlighting annotations of three users.

If there are many annotations, it is evident that the document would look like a mix of fragments of different colours when they are superposed. Another problem appears when annotations intersect. In the first interface every set of annotations was placed over the previous ones, and in this way the last visualized set was covering the first ones. Fig. 2 shows this process. The problem with this approach is that it is possible for a user to cover all the annotations of other users. Also another problem arises from the evidence that we are loosing the possibility of verifying if there are intersection areas between the different highlighting annotations. This is very important because intersections point out that some users have agreed in assigning importance to the same fragments of the document.

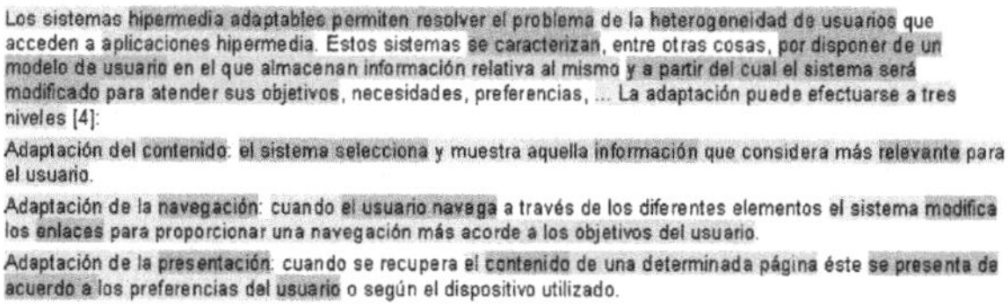

Fig. 2. Overlapping the highlighting annotations of three users.

All these problems required the modification of the strategy applied for visualizing annotations in a comparison mode.

Selecting a style for visualizing annotations

The first task to carry out was to select a good style for visualizing highlighting annotations. We analysed if using others styles for visualization could make the comparing process easier. We analysed the use of icons, background colour variation, underlining and rectangular-form marking. We used prototypes to find the most suitable for the problem. The background colour variation resulted the best of them because it was the most easily perceived thus requiring less effort to the users.

However, as it was exposed in previous sections, just changing the background colour for different sets of annotations has demonstrated not being a solution to our problem of visualization. It was necessary to adapt that strategy to help users compare highlighting annotations. In order to adjust our approach we studied the possible scenarios for comparing annotations.

Activities in the visualization of shared highlighting annotations

The most common activities when visualizing shared highlighting annotations are two: comparing annotations from different users and observing relevance levels calculated from the number of coincidences of highlighted fragments.

Comparing

Highlighting annotations point out which text fragments are interesting for a user. Comparing annotations from many users could help understanding how users see and read the text. Where they agree, by considering a fragment relevant (intersections), or they disagree (fragments with fewer number if intersections), and even if they agree by considering a part of the document to be irrelevant (a fragment never highlighted).

Identifying relevance

Intersections of highlighting annotations point out text areas where various users have agreed in considering those fragments interesting. The more users who highlight a fragment then the more interesting that fragment could be. The problem in this case is how to present this phenomenon to the users in a very easy and natural way.

Selecting a visualization strategy

The background colour variation was the presentation style to be implemented. However, our previous results demonstrated that the appropriate selection of colours was a critical factor for the solution of the visualization problem. An inappropriate selection of colours could lead users to difficult or even erroneous perceptions of the compared highlighted fragments. In order to find the most suitable visualizing strategy we developed prototypes to study each one of the previously described activities.

Comparing

To compare highlighting annotations it is required to be able to identify the source of the annotations (the user who made the annotations), even when annotations overlap. Under this perspective using *primary colours (yellow, red and blue)* for one-user annotations and its combinations to represent intersections seemed to be a good approach. We tried it for visualizing sets of annotations from two and three users. Fig. 3 shows the palette of background colours developed for it.

For example, annotations from User 1 are yellow and annotations from User 2 are red. Orange represent areas were annotations of User 1 and User 2 overlap. Thus, green represents intersections of User 1 and User 3 (blue) and violet represents intersections of User 2 and User 3. The intersection of three users required the use of a special combination because we could not use white as background colour. For this case we selected a combination of light-blue background and red foreground colours in order to emphasise the fact of having a coincidence of three users.

Fig. 3. Background colors and its combinations. Case I: Pseudo-subtractive model

Experimental results were discouraging. Users got confused and they found very hard to distinguish many-user highlighted areas from one-user ones. Users seemed to forget combination rules of *primary colours* and, for example, many times they indicated that texts in red background were perceived as being intersections of annotations. Results were unsatisfactory even in the case of comparing annotation sets from just two users. The application of the combination of this palette is presented in Fig. 4.

Surprisingly, users were able to distinguish three-user intersection areas. But this was because we changed the text foreground color and not because the background color suggested a more important area.

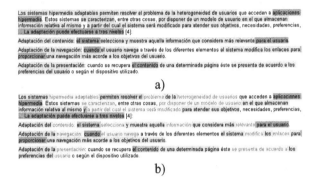

Fig. 4. Visualizing highlighting annotations of two and three users. Case I.

While experimenting with relevance representation, we used a tone variation strategy. The more intense the tonality of the background the more important was perceived to be the text. This fact and the observation of users pointing out, in the previous experiment, that red background represented intersection areas suggested that we were near to a more suitable presentation solution.

We reviewed some of the classical works in order to explain these results [1] [6]. The answers we have found were supported also by more recent and specific studies [8] [15] [19]. These works confirmed our primary observations about tone variation. The key point was in the contrast of colours produced for the variation of tones. When varying tonality we increased the contrast with the general white background color, helping in this way to perceive an area over others.

User 1

Text

Text Text Text

User 2 Text   Text   Text **User 3**

Fig. 5. Background colours and its combinations. Case II: Tone variation model.

As it is shown in Fig. 5, a new palette of background colours was developed. In this case, annotations from User 1 are represented by yellow colour, annotations from user 2 by light-orange colour and the intersection areas of users 1 and 2 by orange colour. User 3 annotations are represented by light-green colour and intersections of User 1 and 3 by green colour. Intersections of user 2 and 3 are represented by blue colour. Finally intersection areas for the three users are represented by light-purple colour. Fig. 6 shows the application of the new palette.

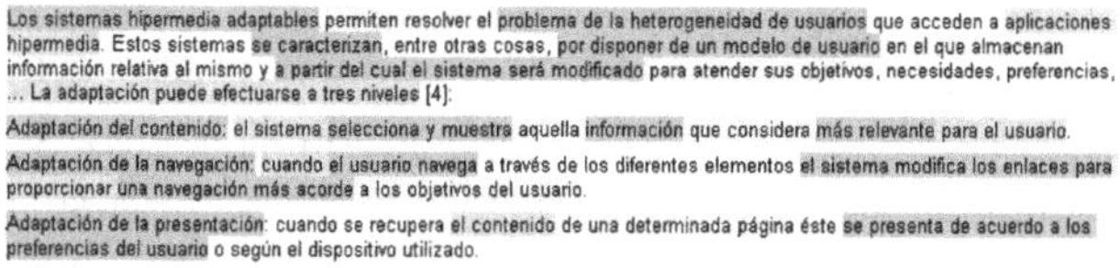

Los sistemas hipermedia adaptables permiten resolver el problema de la heterogeneidad de usuarios que acceden a aplicaciones hipermedia. Estos sistemas se caracterizan, entre otras cosas, por disponer de un modelo de usuario en el que almacenan información relativa al mismo y a partir del cual el sistema será modificado para atender sus objetivos, necesidades, preferencias, ... La adaptación puede efectuarse a tres niveles [4]:

Adaptación del contenido: el sistema selecciona y muestra aquella información que considera más relevante para el usuario.

Adaptación de la navegación: cuando el usuario navega a través de los diferentes elementos el sistema modifica los enlaces para proporcionar una navegación más acorde a los objetivos del usuario.

Adaptación de la presentación: cuando se recupera el contenido de una determinada página éste se presenta de acuerdo a los preferencias del usuario o según el dispositivo utilizado.

a)

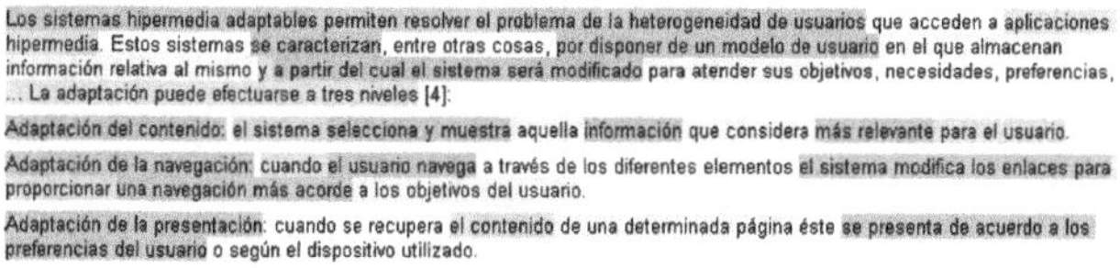

Los sistemas hipermedia adaptables permiten resolver el problema de la heterogeneidad de usuarios que acceden a aplicaciones hipermedia. Estos sistemas se caracterizan, entre otras cosas, por disponer de un modelo de usuario en el que almacenan información relativa al mismo y a partir del cual el sistema será modificado para atender sus objetivos, necesidades, preferencias, ... La adaptación puede efectuarse a tres niveles [4]:

Adaptación del contenido: el sistema selecciona y muestra aquella información que considera más relevante para el usuario.

Adaptación de la navegación: cuando el usuario navega a través de los diferentes elementos el sistema modifica los enlaces para proporcionar una navegación más acorde a los objetivos del usuario.

Adaptación de la presentación: cuando se recupera el contenido de una determinada página éste se presenta de acuerdo a los preferencias del usuario o según el dispositivo utilizado.

b)

Fig. 6. Visualizing highlighting annotations of two and three users. Case I.

The results of applying the last palette were promising, and posteriors experiments showed that it was a good alternative for our visualization problem. However, visualization of sets from four or more users is still a challenge.

Identifying relevance

Our first idea was presenting the relevance levels in a "cold-hot" scale using a range of colours varying from blue to red as it is applied when visualizing thermal images. Experimental results were not satisfactory enough. We explored the more simple possibility of using just one base colour and variations of it to represent different relevance levels. Fragments with a bigger number of intersections could be presented with intense background colours and the others with lighter colours. The application of this model is presented in Fig. 7. Users found this strategy to be less confusing than the application of the blue-red scale.

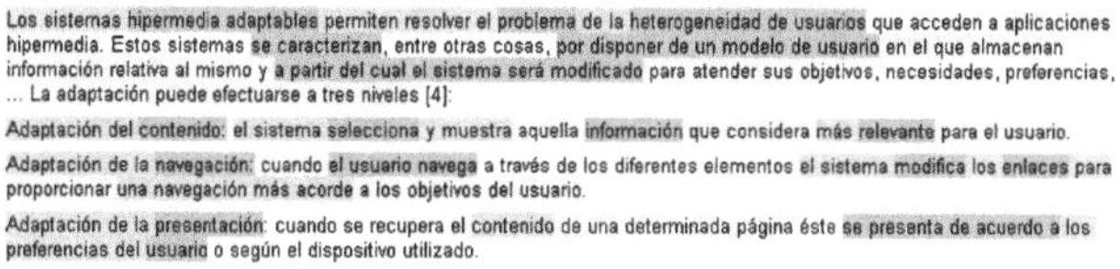

Los sistemas hipermedia adaptables permiten resolver el problema de la heterogeneidad de usuarios que acceden a aplicaciones hipermedia. Estos sistemas se caracterizan, entre otras cosas, por disponer de un modelo de usuario en el que almacenan información relativa al mismo y a partir del cual el sistema será modificado para atender sus objetivos, necesidades, preferencias, ... La adaptación puede efectuarse a tres niveles [4]:

Adaptación del contenido: el sistema selecciona y muestra aquella información que considera más relevante para el usuario.

Adaptación de la navegación: cuando el usuario navega a través de los diferentes elementos el sistema modifica los enlaces para proporcionar una navegación más acorde a los objetivos del usuario.

Adaptación de la presentación: cuando se recupera el contenido de una determinada página éste se presenta de acuerdo a los preferencias del usuario o según el dispositivo utilizado.

Fig. 7. Visualizing three levels of relevance.

Formative evaluation

The user interface of the application was modified in concordance to the results obtained. The visualization facilities can be used in two modes: comparing annotations and observing relevance. Of course, in both cases it is possible to add new highlighting annotations.

The application has been evaluated by a group of users with promising results. They reacted positively to the changes implemented. Some of these users had participated previously in the evaluation of the first prototypes.

Experimentations suggested that it also could be interesting to compare the set of annotations of one user with the rest of annotations but showing the relevance of the others. Another variation comes from the requirement of taking into account the number of annotations independently of the user who has made it in order to enable or to restrict the possibility of one user marking a fragment more than once. Currently one user can highlight many times a text area.

Conclusions

We had analysed different alternatives to deal with the problem of visualizing shared highlighting annotations. The most promising one for this particular context has been selected and a detailed study of how these can be applied to the visualization of shared annotations has been developed. It is relevant that one of the key points of the solution was the adequate selection of colours to present shared annotations. The results obtained are consistent with classical and more recent works on colour theory and colour perception.

The strategy of varying colour tonality has demonstrated to be useful, in order to facilitate the perception of different text areas.

It is necessary to execute a bigger set of experiments to get statistically significant results. It is also necessary to observe the use of the application in real-world situations.

Acknowledgements

This work has been partially supported by MCyT project (TIC2003-09268).

Special thanks to Cristina París (DIIS-CPS, University of Zaragoza) for her helpful comments and patience. The authors would like to thank the anonymous reviewers who provided valuable feedback on a previous version of this work.

References

[1]   Albers J (1967). Interaction of Color. Yale University Press, Revised edition, Nov 1987

[2]   Bernheim Brush A J, Bargeron D, Gupta A, Cadiz J J (2001). Robust annotation positioning in digital documents. CHI 01 Proceedings of the SIGCHI conference on Human factors in computing systems, Seattle, WA USA. ACM Press New York, NY, USA, pp. 285-292

[3]   Bouthors V, Dedieu O (1999). Pharos, a collaborative infrastructure for web knowledge sharing. In Abiteboul S and Vercoustre AM editors, Research and Advanced Technology for Digital Libraries. Third European Conference, ECDL'99, Paris, France: Proceedings, Lecture Notes in Computer Science, Springer-Verlag Inc, pp. 215-233

[4]   Cadiz J, Gupta A, Grudin J (2000). Using web annotations for asynchronous collaboration around documents. In CSCW 2000 Proceeding of the ACM 2000 Conference on Computer supported cooperative work, Philadelphia, PA USA, pp. 309-318. Also in Technical Report 00-44, Microsoft Research

[5]   Golovchinsky G, Price M, Schilit B (1999). From reading to retrieval: freeform ink annotations as queries. In SIGIR' 99, Proceedings of the 22nd annual ACM SIGIR conference on Research and development in information retrieval, Berkeley, CA USA, pp. 19-25

[6]   Itten J (1961). The Art of Color: The Subjective Experience and Objective Rationale of Color. John Wiley & Sons; Revised edition (Dec 1997).

[7]   Levy D, Marshall C (1995). Going digital: a look at assumptions underlying digital libraries. Communications of the ACM, 38(4):77-84

[8]   Meier B J (1988). ACE: a color expert system for user interface design. UIST 88 Proceedings of the 1st annual ACM SIGGRAPH symposium on User Interface Software, Alberta, Canada. ACM Press New York, NY, USA, pp. 117-128

[9]   Marshall C (2000). The future of annotation in a digital (Paper) world. In Harum and Twidale, editors, 35th Annual GSLIS Clinic: Successes and Failures of Digital Libraries. University of Illinois, Urbana-Champaign, pp. 97-117

[10] Kahan J, Koivunen M (2001). Annotea: an open RDF infrastructure for shared Web annotations. Proceedings of the tenth international conference on World Wide Web. Hong Kong. ACM Press New York, NY, USA, pp. 623-632

[11] Nichols D, Pemberton D, Dalhoumi S, Larouk O, Belisle C, Twidale M (2000). DEBORA: Developing an interface to support collaboration in a digital library. In European Conference on Digital Libraries. Lisbon, Portugal, pp. 239-248

[12] O'Hara K, Sellen A (1997). A comparison of reading paper and on-line documents. In CHI-97 Conference Proceedings on Human factors in Computing Systems. Atlanta, GA USA, pp. 335-342,

[13] Phelp T, Wilensky, R (2000). Multivalent documents. Communications of the ACM, 43(6):83-90

[14] Reed D, John S (2003). Web annotator. Proceedings of the 34th SIGCSE technical symposium on Computer science education. Reno, Navada, USA, pp. 386-390

[15] Shubin H, Falck D, Gropius Johansen A (1996). Exploring color in interface design. Interactions, Vol. 3 , N. 4   July/Aug. 1996. ACM Press New York, NY, USA, pp. 36-48

[16] Villarroel M, de la Fuente P, Pedrero A, Vegas J, Adiego J (2000). Una plataforma colaborativa de recuperación de información. In JBIDI'2000 Primeras Jornadas de bibliotecas Digitales. Valladolid, España,pp. 117-128,

[17] Villarroel M, de la Fuente P, Pedrero A, Vegas J, Adiego J (2002). Obtaining feedback for indexing from highlighted text. In The Electronic Library. V.20, N.4, UK, pp. 306-313

[18] Wilson R (2002). The "look and feel" of an ebook: considerations in interface design. In Proceedings of the 2002 ACM symposium on Applied computing. Madrid, Spain, pp. 530-534

[19] Whiteman TA (1997). The Primary Colors Are Not Red, Blue, and Yellow. GATF SecondSight Nro. 53. A reprint from GATFWorld, the magazine of the Graphic Arts Technical Foundation, pp. 1-4

[20] Wojahn P, Neuwirth C, Bullock B (1998). Effects of interfaces for annotation on communication in a collaborative task. In CHI'98 Proceedings of the Conference on Human Factors in Computing Systems. Los Angeles, CA, pp. 456-463

CHILE: A Visual Library Catalog Retrieval Prototype

Mari-Carmen Marcos
Information Science Section, Universitat Pompeu Fabra
Ramon Trias Fargas, 25, 08003 Barcelona. Spain,+34 935422264
mcarmen.marcos@upf.edu

Ricardo Baeza-Yates
Center for Web research, DCC, Universidad de Chile & ICREA-
Dept. of Technology, Universitat Pompeu Fabra
Passeig de Circumval·lació, 8, 08003 Barcelona. Spain, +34
935421452
ricardo.baeza@upf.edu

Carlos Andrés Ardila
Center for Web Research, DCC. Universidad de Chile
Blanco Encalada, 2120, 08003 Santiago de Chile. Chile
cardila@dcc.uchile.cl

1. Introduction

In spite of all the advances in simplifying the access and use of online catalogs (OPACs), in particular with the use of the Web (e.g. metasearch and standard interfaces for programs such as Z39.50), final users still find the same old difficulties: how to find information when they do not know the specific documents that satisfy their needs and how to distinguish which of them are more relevant. This problem comes from the first catalogs and is common to other information retrieval (IR) systems, in particular for subject search.

Research in user interfaces in general has profit from technology advances and the Internet, offering better quality. However, in the world of OPACs, there are few innovative results to improve search interfaces. Ortiz-Repiso and Moscoso [9] show that in spite of the change of media, the organization of the information has been maintained -as Borgman pointed out in 1996 [3]- and there is no special use of the hypertext and multimedia capabilities of the Web.

Looking at standards or guidelines, IFLA (International Federation of Library Associations and Institutions) has elaborated design guidelines for

R. Navarro-Prieto and J. L. Vidal (eds.), HCI Related Papers of Interacción 2004, 205-216.
© 2006 *Springer. Printed in the Netherlands.*

OPAC results [13]. Some authors like Cherry [4] also propose guidelines, but in most cases is work done before the dawn of the Web. A recent result on this problem is due to Babu and O'Brien [1], which also includes a good survey.

Current OPACs, compared to early Web systems, do not show a real evolution regarding access and retrieval techniques, or display of documents. This implies that most users keep having a difficult time finding information needs, particularly in subject searches where they do not know the relevant documents. In this case it is worthwhile to show an overview of the document collection and allow the user to browse.

The main goal of CHILE (Computer-Human Interaction Librarian Experience), is to show a system prototype that includes browsing, clustering and visualization. Our work is an ad-hoc adaptation of the overview-query-preview-answer model for IR [2, 6].

For the development of CHILE, we first did a study of the requirements that a good OPAC interface should have. We defined the phases of the search process (query, display of results and query reformulation), the different interfaces needed and their characteristics [7, 8]. Hence, we propose our own set of guidelines.

The main contribution of our system is the integration of several concepts and techniques to OPAC interfaces. We use structured information from a sample of bibliographic records from the University of Chile main library. The architecture of the system includes control access and the overview and result interfaces use clustering as main visualization technique, like other Web systems already do (e.g. KartOO:http://www.kartoo.com).

2. MODEL

2.1. Retrieval Stages

The information retrieval process is composed by the following stages and sub-stages:

A. Query

• Collection overview. Global view of the collection (or the subset corresponding to the user profile), that is a generic view with the overall content of the collection and the results the user can expect to find. For this step we propose the use of clustering techniques to display the whole collection as a visual map.

- Retrieval by browsing. The user must be able to navigate among related subjects or categories. We also use clustering to create new categories and to visualize them.
- Retrieval by querying. Standard interface for users with well defined information needs.

    B.   *Display of results*
- The resulting set that corresponds to the user query is presented as a visual map that groups document automatically taking in account the Dewey (DDC) classification of the bibliographic records and the subject terms that they contain.
- Each document retrieved shows the basic attributes that identify the document (title, author and year) in addition to the cover image. The user can obtain additional data such as the complete bibliographic record, the summary and keywords, if they are available. We can also offer the comments of users borrowing the document and a list of the most popular documents borrowed by those users.

    C.   *Query reformulation*
- If the user wants to improve the retrieved documents, the system must help him/her restricting or enlarging the results.

Current OPAC models usually only allow:
- Retrieval by querying.
- Display of results in a simple list (sometimes not even sorted by relevance, lexicographical or chronological).
- Does not allow to really reformulating the query (just a new query or some fixed set of options).
- Our ideal OPAC model would follow our retrieval stages:
- Retrieval by querying or browsing using a hierarchical two dimensional overview map.
- Display of results sorted by relevance and also through a two dimensional map grouped by subject similarity, by using subject terms and a MARC (Machine-readable cataloguing) based classification [5].
- Reformulation of the query by adding/deleting search terms, and finding similar documents. This should exploit search terms and MARC metadata.

We are restricted to current catalog data which is usually in MARC format (either binary or lately in XML). Nevertheless, this restricted structured set of fields can be used to allow new ways to access information.

2.2. OPAC Model for CHILE

Now we will describe in detail some of the characteristics that the OPAC model or our system should have (table 1).

2.2.1. Browsing an overview

As we believe that OPACs should help with a first overview of the overall collection, we use automatic clustering techniques using the hierarchical structure of the underlying bibliographic classification. From here the user can browse the main categories and subcategories, in particular when the search terms are not known for the user.

To start the user obtains a list of main topics of the collection. These will be the first 10 categories in the first level of CDU (Universal Decimal Classification) or DDC (Dewey Decimal Classification). From there we can browse up to three levels or less, if we find a period or another character (e.g. quotes) before in the classification codes.

In any of the screens the user can request a document list belonging to a subcategory, sorted by relevance or by an attribute (e.g. title, author, year, type of document, etc.).

After reaching the last level (which in general would have to be collection dependant, based on collection size and thematic breadth), the user will pass without noticing to the display of results stage. That is, from an overview to a preview. In practice, the only difference of both views is that we go from sets of documents to documents, which at the end depends on the sub-collection size.

2.2.2. Display of results (preview)

After posing a query or browsing in the collection, the user can see a list of the relevant documents (textual or graphically). Here we have two different screens: one grouping documents by CDU codes and another one that gives a list of results sorted by relevance.

For relevance ranking we have considered the following factors: query terms in subject descriptors (for query retrieval), most popular documents in the OPAC (complete record viewed and loan statistics), and recommended documents (in case of university libraries). These data is usually available in the integrated library management system.

2.2.3. Visual map for results

After the user obtains a first result, we complement the normal textual list a visual map based in the subject similarity between documents. For this we propose to employ the classification code and the subject terms, to build a two dimensional SOM (self-organizing map).

The visual map would have the following characteristics:

- Documents are represented by small circles grouped by common subject terms, in particular the most frequent of them.
- Just by moving the mouse over each circle opens a window with the title and author.
- By clicking the right button of the mouse we obtain the complete bibliographic record in an overlay window that does not cover the visual map.
- Part of the results can be selected with a zoom-like option, avoiding to loose the context.
- Relevant documents can be marked and extracted in other formats, to save, print or e-mailing them.
- Queries can be stored by the system, such that sessions (or part of them) can be recovered, for example to check for new answers to a query.
- Queries are also stored and can be organized by each user.

2.2.4. Document View

In addition to the traditional bibliographic record, we can offer:

- Comments by other users for a given document, including recommendations by experts.
- Table of contents and index of the document.
- Image of the cover, helpful to remind a known document or to remember later a new document.
- Reference to all documents in the same category that have been borrowed by other users that also had been interested in the current document (e.g. as in Amazon, http://www.amazon.com).

2.2.5. Query Reformulation

As feedback technique a dialog that helps in filtering relevant documents by iterative search. For this, the user may mark relevant documents as well as irrelevant documents, and the system will automatically update the result taking in account the subject and classification code fields.

Each document must allow a query "documents like this one". In the case of visual maps, we can set a point on the 2D space and use a "build new map" option.

Finally, we have a personalization option, where a registered user can select the subjects of his/her interests. This information can be used later for services associated to user profiles, such as initial overviews or news alerts based on their interests.

Table 1 summarizes the different interfaces from our model of OPAC.

Search method		Display of results		Each retrieved document
querying	browsing	list	map	clustering
		Search reformulation		

Table 1. Interfaces for our OPAC model.

3. CHILE PROTOTYPE

3.1. Database

To build the database we selected a random sample of the University of Chile library collection, with the restriction that the document should have subject terms, classification code and the word "Chile" appeared somewhere in the bibliographic record. The sample had 5,523 documents with 3,735 different subject terms. All of them were in MARC format, which made things easy for storing the data in XML-MARC, process and storing them in a relational database using MySQL. Our database only kept the fields and subfields that were needed for the prototype, and was designed to facilitate the querying process and the location of subjects on the visual maps. We used two tables, one for the document attributes and their subject terms, and another one to handle user profiles and personalized searches (Figure 1).

The Web front-end of the prototype was implemented using PHP, because was easy to interface to MySQL and is an efficient tool to manage databases, handle the front to back-end communication, and to generate Web pages. The PHP scripts handle all the updates and queries to the database. Each feature is handled by a separate script, to ease code development and maintenance.

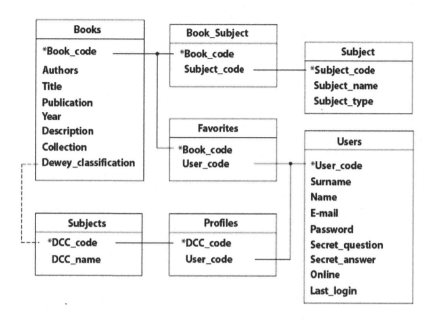

Figure 1. Database structure.

CHILE keeps a log of all subjects and documents queried and viewed by its users, to learn the most frequent subjects and documents requested. An underlying process allows all pages to access the log files, and the news associated to user profiles. This process also does caching to improve the access to previously generated pages (mainly for the frequent visual maps which need more processing time, that is the global overview and the initial overview for frequent users). Figure 2 shows the structure of the Web front-end.

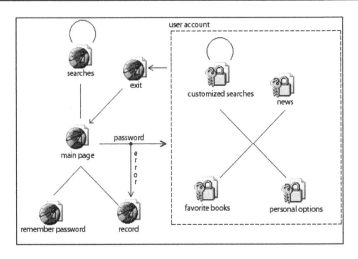

Figure 2. Structure of the Web front-end.

3.2. User Interface

As we mentioned before, we use a visual map for both, the global or user defined overview, and the display of results. A visual map can show many results (much more than 10 as usual Web interfaces) in a reduced space. The proximity of the documents indicates the similarity of subject terms, as we use a variant of self-organizing maps [11], where the location depends on a vector space created from document attributes.

We use a clustering algorithm called PAM (Partitioning Around Medoids) [11], where to find k clusters, a representative object, called medoid, is chosen for each cluster. The medoid must be close to the cluster center and also must contain the subject terms that characterize the cluster. Other objects are classified depending on the proximity to the medoids. Although there are many clustering algorithms, PAM matched well with our retrieval requirements and gave good results. The result of the algorithm over the whole collection (overview) is shown in Figure 3.

The display of results for a query is the same as for browsing the categories, and similar to the overview. In figure 4 we show the result of browsing "Native tribes" ("Pueblos indígenas" in Spanish) plus the subject term "Chile". Notice that new subject terms appear. Queries are handled by standard SQL. For larger catalogs better techniques can be used.

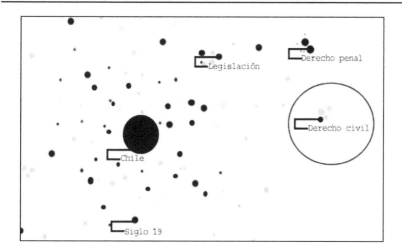

Figure 3. Overview using a visual map.

The algorithm to create a visual map is as follows:
- Search the subject terms that appear in the collection and their statistics.
- Select the most important subject terms that will guide the map, using the frequency of occurrences.
- Find all subject terms that are related to the guiding terms. A circle is drawn with the main subject terms, and each new subject term is positioned in the middle of the largest empty arc in the circle perimeter.
- Put all other subject terms in a random position in the map borders.
- Put all documents in the geometrical center of their subject terms.

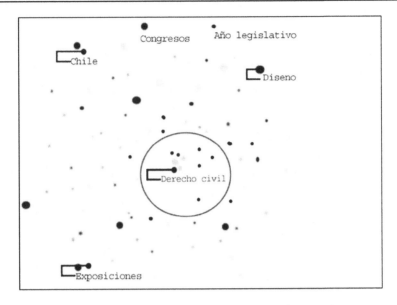

Figure 4. Display of results.

4. CONCLUSIONS AND FUTURE WORK

We have presented a system prototype that allows document visualization based on classification codes and subject terms. The main challenge -and novelty- of CHILE lies in the small amount of information available in OPACs to detect similarities among documents, which is not the case for Web search engines or more complex bibliographic databases with document summaries. We show that in spite of this lack of information, we can avoid useless results thanks to the structured nature of OPAC metadata. Further research is needed to improve interfaces for bibliographic databases.

One problem with our current visual maps is text legibility. We have done no attempts to predict overlaps of subject terms in the screen. As shown in Figure 5, sometimes reading the labels is difficult.

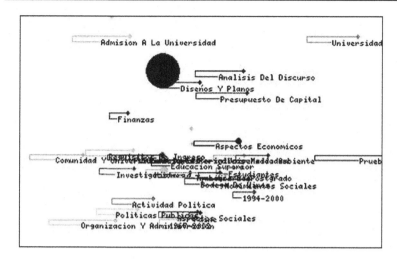

Figure 5. Map legibility problems.

Future work will include:

• Implement all the system requirements, in particular more information about each document in the preview.

• Improve the reformulation stage. Currently, the zoom feature allows redefining the resulting answer but not to pose a reformulated query on that subset or restrict the subject terms.

• Improve the generation and loading time for the main maps. Even caching can be not enough for large maps.

• Change the zoom feature by a fish-eye view such that the context of the visualization is not lost (that is, focus plus context).

• Improve system security. Our current prototype only allows a timeout after which a user must re-enter the user identifier (email address) and password.

REFERENCES

1. Babu, B.; O'Brien, A. Web OPAC interfaces: an overview. Electronic Library, 2000, 18:5, 316-327.

2. Baeza-Yates, R.; Ribeiro-Neto, B. Modern Information Retrieval. Addison-Wesley, 1999.

3. Borgman, C. Why are online catalogs still hard to use? Journal of the American Society for Information Science, 1996, 47:7, 493-503.

4.   Cherry, J. Bibliographic displays in OPACs and web catalogs: how well do they comply with display guidelines. Information Technology & Libraries, 1998, 17:3, 124-137.

5.   MARC Standards. Washington: Library of Congress, http://www. loc. Gov/marc /marcspa.html.

6.   Marchionini, G. Information Seeking in Electronic Environments. Cambridge University Press, 1992.

7.   Marcos Mora, M. C. Human Computer Interaction for OPAC information retrieval interfaces using subject terms, Ph.D. thesis (in Spanish), University of Zaragoza, September 2003.

8.   Marcos Mora, M. C. Interacción en interfaces de recuperación de información: conceptos, metáforas y visualización. Gijón: Trea, 2004.

9.   Ortiz-Repiso, V.; Moscoso, P. Web-based OPACs: between tradition and innovation. Information Technology & Libraries, 1999, 18:2, 68-77.

10.   Pech Palacio, M. A. Adaptation and use of data mining for spatial and non-spatial information. Final degree thesis (in Spanish). Universidad de las Américas-Puebla (México), 2002, http://mail.udlap.Mx/~tesis/msp/pech_p_ma/

11.   Self organizing maps, http://www.cis.hut.fi/research/som-research/

12.   Staley, E. Graphical interfaces to support information search: an annotated bibliography, 2000, http://alexia.lis.uiuc.edu/~twidale/irinterfaces/bibmain.html

13.   Yee, M. Guidelines for OPAC displays. IFLANet, Annual Conference (65th Council and General Conference), 1999, http://www.ifla.org/IV/ifla65/ papers/098-131e.htm

Analysing and modelling user tasks in the DomoSim-TPC system to adapt to mobile device

Ana I. Molina, Miguel A. Redondo, Manuel Ortega

E. S. Informática. University of Castilla – La Mancha
Paseo de la Universidad, 4.13071 Ciudad Real (Spain)
{AnaIsabel.Molina, Miguel.Redondo, Manuel.Ortega}@uclm.es

Introduction

The use of computers in all areas has become more widespread in recent years, accompanied by a fall in prices and an increase in their power and versatility [1]. The same cannot be said about the situation in educational environments, where the penetration of computers is still a very gradual process and has not yet reached the levels needed for the qualitative leap that their wide scale introduction could bring.

The main goal of the work in which this article is situated is to incorporate the ubiquitous computing paradigm in the teaching and learning of domains with a high experimental degree in order to take into account mobile computing possibilities. Thus, we are going to study the methods that allow us to systematize these tasks. We will take as a starting point a collaborative e-learning environment based on the desktop metaphor, following the [2, 3]so-named "Domosim-TPC" system. This system is used to support the learning of the design of automated control facilities in buildings and housing, also called Domotics. We present the process followed to obtain a PDA-based (PDA, Personal Digital Assistants) version of DomoSim-TPC system in order to support learning tasks by using mobile devices. In particular, we focus the discussion about the process to design the user interface for PDA-type devices. We describe the analysis of the main tasks supported in Domosim-TPC. These are necessary for adapting the interface to mobile computing.

The paper is organized in this way: in the following section, dealing with background, the concept of ubiquitous computing is introduced; next, we describe the main features of the Domosim-TPC system and some ideas about automated generation of user interfaces and task modelling. In the following section, the stages necessary to develop a ubiquitous version of the aforementioned system are enumerated. And finally, we show the

R. Navarro-Prieto and J. L. Vidal (eds.), HCI Related Papers of Interacción 2004, 217-227.
© 2006 *Springer. Printed in the Netherlands.*

first results in the evolution process of the asynchronous learning tasks supported in Domosim-TPC towards PDA devices and we will draw some conclusions and outline the future work we will develop.

Background

Ubiquitous Computing

Ubiquitous computing as an interaction paradigm [4, 5] creates a shift in the concept of the computer by distributing a multitude of low power computers throughout the environment and trying to make their presence and use as unobtrusive as possible. In other words ubiquitous computing aims to extend computing capacity to the whole environment by means of the distribution of small and highly varied devices of an interactive nature, all connected to higher powered servers. The solution put forward by Weiser consists of deploying wireless networks of computers which exchange information with each other and serve as a mechanism of interaction.

Our research group [6] advocate the introduction of this new paradigm in the classroom for educational purposes, pointing out some of the educational benefits its use would provide. Soloway and his collaborators [7] believe that handheld or PDA devices will help to promote discovery learning, having carried out experiments based on the principles of the ubiquitous computing paradigm. They propose that devices and peripherals should be designed to be used to capture real world data with *handheld* devices. This data would subsequently be sent to a server to be presented for group discussion.

Domosim-TPC

The domain where our investigation is being applied is the learning of the design of automated control facilities in buildings and housing, also called Domotics. The term Domotics is associated to the set of elements that, when installed, interconnected and automatically controlled at home, release the user from the routine of intervening in everyday actions and, at the same time, provide optimized control over comfort, energy consumption, security and communications. In this kind of training, the realization of practical experiments is specially important. In order to soften this problem by means of the use of technology, we have developed a distributed environment with support for distance learning of domotics design: DomoSim-TPC.

In DomoSim-TPC the teacher carries out a presentation of theoretical contents. Next, the students are organized in small groups whom the teacher assigns the resolution of design problems. The students use an individual workspace to design the models that they consider will satisfy the requirements of the proposed problems. Later on, they discuss, comment and justify the design decisions taken, building a shared knowledge base.

This system is based on Abstract Assisted Interaction [8] and Direct Manipulation paradigms; and it is based on the desktop metaphor.

Automated Generation of User Interfaces based on task Modeling

Due to the great demand of new technologies and the massive growth in information access, the design and creation of user interfaces is of increasing importance. The user interface is a fundamental part in the development of applications. It is essential to realize a correct design suitable to the needs of the final user.

Generation tools based on models include all necessary information to develop declarative models (structure and behavior specifications of a software element with no code included, but with descriptions of a high level of abstraction).

An interface model for separating the user interface from the application logic and the presentation device is necessary. There are several markup languages that help in this purpose (UIML [9], XML,...). This kind of languages allows the production of device-independent presentations for a range of devices. But these solutions do not provide high-level guidance, guaranteeing quality across multiple versions of applications. We propose the use of a model-based design of GUI, which focuses on the tasks supported. The idea is that task analysis provides some structure for the description of tasks or activities, thus making it easier to describe how activities fit together, and to explore what the implications of this may be for the design of user interfaces. A number of approaches to task modeling have been developed (GOMS [10], HTA [11], CTT [12, 13],...). The logical decomposition of tasks is reflected in the selection, consistency and grouping of elements in the GUI obtained.

The success of model-based systems has been limited. Several systems have attempted to automatically generate user interfaces in a model-based environment (UIDE [14], Mecano [15], Trident [16],...). The idea of these systems was to try to automate as much as possible the interface generation process from a task model, but these interfaces are very closed in specific domains.

Evolution of Domosim-TPC to Ubiquitous Computing

Our purpose is to improve the traditional classroom environment with the collaborative and the ubiquitous computing paradigms. We intend to implement a prototype in a particular environment for collaborative learning (Domosim-TPC). We have to adapt the asynchronous tools of Domosim to the characteristics of mobile devices. To do this, it is necessary to restructure the user interface and adapt it to the constraints of size and functionality of this kind of appliances.

If we want to generalize this process to the learning environment of other disciplines, we can automate the transformation process of the user interface. For CSCL tools developers, this introduces the problem of constructing multiple versions of applications for different devices. There are many dimensions to consider when designing context-dependent applications (environments, platforms, domain, users,...). We intend to identify similar tasks in CSCL tools to automate the attainment of a ubiquitous version of a collaborative design environment.

We have chosen the graphical ConcurTaskTrees (CTT) notation [12, 13] for analyzing tasks in Domosim-TPC. Some important features are supported in CTT: hierarchical logical structures, temporary relationships among tasks, and cooperative tasks modeling (multi-user cooperation). Also, a automatic tool for task-based design (CTTE) [17] is available.

Stages in evolution process

The evolution process of Domosim-TPC to incorporate PDA-based access to the DomoSim-TPC system consists of several stages:
1. Analysing tasks that can be improved in a mobile computing scenario.
2. Design of tasks taking ubiquitous computing paradigm principles into account. Modelling and the design of certain tasks must be reconsidered. The devices and protocols necessary for materializing these tasks must be decided.
3. *Implementing a prototype* that applies the theories proposed.
4. *Evaluating the prototype in real contexts.*

5.*Identifying the task patterns* that could be common in CSCL environments, based on the resolution of proposed problems and simulation of solutions contributed by students.

6.*Creating a tool that*, from a model of tasks in a CSCL application, allows obtaining the equivalent interface for several mobile devices in a semiautomatic way.

Currently, we are in stage (3). We are developing PDA-based asynchronous tools in order to increase the realism and flexibility of the tasks supported in Domosim-TPC.

Supported Tasks in Domosim-TPC

Next, supported tasks in Domosim-TPC system are described:

- *Specification of models and planning* of their design strategy. In this stage the students, in an individual way, reflect and plan the steps to build a model satisfying the requirements proposed in the problem formulation. The strategy traced by the user is dynamically contrasted with an optimal plan of design for this problem.

- *Discussion, argument and search of consent* in the characteristics of the models individually built. In this stage, the participants discuss about the models built, about their types and about the steps carried out to obtain them. From this process a proposal (model) is obtained reflecting the viewpoint of each participant.

- *Detailed design and simulation in group*. Before checking the validity of the proposed solution, the apprentices should detail and organize the attributes associated to the objects that form the model. Later on, they consider the hypothesis and case studies that should be contrasted by means of the Collaborative Simulation of the behavior of this model.

An example of the generation of the user interface for PDA

We are interested in the effective use of such mobile computing devices for collaborative learning. There are tasks in the system Domosim-TPC which are susceptible of improvement through mobile computing. In particular, the Collaborative Planning of Design is an asynchronous and reflexive task which could be improved using mobile devices.

In this section, we describe the analysis of the main tasks in the asynchronous workspace of Domosim-TPC. This analysis should be done at low level. It has to determine the kind of interaction task (for example, enter text, select a Boolean value, select a numeric value) and the kind of domain application objects manipulated by the tasks. This information facilitates the identification of the visual component (*widget*) that best allows the realization of a particular task, taking target device restrictions into account.

The Mapping Problem

The process of generating a user interface in a model-based system can be seen as that of finding a concrete specification given an abstract one (*the mapping problem*) [18]. Once the elements of the abstract task of the user interface have been identified, every interactor has to be mapped into interaction techniques supported by the particular device configuration considered (operating system, toolkit, etc.).

The new context of use implies reconfigurations of the UI that are beyond he traditional UI changes [19, 20] such as the redistribution of widgets across windows or tabs in a tabpanel, the reduction of a full widget to its scrollable version, without using a sophisticated widget, to replace an interactor with a smaller alternative, etc. The technique of automatically selecting an appropriate interactor while considering screen resolution constraints has already been investigated and shown to be feasible [21].

Obtaining the interface for PDA of the individual planning space

We intend to obtain the ubiquitous version, and in particular, for PDA, from the tasks analysis of the individual plan edition space in Domosim-TPC. Figure 1 shows the user interface of the plan editor. This is structured in separate areas: the problem formulation, the list of tasks to realize (tasks which give structure to the problem), the icon bars representing design actions/operators, the sequence of design actions already planned, the current action under construction and a set of buttons dedicated to supporting several general functions.

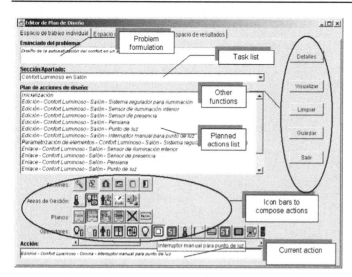

Fig. 1. Plan editor user interface

In figure 2 we can see the task model in CTT notation for individual planning. Figure 3 gives details about the abstract task of *PLANNING*.

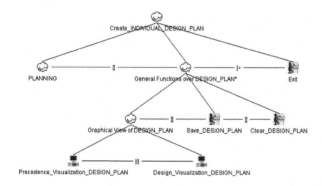

Fig. 2. Tasks modelling of space for individual planning in Domosim-TPC

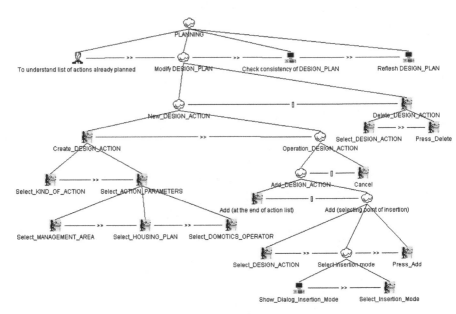

Fig. 3. Modelling of the *PLANNING* abstract task

To obtain the version for PDA of the individual workspace, temporary relationships among the tasks and the domain application objects manipulated to perform them must be taken into account. This information allows creating the interface in which both the widgets (user interface objects) that show domain application objects (internal objects) and the widgets that allow executing certain actions applicable to these internal objects must appear together. In the editor of plans of design (the individual workspace) two internal objects are handled: the *design action* and the *design plan* (a collection of design actions). In figures 2 and 3 the names of both objects are written in uppercase. They are part of the name of the tasks that manipulate them.

The diagram in figure 2 shows the general functions that can be performed on the design plan. It can be shown graphically. There are two modes of *visualization*: a list of nodes (a node represents a action) connected by arrows (that represent precedence relationships); and the design of the scene created to execute the planned actions list. Also we can *save* the design plan. The option *Clear* eliminates all the information contained in the actions list. These actions are applicable to the *plan design* object. These must appear in the user interface next to the object related (the list box that shows the sequence of steps in the plan). The resulting interface for PDA of these subset of tasks is shown in figure 4.

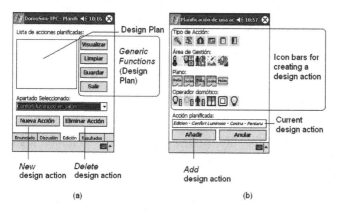

Fig. 4. PDA version of the interface to individual plan edition. (a) Interface that allows showing and performing actions on the *Design_Plan*. (b) Dialog box that allows the creation of a new *Design_Action*.

In addition, the individual plan editor handles *design action* objects. In the diagram shown in figure 3 the *Add_DESIGN_ACTION* and *Delete_DESIGN_ACTION* actions are included. The first one has a certain complexity. When a task (that means an operation over an internal object) is of the interaction type, the mapping to a perceptible object (a widget in the interface) is more direct. This kind of operations can be represented by means of buttons, options in a menu or a contextual menu. It has been applied to the mapping of the *Delete_DESIGN_ACTION* operation, or the aforementioned generic functions, which the user can perform on the *DESIGN_PLAN* object.

However, when a task has a certain complexity, i.e., when a task is represented by an abstract task, with several abstraction levels and several interaction tasks (this occurs in the *New_DESIGN_ACTION* task), more complex visual components are necessary (a panel, in a PC version of the interface; or in a PDA, where there are display resolution constraints, a dialog box is a better choice). This occurs in the task that allows creating new design actions, as we can see in figure 4. This dialog box appears whenever a new design action is created.

Conclusions

Using mobile computing devices in collaborative learning scenarios we could improve the effectiveness of the learning process. In this paper we have shown its application to a case study: domotics learning by problem solving. To achieve our goal, we have analyzed the tasks which are susceptible of improvement through mobile computing. To do this, it is necessary to restructure the desktop user interface to adapt it to the constraints of size and functionality of this kind of appliances. We use graphical ConcurTaskTrees (CTT) notation for analyzing tasks in Domosim-TPC. Nevertheless, CTT does not provide optimal support for specifying collaborative aspects. This is an important deficiency in this notation. We intend to extend CTT notation to supporting representation of collaborative tasks. Additionally, we intend to identify common high-level task patterns in CSCL environment and guidelines that allow creating a complete semi-automatic environment that generates CSCL and mobile tools, independent of the study domain and platform.

Acknowledgement

This work has been partially supported by the Junta de Comunidades de Castilla – La Mancha and the Ministerio de Ciencia y Tecnología in the PBI-02-026 and TIC2002-01387 projects.

References

1. Sharples, M., Disruptive Devices: Personal Technologies and Education, in Educational Technology Research Paper Series 11. 2000: Birmingham: The University of Birmingham.
2. Bravo, C., Un sistema de Soporte al Aprendizaje Colaborativo del Diseño Domótico Mediante Herramientas de Modelado y Simulación., in Dpto. de Informática. 2002, Universidad de Castilla - La Mancha.
3. Redondo, M.A., Planificación Colaborativa del Diseño en Entornos de Simulación para el Aprendizaje a Distancia, in Departamento de Informática. 2002, Universidad de Castilla-La Mancha: Ciudad Real. p. 334.
4. Weiser, M., The computer for the twenty-first century. Scientific American, 1991: p. 94-104.
5. Weiser, M., The future of Ubiquitous Computing on Campus. Comm. ACM, 1998. 41-1.
6. Ortega, M., et al., AULA; A Ubiquitous Language Teaching System. Upgrade II, 2001. 5: p. 17-22.
7. Soloway, E., et al., Science in the Palms of their Hands. Communications of ACM, 1999. August 1999, 42-8: p. 21-26.

8. Bravo, J., et al. Interacción asistida abstracta: un complemento a la manipulación directa en problemas de diseño. in INTERACCION 2001. 2001.
9. Abrams, M., et al. UIML: An appliance-independent XML user interface language. in 8th International World-Wide Web Conference WWW'8. 1999. Amsterdam: Elsevier Science.
10. Card, S., T. Moran, and A. Newell. The Psycology of Human-Computer Interaction. 1983. Hillsdale.
11. Annett, J. and K.D. Duncan, Task Analysis and Training Design. Occupational Psychology, 1967. 41: p. 211-221.
12. Paternò, F., C. Mancini, and Meniconi. ConcurTaskTree: A diagrammatic notation for specifying task models. in IFIP TC 13 International Conference on Human-Computer Interaction Interact'97. 1997. Sydney: Kluwer Academic Publishers.
13. Paternò, F., C. Santoro, and S. Tahmassebi. Formal model for cooperative tasks: Concepts and an application for en-route air traffic control. in 5th Int. Workshop on Design, Specification, and Verification of Intractive Systems DSV-IS'98. 1998. Abingdon: Springer-Verlag.
14. Foley, J., et al., UIDE-An Intelligent User Interface Design Environment, in Intelligent User Interfaces. 1991: p. 339-384.
15. Puerta, A.R. The MECANO Project: Comprehensive and Integrated Support for Model-Based Interface Development. in CADUI96: Computer-Aided Design of User In-terfaces. 1996. Numur, Belgium.
16. Vanderdonckt, J.M. and F. Bodart. Encapsulating Knowledge for Intelligent Automatic Interaction Objects Selection. in InterCHI'93. 1993: ACM Press.
17. Paternò, F., CTTE: Support for Developing and Analyzinf Task Models for Interactive System Design. IEEE Transanctions on Software Engineering, 2002. 28(N° 9).
18. Puerta, A. and J. Eisenstein. Towards a General a Computational Framework for Model-Based Interface Development Systems. in IUI99: International Conference of Intel-ligent User Interfaces. 1999. Los Angeles.
19. Eisenstein, J., J. Vanderdonckt, and A. Puerta. Adapting to mobile contexts with user-interface modeling. in IEEE Workshop on Mobile Computing Systems and Applications WCSMA'2000. 2000. Los Alamitos (Monterey): IEEE Press.
20. Eisenstein, J., J. Vanderdonckt, and A. Puerta. Applying model-based techniques to the development of user interfaces for mobile computers. in ACM Conference on Intelligent User Interfaces IUI'2001. 2001. Alburqueque.
21. Eisenstein, J. and A. Puerta. Adaptation in Automated User-Interface Design. in IUI'2000. 2000. New Orleans.

Microworld Approach to Supervision Activity Modelling in Industrial Process Control

Pere Ponsa Asensio
Knowledge Engineering Research Group (GREC)
Technical University of Catalonia, EPSEVG
Av. Víctor Balaguer s/n 08800 Vilanova i la Geltrú
pedro.ponsa@upc.edu
+34 938967231

Marta Díaz Boladeras
Knowledge Engineering Research Group (GREC)
Technical University of Catalonia, EPSEVG
Av. Víctor Balaguer s/n 08800 Vilanova i la Geltrú
marta.diaz@upc.edu
+34 938967753

1. INTRODUCTION

In recent years, control systems and the role of control room operators have changed dramatically. Operator activity has evolved from manually performing the process, to control system supervision (see Fig 1). Today, the operator requires an in-depth knowledge of the process that he/she is overseeing and the ability to make effective decisions within demanding constraints.

The increased complexity of industrial process control calls for a new methodological approach (for research and design purposes), which reproduces the essential components of current control systems: the environment, the task at hand and operator activity.

The use of process simulators in power plants, air traffic control rooms and the oil industry is relatively commonplace (Woods et. al. 1987). We can distinguish between two kinds of simulators: those geared to plant design, and Process Training Simulators (PTS) (Malik 1996). A particular type of PTS is the Full-Scale Simulator (FSS) that reproduces the appearance

R. Navarro-Prieto and J. L. Vidal (eds.), HCI Related Papers of Interacción 2004, 229-242.
© 2006 *Springer. Printed in the Netherlands.*

and function of a central control room. A FSS is a useful tool to train operators in fault diagnosis and process operation.

However, there is still a need for a simulation tool, which simulates a
setting from which to study the human performance of operators as they
carry out supervisory control tasks. At present, the most accepted model of
plant operator activity is the perception-reasoning-action cycle (Rasmussen
et. al. 1994; Vicente 2000).

Microworld is a simulation tool, which could help bridge the gap
between laboratory and field studies in cognitive systems engineering
research. *Microworld* presents advantages as regards flexibility and repro-
ducibility, while maintaining acceptable realism. *Microworld* is based on a
simulation of systems that change dynamically. The systems' profiles
change as a result of the subject's actions, and to a certain degree, they can
change autonomously.

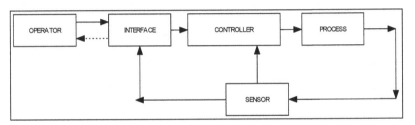

Fig. 1. Supervisory control scheme

2. MULTIDISICPLINARY APPROACH

The complexity of industrial process supervision makes it necessary to
supplement the Human Factors approach and the Human-Computer Interaction approach with a cross-disciplinary cooperation in order to integrate
knowledge and methods from other fields, especially Cognitive Ergonomics, Automation and Artificial Intelligence (Arnau 1996; Barthélemy et al.
2000; Martinez 2002). Our view is that complete control system engineering must encompass all these approaches.

Ergonomics is concerned with the adaptation of technology to suit
operator need and ability so as to achieve effectiveness, efficiency and

user/worker satisfaction and comfort (Ivergard 1989; Sanders and McCornick 2000).

Romera defines Automatics as the set of methods and procedures that replaces human work in previously programmed mental and physical tasks (Romera et. al. 1994). According to this definition, Automation is commonly considered to be the application of Automatics to industrial control processes.

Provided that even in automated systems the shift to manual mode is often required (when adjustments in the control algorithm are required, or some failures or malfunctions in the process appear), the point of automation is not *how* to replace operators with artificial controllers, but how to make them cooperate correctly.

Above the automation level there is supervision task. Colomer defines supervision as the activity that achieves *optimal system functionality* even in anomalous situations. In this context optimal functionality is the performance that takes place under a periodically verified and tested control algorithm that leads to desired results and satisfaction, both in product quality and developed control (Colomer et. al. 2000). An industrial environment, unpredicted events can deviate the controlled system from a prior set point and, eventually deteriorate system performance. Basically, a supervision system carries out the following activities:

- Data acquisition and storage
- Monitoring (or surveillance) of the main process variables.
- Supervisory control over automatic controllers and industrial regulators (Aguilar 1998)
- Fault detection and diagnosis (Hamsher et. al. 1991; Patton 1997)
- Reconfiguration.

Supervisory control is the set of activities and techniques developed over a set of controllers (programmable logic controllers and industrial regulators) which ensures the fulfilling of control goals. Communication protocol configuration, network management, data sampling and displays are very common tasks in supervisory oriented programs.

In this activity a certain level of automation is required to help supervisor decision making. It is not possible to design architectures in which human supervision is still present and architectures in which human supervision is replaced by artificial expert programs. In both cases, we must not forget that one of the main goals is to prevent possible plan malfunctions that can lead to economical loses and/or result in damage. For this reason, other fields of knowledge concerned with manufacturing systems perform-ance – such as maintenance and industrial security- are complementary in the study of supervision systems.

Recently, there has been a move to integrate supervision applications and Artificial Intelligence (AI) (Rodriguez 2002). Artificial Intelligence adds a fourth desired feature to ergonomics, supervision and automatic control in an industrial process, that is, *decision support aid system* (Rios et. al. 2002; Gentil 1995). Integration becomes important in factories in order to add flexibility to the changing requirements of production like safety, efficiency, product change and technological progress. It is also necessary to define synergic policies.

3. PREVIOUS RESEARCH

In this section we will briefly review the latest research on cognitive behavioural studies related to control and supervision tasks. Table 1 shows the relationship between field study and laboratory research and diverse hardware, devices, dynamic simulations and *microworlds*.

In power plants, the study of the operator's control room is based on the application of a questionnaire to obtain the Decision Ladder. From this point of view human operator behaviour develops a perception-reasoning-action cycle. The final purpose of this study is to increase efficiency and safety in power plants (Rasmussen et. al. 1994).

Another approach is the study of modelling and prediction of human behaviour in car driving. The identification of cognitive driving styles is a good indicator to reduce the risk of accidents. Some studies focus on the driver's hypovigilance detection, related to factors like fatigue or stress, applying artificial intelligence techniques (i.e. neural networks Radial Basis Function) to the subject's classification (Hernández-Gress 1998).

Other studies obtain cognitive driving styles and predict the subsequent actions of automobile drivers based on their initial preparatory activity in a virtual vehicle prototype (Pentland and Liu 1999).

However, the purpose of behavioural cloning is to make use of the operator's skill in the development of an automatic controller. In this case, the instrumentation is dynamic control simulations like F-16 fly simulation or container crane simulation. Then researchers apply qualitative reasoning techniques to symbolic reconstruction of operator trajectories (i.e. control strategies) (Bratko et. al. 1997).

Microworlds are based on the simulation of a task changing dynamically (Ritter and Young 2001). The example of a *microworld* is *Firechief* Quesada et. al. 2000; Cañas et. al. 2003). This framework mimics a forest where the fire is spreading. The task of the subject is to extinguish the fire as soon as possible. The *microworld Épure* is a water purification plant simulation designed to analyze temporal complexity and causal actions (Carreras et. al. 1999).

Table 1. Behavioural studies

Instrumentation	Research
Field Study in power plant control: a questionnaire to operator control room	Activity analysis
	Decision making
Multi sensorial vehicle prototype (ECG, EEG measures, eye tracking)	Hypovigilance detection of a vehicle driver
	Factors: fatigue, stress, drugs
Vehicle prototype and virtual driving simulation	Modelling and prediction of human behaviour with hidden Markov models and Kalman's filter
	Cognitive driving styles
Computer control tasks: F-16 fly simulation, container crane simulation	Behavioural cloning
	Qualitative reconstruction of operator control strategies
	Automatic controller design
Microworld: dynamic processes control simulations (chemistry industries, manufacturing plants)	Temporal complexity
	Organization of actions
	strategy analysis

ECG electrocardiogram, *EEG* enchephalongram

4. MICROWORLD RESEARCH

In this section we will briefly review t*microworld* research and will highlight the *microworld* attributes as an experimental task to assess supervision activity (Brehmer and Dörner 1990).

The most important differences between *microworlds* and field studies are:

- *Time is contracted.* In some simulations the interaction is defined within few minutes or seconds.
- *The tasks are simplified.* It is very difficult to make a complete model and a complete simulation of any dynamic task. For example, it is difficult to model stochastic events that occurred in industrial plants.
- *Virtual versus real world.* The simulation is a game and it is difficult to assess subject decisions when faced with a simulated problem in a critical industrial context.
- *Isolated interaction* The interaction is typically one subject versus one *microworld*. Some researchers are working on distributed decision making over a set of subjects.

Examples of microworlds used as experimental task in research are:

- *Lohhausen.* In this simulation the subject has to assume the role of mayor with dictatorial powers for a small German town called Lohhausen.
- *Dynamic Environment Simulation System* (DESSY). It was developed in Uppsala University as a methodology for designing *microworlds*. The model provides different demanding situations to cope with such as forest fire fighting, battles, epidemics and floods.
- *Dual Reservoir System Simulation* (DURESS). In this case the system to manage is a thermal and hydraulic multivariable system with water level control and temperature control. Researchers apply cognitive work analysis to find differences between novel and expert subject performance, and strategy analysis according to cognitive systems engineering methods (Vicente 2000).

There are many different kinds of *microworlds* but they have some general characteristics in common:

- *Complex.* The subject must consider many goals, some of which may be contradictory. Some industrial applications have dual processes and subjects must choose frommany possible courses of action.
- *Dynamic.* The current state is a function of the history of the interaction between the subject and *microworld* interface. There are irregular intervals of subject actions and subject *non-action* (inactivity).
- *Opaque.* Typical *microworld* architecture presents a set of levels, from subject interface to instructor configuration interface. From subject position some aspects of the dynamic system are neither explicit nor obvi-

ous, so some dynamic aspects of the simulation system have to be inferred to interact effectively.

- *Expertise*. The *microworld* may or may not be in agreement with the subjects' previous knowledge.
- *Goals*. *Microworlds* may also differ with respect to the goals subjects must achieve. Multiple goals increase the cognitive and emotional demands. In industrial domains, time pressure is a usual constraint in operator decision making.
- *Learning*. Subjects must learn to perform efficiently with *microworlds* during experimental interaction.

Microworld interaction requires a high level of complex cognitive activity. In this sense *microworlds* clearly overpass conventional experimental cognitive tasks that are focused on one particular cognitive skill. On the contrary, managing complex dynamic *microworlds* demands a high level of activity planning that involves reasoning, problem solving and decision making.

Research with *microworlds* has followed three different approaches: the individual differences approach, the case study approach, and the system characteristics approach. Studies of individual differences have diverse goals:

- To find ways of predicting performance
- To find and characterize individual variability. To find not only differences in the degree to which subjects are able to reach the goals, but also differences in how they perform, i.e. decision making strategies

Subjects who show good performance in problem solving tasks also make errors. The errors that the subjects make are of particular interest for understanding the characteristics of the information processing system.

In the use of *microworlds*, the errors can be explained in terms like:

- *Forgetting*. It is difficult for the subject to find regularities over time.
- *Capacity limitations*. Subjects can only process small amounts of information rather slowly. There is a tendency towards concentration on central aspects, i.e. the *key in a hole effect* in power plant control rooms (Choi et. al. 2001).
- *Protection of competence*. To act, a person needs to be convinced that he or she can act successfully.

In the use of industrial supervision interfaces in control rooms, the errors can be explained in terms like:

- Classification of human errors in lapses, slips and mistakes
- Relationship between errors and execution levels: knowledge, rules, and skills

During unfamiliar situations for which no know-how or rules for control are available from previous encounters, the subject must develop new strategies over stochastic events. At the rule based level, the operator can use *the operator manual* to follow a priori specifications and control planning. In skill-based control, the sensory-motor skill level is very important and it is easy to detect incorrect actions when controlling devices.

5. METHOD

During the last four years, our research group *Knowledge Engineering Research Group* (GREC) has been developing a method for modelling and assessing supervisory activity. The main issues of this study have been *microworld* design and testing, artificial controller implementation and experimental setting (Català et. al. 2000; Diaz and Ponsa 2001; Diaz et. al. 2001; Raya 1999).

The *microworld Microworld Knowledge Engineering Research* (MOREC in Catalan tool) was designed and inspired by the Worlds for Assessing Human Reasoning Process Supervision (WAHRPS) project (Pastor et. al. 1998). The industrial plant representation consisted of a set of open tanks connected to pipes, which are controlled by binary valves (on/off). The experimental session consisted in presenting the *microworld* display to the subject together with an instruction. The instruction was: *Move water from the top tank to the bottom tank as quickly as possible without it overflowing.* The purpose of the present study is to model control behaviour when copying with MOREC and to define relevant performance measures in this context (Fig. 2).

Now we are working on the second version of MOREC (MOREC II) that includes the possibility of introducing random events and perturbations such as a sudden increase in water flow or unexpected valve breakdown. MOREC II is more realistic than MOREC in the sense that it includes stochastic events. In the short term, our aim is to analyse the changes in activity strategy as the operator copes with unexpected events, and to analyse the cognitive ability of operators to shift from one operational mode to another (cognitive flexibility).

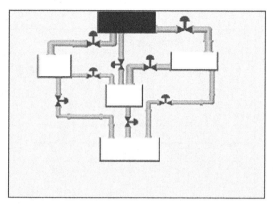

Fig. 2. *Microworld* MOREC (Microworld for Knowledge engineering research)

The controller design follows the human reasoning model. The *Perception-Reasoning-Execution* (PRE) controller is based on human problem solving activity from the Decision Ladder scheme. Best results are those of an artificial supervisor able to use 5 different strategies and 27 courses of actions dealing with the MOREC *microworld*.

In this context it is possible to implement a *Naïve Qualitative Controller* (NQA) based on rules that assess qualitative human activity in comparison to artificial problem solving patterns (Travé-Massuyès et. al. 1999). After a preliminary experimental test we changed the first MOREC interface to adapt the simulated plant dynamics to subject activity (in this case engineering students) to make it more sensitive to different copying strategies (Ponsa 2003).

Then 31 students performed a series of 20 trials in the *microworld* MOREC and then answered an adapted version of the *Task Load Index* (NASA-TLX) questionnaire to assess the mental workload associated with the task. Finally they answered the Eysenck Personality Questionnaire (EPQ-A) in order to control personality variability (Diaz et. al. 2001). These preliminary results do not show a significant relationship between mental workload and successful performance in terms of execution time and in the number of actions. Personality differences do not seem to affect effective supervision in our *microworld*. After analysing the results we lieve that quantitative parameters of execution were not relevant to capturing the essential differences between subjects and that performance should be measured in terms of the strategies developed. Therefore, we reviewed our experimental approach and switched to the operation mode approach

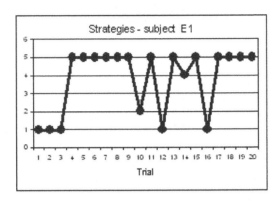

Fig. 3. The subject E1 does 20 trials on MOREC. The graphic shows the strategies changing from one trial to the next. The identified strategies are numbered from 2 to 5. Case 1 is not classified as a strategy

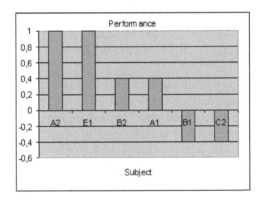

Fig. 4. Subjects Performance (normalized between values -1 and 1) of the best trial on MOREC

following the works of Vicente and Rasmussen on strategies analysis (Vicente 2000). In the latest experiments we have focused on obtaining a qualitative behaviour pattern that enables us to estimate the observed differences in performance depending on strategies and operation modes rather than on execution measures (Fig. 3). In this context we try to obtain the behaviour trace beyond the recorded execution trace. This approach implies moving from the execution domain of physical operations over

Moeller, M. L. (1996): Selbsthilfegruppen: Anleitungen und Hintergründe. Rororo-Sachbuch : Psychologie aktiv, Rowohlt, Reinbek bei Hamburg 1996.

Nielsen, J. (Ed.) (2002): Coordinating user interfaces for consistency (reprint from 1989). San Francisco 2002.

Nonnecke, B.; Preece, J. (2000): Lurker Demographics: Counting the Silent. In: Proceedings of the ACM CHI 2000, S. 73-80, The Hague, NL.

Norman, D. A. (1988): The psychology of everyday things. Basic Books, New York 1988.

Norman, D. A. (1992): Turn signals are the facial expressions of automobiles. Addison-Wesley, Reading 1992.

Peppers, D.; Rogers, M. (1997): Enterprises One to One: Tools for Competing the Interactive Age. New York 1997.

Preece, J. (1999): Emphatic communities: balancing emotional and factual communication. In: Interacting with Computers, Vol. 12 (1999), pp. 63-77.

Preece, J. (2000): Online Communities - Designing Usability, Supporting Sociability. John Wiley and Sons, Chichester, 2000.

Preece, J.; Ghozati, K. (2001): Observations and Explorations of Empathy Online. In: Internet and Health Communication: Experience and Expectations. Eds.: Rice, R. R.; Katz, J. E., Sage, Thousand Oaks 2001, pp. 237-260.

Preece, J.; Maloney-Krichmar, D. (2003): Online Communities: Focussing on Sociability and Usability. In: Handbook of Human-Computer Interaction. *Eds.*: Jacko, J.; Sears, A., Lawrence Earlbaum Associates Inc., Mahwah (NJ) 2003.

Rafaeli, S.; LaRose, R. J. (1993): Electronic Bulletin Boards and "Public Goods" - Explanations of Collaborative Mass Media. In: Communication Research, Vol. 20 (1993), No. 2, pp. 277-290.

Ruprecht, T. M. (Ed.) (1998): Experten fragen - Patienten antworten : Patientenzentrierte Qualitätsbewertung von Gesundheitsdienstleistungen ; Konzepte, Methoden, praktische Beispiele. Asgard-Verlag, Sankt Augustin 1998.

Schubert, P. (1999): Virtuelle Transaktionsgemeinschaften im Electronic Commerce: Management, Marketing und Soziale Umwelt. Electronic Commerce, Josef Eul Verlag, Lohmar, Köln 1999.

SEKIS (2000): Nutzeranliegen an Patienteninformation - Auswertung des Expertendialogs und der Fragebogenerhebung zum Informationsbedarf aus Patientensicht. SEKIS Selbsthilfe Kontakt- und Informationsstelle, Berlin 2000.

Shuyler, K. S.; Knight, K. M. (2003): What Are Patients Seeking When They Turn to the Internet? Qualitative Content Analysis of Questions Asked by Visitors to an Orthopaedics Web Site. In: Journal of Medical Internet Research, Vol. 5 (2003), No. 4.

Spolsky, J. (2001): User interface design for programmers. Apress, Berkeley 2001.

WEBforALL (2004a): Die Bedeutung des Internets für Behinderte. In: http://www.webforall.info/html/deutsch/bedeutung_des_internet.php, zugegriffen am 10.10.2004, VbI e.V. - Vereins zur beruflichen Integration und Qualifizierung e.V.

WEBforALL (2004b): Empfehlungen für ein barrierefreies Webdesign. In: http://webforall.info/html/deutsch/empfehlungen.php,   zugegriffen   am 10.10.2004, VbI e.V. - Vereins zur beruflichen Integration und Qualifizierung e.V.

Zemore, R.; Shepel, L. F. (1987): Information Seeking and Adjustment to Cancer. In: Psychological Reports, Vol. 60 (1987), pp. 874.

How to Win a World Election: Emergent Leadership in an International Online Community

Justine Cassell[+], David Huffaker[+], Dona Tversky*, Kim Ferriman[+]
[+]Northwestern University, *Stanford University
{justine, d-huffaker, kferriman}@northwestern.edu, dtversky@stanford.edu

Introduction

In light of the recent U.S. presidential election, our attention is once again focused on the characteristics that determine perceptions of leadership and the factors that determine elections. It appears that style, appearance and language are at least as important as the issues and beliefs of the candidates. With television, for instance, discourse may largely be conducted through visual imagery (Postman 1985), in which physical appearance and nonverbal behaviors magnify the political platform of the respective parties. In fact, for presidential candidates, happy/reassuring facial displays during television interviews elicit more change in the electorate's attitudes than party identification, position on campaign issues or assessment of leadership capability (Sullivan and Masters 1988). Similarly, an experimental study of women's images shows that the manipulation of *attractive-ness* in photographs on campaign flyers affect election results (Rosenberg, Kahn et al. 1991).

In the early days of the Internet, much was made of the fact that superficial characteristics such as height and weight would not – could not – play a role in interpersonal relationships. As our experiences with the online world have increased, it has become clear that some of these characteristics are not in fact skin-deep. Communication online is as gendered as it is in the real-world. And

P. van den Besselaar et al. (eds.), Communities and Technologies 2005, 149-169.

power is reproduced faithfully, even when physical strength is irrelevant. Little research, however, has returned to an examination of the correlation between individual traits and leadership, in contexts where sight and sound do not play a role.

What happens, then, when elections take place online, in an environment where we can no longer see the physical appearance or nonverbal behavior of the candidates? Does language become the predominant factor in perceiving leadership? If discourse is all that is left to judge the potential leaders of a virtual group, what linguistic characteristics serve as criteria for electing a leader? In order to address these questions, we examine data from the JUNIOR SUMMIT, an online community composed of 3000 children from 139 different countries who had to choose 100 delegates to attend a highly coveted week-long symposium in the U.S.

Without ever seeing each other face-to-face, and in a community almost entirely free of adult intervention, these children traded messages in an online forum about how technology could improve life for young people around the world. They then elected leaders to represent their community in a real-world meeting with political and industry leaders from around the world (Cassell 2002). From the children's messages to one another in the months leading up to the election, we are able to examine the linguistic cues and language use that predict who emerged as a leader in the group and how leaders were perceived by the group.

The Junior Summit

The JUNIOR SUMMIT's goal was to connect and empower motivated youth from around the world to make their voices heard. Eighty-thousand calls for participation, translated into 16 languages, were sent out worldwide with the goal of attracting participants with a passion for changing the world. Ultimately, the hosting institution, the Massachusetts Institute of Technology (MIT), received over 8000 applications in 30 languages, and from a broad variety of urban and rural contexts, high- and low-socio-economic strata. Ultimately 3062 young people from 139 different countries were accepted – some participated as individuals and some in groups or school classes such that there were 1000 log-ins. Computers and internet connections were given to those participants who needed them. The forum was neatly divided between girls (55%) and boys (45%), and the ages of participants ranged from 10 to 16.

Timeline

The main activities of the JUNIOR SUMMIT took place over a 3-month period: one month in homerooms, two months in topic groups. During the topic groups, the participants elected two delegates per group to attend an in-person summit in devices to the conceptual domain of state of knowledge proposed by Rasmussen (Rasmussen et. al. 1994).

This new frame makes the *microworld* studies consistent with Rasmussen cognitive systems engineering approach and with the methodological proposals on complex activity studies of Brehmer and Dörner. We assume that the operational mode approach or strategy approach would prove to be more pertinent in capturing differences in complex activities like dynamic systems control processes, both in a laboratory (*microworld*) and in the field (Fig. 4).

6. CONCLUSIONS

In recent years there has been extensive research on operators activity based on simulated environments in very specific workplace contexts such as nuclear power control rooms or air traffic control. However, there are few references to applying simulation methodology to more frequent industrial processes.

We consider that expanding simulation methodology to all kinds of industrial computer-mediated supervision processes would be useful in order to increase the scope of practical applications in workplace improvement.

In this context we think it would be useful to develop tools and methods to study human behaviour in industrial supervisory tasks. *Microworlds* and qualitative reasoning based artificial controllers seem to be a fruitful approach in industrial contexts.

Microworlds provide a very flexible tool which is easy to adapt to diverse experimental conditions. *Microworld* specifications could easily be modified to reach experimental demands and to adapt to specific subjects. Flexibility and precision in behavior recording make *microworld* a very valuable tool for interface ergonomic evaluation in laboratories. In this respect the present study assesses the pertinence of MOREC and MOREC II – this second in its preliminary phase- in supervisory behaviour assessing and modelling in industrial domain. According to our preliminary results MOREC has proved to be useful in obtaining behavioural data under diverse interface conditions.

In addition to *microworld* human performance analyses, another line of research is to design optimal controllers to manage *microworld* dynamics and to emulate the different strategies operators adopt. The final application would be related to classic topics in human engineering: optimal task allocation between people and artificial agents.

Now we are working on the design of a controlled environment in which many operators can work simultaneously. This format would allow the study of collaborative work. Furthermore, it would facilitate online behavioural analysis and online control of task conditions.

A future approach could be the application of field studies in control rooms in industry domain. In this way, the study of human behaviour in supervisory control tasks enables us to develop future computer systems to aid and cooperate with plant operators to reduce the mental workload, to optimize the graphical interface (ecological approach), to prevent errors and to maximize the performance of the global system (human supervision and advanced automatic controllers in industrial plants).

REFERENCES

1. Acebes LF, Achirica J, Garcia MA, De Prada C (1995) A Simulator to train plant operators of a beet-sugar factory. In: Proceedings of the IMACS Symposium on Systems Analysis and Simulation SAS'95, pp 659-662
2. Aguilar J (1998) Supervisión de procesos industriales, razonamiento y autómatas híbridos In: www.laas.fr/~aguilar/supira.htm
3. Arnau J (1996) Mètodes, dissenys i tècniques en investigació psicològica. Edn UOC, Psicopedagogia
4. Barthélemy JP, Bisdorff R, Coppin G (2000) Human Centered Processes and Decision Support Systems. EURO2000: HCP Working Group Creation, Budapest. In: http://www-hcp.enst-bretagne.fr/
5. Bratko I, Urbancic T, Sammut C (1997) Behavioural clonning of control skill. In: Michalski RS, Bratko I, Kubat M (eds) Machine Learning and Data Mining: Methods and Applications.John Wiley and Sons
6. Brehmer B, Dörner D (1990) Experiments with computer simulated microworlds: escaping the narrow straits of the laboratory as well as the deep blue sea of the field study. In: First MOHAWC Workshop: Taxonomy for Analysis of Work domains, Liège, 15-16 May
7. Cañas JJ, Quesada JF, Antolí A, Fajardo I (2003) Cognitive flexibility and adaptability to environmental changes in dynamic complex problem solving tasks. Ergonomics 46, pp 482-501

8. Carreras O, Vallax MF, Cellier JM (1999) Réduction de la complexité tempo-
    relle dans le contrôle d'un micro-monde dynamique. Collection Le Travail
    Humain 4 T.62, Presses universitaries de France, Paris
9. Català A, Ponsa P, Travé-Massuyès L (2000) Artificial reasoners for human
    process supervision. Revista Iberoamericana de Inteligencia Artificial 9
    Invierno /2000 (II/00), AEPIA (eds), pp 76-84
10. Choi S, Byun S, Lee D (2001) Cognitive activities of main control room op-
    erators on emergency operations in nuclear power plants. Proceedings on
    Computer Aided on Ergonomics and Safety, Maui, USA
11. Colomer J, Meléndez J, Ayza J (2000) Sistemas de Supervisión. Cuadernos
    CEA-IFAC 1, CEA-IFAC eds
12. Díaz M, Ponsa P (2001) Mental workload assessment from performance
    analysis on a simulated process control system. In: Proceedings of the
    International Conference on Computer-Aided Ergonomics and Safety
    (CAES'01), Maoui, Hawaii 29th july-3d August
13. Díaz M, Ponsa P, Dalmau I (2001) Performance analysis on a process control
    micro-world: an approach to mental workload assessment. In: Proceed-
    ings of the International Conference on European Academy of Occupa-
    tional Health Psychology (EA-OHP'01), Barcelona, Spain, 24-27 October
14. Gentil, S. Systèmes d'aide à la supervision. En *Supervision de processos à
    l'aide du système expert G2.*Coordinadors N. Rakoto-Ravalontsalama &
    J. Aguilar-Martin, Editors Hérmes, Paris, 1995
15. Hamsher W, Console L, De Kleer J (eds) (1991) Readings in model based
    diagnosis. Morgan Kaufman
16. Hernández-Gress N (1998) Systeme de diagnostic par réseaux de neurones et
    statistiques: application à la détection d'hypovigilance du conducteur automobile.
    Ph.D. thesis, Institut National Polytechnique de Toulouse. Rapport LAAS
    98571
17. Ivergard T (1989) Handbook of control room design and ergonomics. Taylor
    and Francis Cop.
18. Malik TI (1996) Process Training Simulators (PTS), a comparison of different
    types. In: Measurement +control, vol 28, December/January
19. Martinez EC (2002) Intelligent Process Supervision using Reinforcement
    Learning and Temporal Abstraction. In: Proceedings of the B'02. XV IFAC
    IFAC World Congress. Barcelona, Spain, 21-26 July
20. Merino A, Pelayo S, Alves R, Garcia A, Acebes F, De Prada C, Gutierrez G,
    Garcia M (2003) Un simulador de alcance total para la formación de los
    operarios de sala de control de factorias azucareras, XXIV Jornadas, Automática
    Leon, September
21. Pastor J, Agniel A, Celsis P (1998) Artificial reasoners for the cognitive
    assessment of patients with parkinson's disease. In: 13th European Conference
    on Artificial Intelligence (ECAI'98), Prade H ed, pp 119-123, John Wiley & Sons
22. Patton RJ (1997) Fault tolerant control: the 1997 situation. In: Proceedings of
    IFAC Safeprocess, pp 1033-1055, Hull, GB

23. Pentland A, Liu A (1999) Modelling and prediction of human behaviour. Neural Computation 11, pp 229-242

24. Ponsa P (2003) Behavioural patterns study applied to processes supervision. Ph.D. theis, Technical University of Catalonia

25. Quesada JF, Cañas, JJ, Antoli A (2000) An explanation of human errors based on environmental changes and problem solving strategies. In: Wright P, Dekker S, Warren CP (Eds.) ECCE-10: Confronting Reality. Sweden: EACE

26. Rasmussen J, Mark A, Goodstein, LP (1994) Cognitive systems engineering. John Wiley and Sons

27. Raya C Microworlds design with LabVIEW. Internal report, Technical University of Catalonia, 1999

28. Ríos S, Bielza C, Mateos A (2002) Fundamentos de los Sistemas de Ayuda a la Decisión. Ra-Ma edn

29. Ritter FE, Young RM (2001) Embodied models as simulated users: introduction to this special issue on using cognitive models to improve interface design. In: International Journal Human-Computer Studies, vol 55, pp 1-14. Academic Press

30. Rodriguez, RO (2002) Aspectos formales en el razonamiento basado en relaciones de similitud borrosas. Ph.D. thesis, Departamento de Lenguajes y Sistemas Informáticos. Technical University of Catalonia

31. Romera JP, Lorite JA, Montoso S (1994) Automatización: problemas resueltos con autómatas programables. Paraninfo edn

32. Sanders MS, McCornick EJ (2000) Human factors and design. McGraw-Hill edn

33. Travé-Massuyès L, Prats F, Sánchez M, Agell N, Pastor J (1999) A qualitative agent approach for assessing dynamic process human supervision. In:The Thirteenth International Workshop on Qualitative Reasoning, (QR'99), p 221. Loch Awe, Scotland, 6-9 June

34. Vicente KJ (2000) Cognitive work analysis. Lawrence Erlbaum associates, publishers, 2000

35. Woods DD, O'Brien JF, Hanes LF (1987) Human factor challenges in Process Control: the Case of Nuclear Power Plants. Handbook of Human factors, John Wiley and Sons

Incorporation of users in the Evaluation of Usability by Cognitive Walkthrough

Granollers, T. and Lorés, J.

University of Lleida (Spain). GRIHO: HCI research group.

1. INTRODUCTION

Evaluation is an activity of vital importance in any development of interactive systems, enabling the testing of certain system-related aspects.

It is well-known that User-Centred system Design methods, UCD, [8] encourage the constant application of evaluation methods or techniques from the very outset of development in order to test a system's usability and accessibility, in addition to the testing of functional aspects.

The different evaluation techniques are usually classified according to diverse criteria such as the place where the evaluation is hold, the kind of technique, the degree of automation or the involvement or non-involvement of users and/or session-participants.

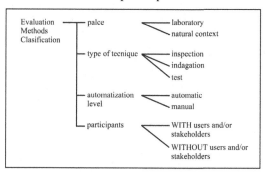

Fig. 1. Different ways of classifying the (usability) evaluation methods.

If the kind of technique used is the sole reference then the usual classification system is to separate the different methods into three categories: inspection, indagation and test.

Despite, the classification that usually prevails in the related bibliography is the one to choose the criterion of the type of used technique, obtaining therefore the separation of the different methods in *inspection*, *investigation* and *test* categories.

243

R. Navarro-Prieto and J. L. Vidal (eds.), HCI Related Papers of Interacción 2004, 243-255.
© 2006 *Springer. Printed in the Netherlands.*

a) *Inspection* is a generic name for a set of methods whose main common characteristic is that there are experts, known as evaluators, that examine (inspect) interface aspects related to the usability and the accessibility that the system offers to its users. Although the different methods for inspection have slightly different objectives, but all of them take into consideration the opinions, judgements and reports of the evaluators on specific elements of the interface as a fundamental factor in the evaluation of usability [10].

b) *Indagation* methods are carried out by speaking with the users, observing them, using the system in real work, or obtaining answers to questions verbally or in writing.

The goal is to obtain data about the user preferences, complaints, necessities, … and, fit al these data into the system requirements. Therefore, is necessary to discover, to learn and to generate design ideas of the system that improves the usability and the accessibility information of the system.

c) And, in the methods of evaluation by *test* we dispose of representative users trying to solve concrete tasks while they use the system or a prototype. Then the evaluators analyze the results in order to know how the user interface gives support to the users with its tasks.

Centring us in the methods by inspection, the *heuristic evaluation* (described as the process that a small set of evaluators examine the interface and judge its compliance with recognized usability principles) [9][10] is the most popular method. However, *walkthroughs* [10] constitute a valuable alternative also very extended.

But *both techniques intend to predict and/or to detect usability problems without the presence of end users*, and we ask *why do not include users?*.

2. COGNITIVE WALKTHROUGH METHOD

The Cognitive Walkthrough (CW) is a usability inspection method centred on evaluating a design's ease of learning. It uses a more explicitly detailed procedure to simulate a user's problem-solving process at each step through the dialogue, checking if the simulated user's goals and memory content can be assumed to lead to the next correct action. The motivation is the observation that many users prefer to learn software by exploring the possibilities that it has to offer [13][10].

Formally, the steps to be followed when evaluating a system using this technique are as follows:

a) Definition of the data necessary for the walkthrough
    i.   Identify and document the users' characteristics. *Who will be using the system?*
        The description of the users should include the specific accumulated experience and the acquired knowledge as determining factors in the testing of the "cognitive" factor during the walkthrough.
    ii. Describe in detail the system *prototype* to be used in the evaluation.
    iii. Enumerate the specific *tasks to be performed.*
        For each task implement the complete list of necessary actions to be carried out with the described prototype. This list consists of a repetitive series of action pairs (the user's) and responses (the system's).
    iv. For each task *implement the complete list of necessary actions to be carried out with the described prototype.* This list consists of a repetitive series of action pairs (the user's) and responses (the system's).

b) Walk through the actions: *the evaluators should carry out each of the previously determined tasks following the specified steps and using the described prototype.* In this process the evaluator will use the information on the users' cognitive factor (experience and acquired knowledge) to test if the interface is suitable for them. This review must be meticulous for all of the actions specified as necessary for the achievement of the task.

Hence the evaluator will be critical with every action of the system by answering the following questions [5]:
    i.   Are the available actions suitable for the user's experience and knowledge?
    ii. Will the users be aware that the correct action is available? This is related to the visibility and comprehensibility of the actions on the interface. Whether the action is in the appropriate place or not will not be discussed here, but rather if this is present and visible.
    iii. Once the action has been found on the interface, will these users associate the correct action with the achieved effect?
    iv. Once the action has been carried out, will the users understand the system's feedback? (whether the action has been carried out successfully or not).

c) Document the results.
    i.   The evaluator will note down the system's response and his own notes for each action

ii. The document will include a special appendix, known as the *"Usability Problem Report Sheet"* [5] detailing the negative aspects of the evaluation and assigning them a degree of severity that enables distinction between those errors which are most harmful and those which are less so.

2.1. Observations about Cognitive Walkthrough

The great virtue of this technique is that by being so focused on the execution of specific tasks it manages to detect a high number of problems, inconsistencies and improvements.

It has, however, a series of problems that if we are capable of solving will establish this method as one of the most efficient.

These problems are:

– The absence of users in the evaluation sessions is a common deficiency in all of the methods that are based solely on the criteria of experts to decide on aspects concerning third persons (the users). This factor is very important because, as expert as the evaluators may be, there will always be aspects that only the really interested parties will discover. Therefore the cognitive walkthrough has this deficiency, being as it is a method with no user involvement.

– Furthermore, in order to constantly walk through the actions the evaluator must be capable of answering questions of the type *will the users of this application be able to understand a particular icon or metaphor?, or will they know enough when they access a specific function?*. Questions that should be answered on the basis of the description of the users' characteristics in terms of their acquired knowledge and accumulated experience, carried out in the first stage of the method.

   The evaluator, therefore, must trust in this description to assess whether the tasks are suitable or not, which introduces a first level of possible uncertainty. And even if the descriptions were absolutely correct the final assessment always depends on the evaluator, adding a second level of error.

– And, a third problem also derived from the absence of users (and therefore applicable to the rest of inspection methods), is that does not favour the so important *participative design* [9] from the Human-Computer Interaction discipline point of view.

3. NEW PROPOSAL: COGNITIVE WALKTHROUGH WITH USERS

The new proposal presented here arises as a result of the work carried out by a HCI University research team which bases almost all of its research on systematically applying the known prototyping and evaluation techniques to the development of real interactive systems. The real cases are the validation methodology that contributes the empiric basis on which all the results and posterior conclusions stand.

Fully aware, in the context described, of the advantages of cognitive walkthroughs, but also aware of their main drawbacks we decided to check how efficient it would be to extend the aforementioned evaluation technique by incorporating users and thereby overcoming the deficiencies explained in the previous section.

Nevertheless, such incorporation cannot be carried out lightly. It should be borne in mind that, among other factors, every person has a separate point of view and their own ideas; everyone carries out certain actions in a spontaneous, routine or subconscious manner, while others are carried out knowingly in private; this fact means that, paradoxically, oneself is not the most appropriate person to reveal one's own thoughts! [12]. Therefore at certain times the answers that a user can give will not be as good as those of the experts. When evaluating user interfaces the expert may know what the users are thinking better than they themselves do [4].

Furthermore it should also be borne in mind that people who fit all the possible defined user profiles are not usually available for the evaluations, which will influence the kind of tasks proposed for each session.

All this leads us to propose the new way of carrying out the evaluation by means of Cognitive Walkthrough with Users (CWU), starting out from the traditional cognitive walkthrough methodology (as mentioned above) and then proceeding to carefully incorporate users in such a way that the fact of solving some deficiencies does not lead to the appearance of others.

The proposed process is as follows:

a) Carry out the cognitive walkthrough in the traditional manner.

b) When the previous point has been concluded users will be incorporated in the following way:
   i. Recruit users who are representative of the profile to be evaluated.
   ii. After an introductory explanation of the test, the method, the objectives and the prototype every user is asked to individually

carry out the group of tasks defined in the walkthrough as corresponding to their user profile.

The users are asked to express their thoughts, feelings and opinions about any aspect (interactivity, design, functionality,...) out aloud while they interact with the system or the prototype; a feature adopted from the method of thinking aloud [10].

Every user will carry out the tasks without receiving any further explanations and on finishing each task must complement the information making note of the main defects detected.

iii. In addition, once the user has finished the tasks the potential problems identified at point (a) can be commented on in order to know his/her point of view.

This point, although additional, is highly recommendable.

c)   The expert(s) will a posteriori go over the questions formed at stage (b).

3.1 Rationale

Looking at the procedure it appears that after the incorporation of the users the traditional walkthrough of point (a) is no longer necessary. Nevertheless, the reasons for maintaining this activity are:

– To allow an "unbiased" walkthrough to be carried out, without intervention from real users. We must be sure that the expert discovers different problems from those than he would discover after the intervention of the users.
– To provide an "entry point" for stage (b) enabling the evaluator to observe the points that were most confusing or erroneous for him.

As for point (b) the reasons for putting (ii) before (iii) seem obvious: for one thing part (iii) is optional and for another if the order were inverted it would be the user who would not carry out an unbiased walkthrough.

4. CASE STUDIES

With the main objective of checking if the results obtained by the new method are an improvement on those obtained by the traditional method, the new proposal (as described) has been applied in various evaluation sessions corresponding to various applications, two examples of which follow hereafter.

As the first step of the method consists of carrying out the starting point properly it will be very easy to check if a greater effort is really required.

The interactive systems presented as an example of the application of the described variant are:

4.1. "Haemoglobin" Program

This deals with an application whose main functional objective is to act as supporting material for teaching practice of certain subjects for the faculty of Medicine of the University of Lleida. The system enables some of the students of these subjects to carry out a number of the tests that they would normally do in the laboratory (with microscopes and related material) directly on their personal computers.

Fig. 2. One image of the digital mock-up used in the evaluation of the medicine project.

In the first stage of the project an application is developed to enable the students (users) to carry out a test counting base cells in a blood sample. The test must simulate its execution with the laboratory microscope and also offers contextual help that enables familiarisation with cell typologies as well as an end evaluation of whether the test has been carried out correctly or not.

This application will solve the typical problems of laboratory overcrowding for simple tests that require many hours of learning.

The cognitive walkthrough with users in this project was carried out at a relatively early stage in the development life cycle of this application; it being a paper prototype [11] carried out using digital mock-ups [3] for the evaluation sessions.

After elaborating the descriptive document with the knowledge acquired by the possible users, their own experience, the prototype used and the tasks to be carried out, by means of a traditional cognitive walkthrough an expert evaluated the prototype (1rst CWU step), and afterwards individual sessions with 10 students, future users of the system, were held (2nd CWU step).

In table 1 we can see that the number of problems and improvements detected by the expert evaluator with the traditional walkthrough is considerably lower than those detected after the trial with the students of medicine.

Table 1. Problems and improvements detected in the first example.

	Problems	Improvements	Total
1rst step (a) "evaluator"	3	2	5
2nd step (b) "users"	8	6	14
detected in both cases	2	1	3
increase with respect to the traditional CW	+6	+5	+11

The table, obtained from the document written up by the expert (3rd CWU step), shows that the evaluator was able to detect 3 problems and 2 possible improvements by the traditional cognitive walkthrough whereas the users detected 8 problems (two of which agreed with those of the evaluator) and 6 improvements (a coincident one with one of the evaluator), which supposes a total increase of +11 error-improvements (+120%) with respect to the initial data found by the evaluator.

4.2. Scientific event web + event manager

On the occasion of the hosting of a certain scientific event its own web site has been created, which enables its organizers to offer all of the event-related information. At the same time a related tool has been developed enabling the performance of all of the administrative tasks related to the processing of documents, the reviewers of these documents and the observations or comments that they make.

Both projects have been developed as if they were one and the same and have been carried out according to the Usability and Accessibility Engineering Process Model, u+aEPM [7], which proposes a formalized User-Centred interactive systems Design.

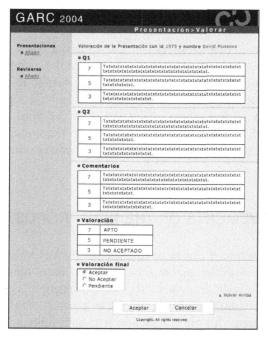

Fig. 3. One screen-shot of the developed system.

In this project the new proposal of the cognitive walkthrough with the incorporation of end users has been experimented with, using in this case software prototypes with some functions implemented almost to the full.

As explained in the method the appropriate documentation was employed so that an expert could carry out the evaluation in his usual way. After that three different users corresponding to different identified user profiles were chosen to carry out their profile-related tasks.

There were seven evaluated tasks in total and the results obtained in this case are summarised in table 2.

Table 2. Problems and improvements in the second example.

	Problems	Improvements	Total
1rst step (a) "evaluator"	4	5	9
2nd step (b) "users"	7	9	16
detected in both cases	0	2	2
increase with respect to the traditional CW	+7	+7	+14

Improvement that it increases in +14 (55%) the number of errors detected by the evaluator at first stage, or that is the same, with traditional Cognitive Walkthroug.

4.3. Aspects related to both projects

It can be observed that ten users where used in the first study whereas they were only three in the second. To be honest in the second project the call to the participation had a very low response, despite this factor does not have much importance since in the first example we stated that the number of new problem-improvements detected from the third or fourth user is practically null. Consideration reinforced with the study made by Nielsen and Landauer that determine the optimal number of evaluadores between 3 and 5 [11].

5. IMPROVEMENTS OF THE NEW PROPOSAL

In the first example it can be seen that the number of improvements and errors detected with the new method is twice that of those found with the usual cognitive walkthrough. In the second example although there is a significant increase the difference is not as great. It seems evident that the proposal's capacity for error detection is considerably greater than that of its predecessor.

Although two examples are too few to demonstrate the absolute validity of a method the results obtained allow a glimpse of what was intuited when it occured to us to incorporate users in the execution of this method.

In addition to the numerical improvements incorporated into the wide spectrum of usability evaluations by the new procedure we believe that there are further factors which allow us to affirm that this method surpasses its predecessor. These are:

– If we agree that a real DCU should incorporate users [1] then we will agree that the methods that do not incorporate users need to complement their results with results obtained by other techniques in which end or representative users intervene.

– The presence of users encourages participative design [6] and with it the formation of the multidisciplinary teams which are so important in the discipline of Human-Computer Interaction.

– With the material previously prepared for the cognitive walkthrough and thanks to the technique of thinking aloud the user's participation is more fluid than placing him in a laboratory where he is inhibited by the feeling of being observed.

– The doubts or errors that may have arisen in the first stage of evaluation can be rapidly cross-checked with end users, thereby avoiding creating indecisions which are harmful to the project.

– Often the evaluator is not able to detect the errors correctly because the specifications of the experience and knowledge of the users are inexact or incomplete. Complementing the evaluation with the users will also help to corroborate, complete or simply improve these descriptions.

In contrast it could be pointed out that the execution of the method requires more resources: the evaluator needs much more time and it is necessary to recruit users and dedicate the necessary time to them. Nevertheless we believe that the considerable improvement obtained justifies this increase.

5.1. Objections to the method

Another known method of inspection of the usability of interactive systems is that known as the *Pluralistic Usability Walkthrough*, PUW, a method developed in the laboratories of IBM [2] that shares some characteristics with traditional walkthroughs but has some of its own defining characteristics, among which the most notable is the involvement of end users.

– It may seem that the previously explained proposal is nothing more than a PUW called by another name. Far from it. Below we will see what the main differences that make the proposed method worthy of separate consideration are.

– In PUW three kinds of participants intervene, all of them taking on the role of the user to carry out the walkthrough tasks, while in our proposal only two kinds of users intervene and neither of them play the part of the other, a part which furthermore would be difficult for them to develop correctly.

– The PUW method ends with a questionnaire about aspects of usability that every participant should answer, leading to conclude with a final debate among all involved. We believe that with the contribution of the users and the experience of the experts such activities which only prolong the process without making significant contributions are unnecessary.

– A possible argumentation to the method is that the system designed improves incorporating the users not so that they are users but because in general more people have evaluated the interface. We have not solved this aspect because we would have an experiment with two groups, one with users and another one with more evaluators and equal number of evaluators by interface. In future work we will experiment.

– To finish we should point out that the PUW method is a method with a collective focus, where everyone participates in all of the activities whereas the method proposed here is an individual one.

It can be seen therefore that there are a good many differences between both methods for them not to be considered as one and the same.

Another possible objection to the method can come from the greater required time to carry out the new proposal, which have direct repercussions against the economic impact of the evaluation. Despite the number of detected error-improvements is so greater that the return on the investment is, from the usability viewpoint, justified.

6. CONCLUSIONS

This article explains a variant of the usability evaluation method called Cognitive Walkthrough, which is in the group of inspection methods. The new variant which can be regarded as a new method with its own identity incorporates users in way that combines the advantages of the initial method with those contributed by the availability of end users in the evaluation of interactive systems.

The benefits that the method is reported to contribute to the field of usability evaluations are demonstrated and verified with two examples applied to different situations with distinct prototypes, which show with empirical data the quantative increase in errors detected and with logical data the qualitative increase.

The new method goes by the name of Cognitive Walkthrough with Users and can be classified as one of the methods of inspection and testing, incorporating the advantages of each one of these groups of techniques.

ACKNOWLEDGEMENTS

We are particulary grateful to Alan Dix for his disinterested support in the conception of the method presented. His suggestions as to how we should proceed to efficiently incorporate the users have been very useful.

REFERENCES

[1]   Bevan N., Curson I. (1998). Planning and Implementing User-Centred Design. CHI98 Tutorial (ACM).

[2]   Bias, R. G. (1994). The Pluralistic Usability Walkthrough: Coordinated Empathies. IBM Corporation. In [10] chapter 3 (pag. 63-76).

[3]   Brink, T.; Gergle, D.; Wood, S.D. (2002). Design web sites that work: Usability for the Web. Morgan-Kaufmann.

[4]   Dix, A.; Ramduny, D., Rayson, P.; Onditi, V.; Sommerville, I.; Mackenzie, A.   (2003). Finding Decisions Through Artefacts. Human-Computer Interaction: theory and Practice (volume 1). Lawrence Erlbaum Associates.

[5]   Dix A., Finlay, J., Abowd G., Beale R. (1998). Human Computer Interaction. Prentice Hall, Englewood Cliffs, NJ (2nd edition)

[6]   Gaffney, G. (1999). Usability Techniques series: Participatory design workshops. Information & Design.

[7]   Granollers, T. (2003). User Centred Design Process Model. Integration of Usability Engineering and Software Engineering. Proceedings of INTERACT 2003 (Doctoral Consortium), Zurich (Suiza), Septiembre 2003.

[8]   International Standard (1999). ISO 13407. Human-centred design processes for interactive systems.

[9]   Molich, R.; Nielsen, J. (1990). Improving a human-computer dialogue. Communications of the ACM Volume 33 Issue 3.

[10]   Nielsen, J.; Mack, R.L. (1994). Usability Inspection Methods. John Wiley & Sons, New York, NY.

[11]   Rettig, M. (1994). Prototyping for Tiny Fingers. Communications of the ACM, April 1994/Vol. 37, No. 4 (pag. 21-27).

[12]   Sutcliffe, A. (2002). User-Centred Requirements Engineering. Theory and Practice. Springer-Verlag.

[13]   Wharton, C. (1992). Cognitive Walkthroughs: Instructions, Forms and Examples. Institute of Cognitive Science. Technical Report CU-ICS-92-17. University of Colorado, Boulder.

User-Centered Adaptive Web Sites: A Proposal for the Near Future

Antonio Fernández-Caballero
Arturo Peñarrubia
Pascual González
Instituto de Investigación en Informática de Albacete
Laboratory of User Interaction and Software Engineering (LoUISE)
Universidad de Castilla-La Mancha, Albacete, Spain
caballer@info-ab.uclm.es
+34 967599200

1. INTRODUCTION

Recently, Human Computer Interaction (HCI) is awakening a growing interest from different perspectives and especially from Software Engineering [3] [10]. The need to facilitate access to more and more complex systems is causing a un-precedent development in this research area. In addition, especially web-based applications, as they must manage a big quantity of data with complex structures due to the wideness and heterogeneity of the Internet, are those that require a most important treatment with regard to interaction.

It is not a trivial task for a user to find out in an easy manner what he is looking for. Especially, when accessing such a large and complex information system. In addition, this is even truer if performing this task in a handy and effective way [2]. Nowadays, a user with certain information requirements starting a navigational web session already finds tools able to make specific navigational aspects easier. For instance, some excellent browsers available to date provide a great number of documents containing certain searched terms. They even support searches of simple expressions based on these same terms. Most of these browsers also permit to access the information included in the web through a thematic tree. However, the tools offered neither makes the user-system interaction easier, in a broad sense, nor do they solve the user's concrete problems, as they provide too generic solutions. Thus, there is a real need for adaptive web sites. In the following sections, our proposal for the near future is introduced in detail.

R. Navarro-Prieto and J. L. Vidal (eds.), HCI Related Papers of Interacción 2004, 257-265.

2. WEB INTERFACE ADAPTIVITY

2.1. User Profiling

In a broad sense, many HCI aspects have experienced much progress in recent years, but only in comparison to other kinds of information systems. This is especially true in research related to user interface adaptivity [6] [11]. Obviously, when there is no adaptivity to user's skills or preferences, the interface designed for a wide group of users reduces the satisfaction degree for most of them. Consequently, to obtain more usable interfaces, it is necessary to know how these users are and in which way they behave in front of the interface. This is the reason why the so-called user profiles are established [1] [7]. These profiles allow grouping potential users in different sets by some common features. These features usually incorporate certain behavioral norms about the user interactions with the system. The inclusion of a user in a profile implies the adaptation of the application inter-face to this profile all the time, with the intention to make the interaction easier. However, the question is now if this general approach can be useful when applied to the Internet.

When a user browses a web, he tends to follow some repetitive guidelines ac-cording to the information requirements at any moment. It is not our purpose to establish the way in which these guidelines develop, neither to define them in a detailed way. Simply, we start from the idea that these guidelines exist. When basing our reasoning on a coherence principle, the conclusion is that a certain connection between the user information requirements at a given moment and the information he has received along the session exists. This very valuable information is filtered to improve the future navigation.

Hence, it is not our desire at this moment to identify a specific user and to ac-cumulate this information for use in the future, but rather to establish anonymous user profiles. This is non-persistent (or temporary) information used in the adaptation of the interface to the user requirements. The first point to establish is which kind of information about the learning session to collect. Actually, all web browsers include mechanisms – help in the address bar, or link lists, for instance – for accessing the last recently visited pages in an easier way. They also offer support for the most frequently visited addresses by means of bookmarks. However, the intention of our research is to go a step further, making the access to recently visited contents easier. This is an ambitious starting point, because it is not easy to extract thematic information from the web documents as designed at this moment.

2.2. Semantic Web and Metadata

For this purpose, we need to engage into the quite new approach to the web called Semantic Web [13] [19]. This emergent web suggests enriching the information present in the traditional web with meta-information, which describes the more basic information [9]. In this sense, there are many projects in progress [17] [18], but nowadays most of the documents available on the web lack in describing metadata.

Some projects define their own label set for metadata, being one of the most accepted the Dublin Core (DC) [4]. Dublin Core defines a set of 15 labels, although some people prefer a more extended set. The labels have names like *Title, Creator, Subject, Description*, etc. (see Table 1). The *Subject* label is of a special interest to our purpose. However, some questions remain open. How can we interpret this field? Is this information useful by itself to our purposes?

Title	Publisher	Format	Relation	Creator
Contributor	Identifier	Coverage	Subject	Date
Source	Rights	Description	Type	Language

Table 1. Dublin Core labels

2.3. Ontologies

Apparently, there has been little advance since some search sites approaches such as Google [8] appeared in the market. The real relevant terms about the document content are present, but there is no possibility to interpret their sense. When a user browses a polysemic term in Google, the tool returns all the pages that contain this term in any of their senses.

On the other hand, the web browser forces a perfect lexical match, because it looks just for strings, ignoring their semantic interpretation. However, the Semantic Web allows preventing this lack of semantic interpretation, by introducing the ontology concept [12] [14] [16]. An ontology establishes relations between all the terms that appear in the document descriptions. An ontology like RDF [15] establishes a sentence format, *<subject> <verb> <predicate>*, in which every field is expressed in the sentence by means of the URL of the document that contains this element description. This allows, for example, defining term equivalences, as well as other kinds of relations. It is precisely this simplicity what makes RDF a very flexible ontology.

Actually, there are other ontologies, some of them designed for very different purposes in the Semantic Web. Recently, research teams from various European universities have developed a multilingual lexical database called EuroWordNet [5] from the previous monolingual large lexical database project developed in the USA denominated WordNet [21]. EuroWordNet builds on an ontology that is stricter than RDF. Its minimal information unit is the *synset*. A *synset* is a set of words – nouns, verbs, adjectives or adverbs – at the same grammatical category and with the same meaning in a given context. With these elements, and using a limited relational set, EuroWordNet establishes a semantic lattice. Some of the default relations are synonymy, antonymy, hyponymy, meronymy, etc. (see Fig. 1). This ontology provides enough expressiveness to help achieving our objectives and allows to efficiently processing the information.

Now, starting from an ontology like EuroWordNet, it is possible to associate pages where semantically related terms appear, that is to say, those pages that not necessarily represent the same lexical terms. We will be able, for instance in an organic chemistry context, to allow the user the access to pages about saturated hydrocarbons, where these pages do not really contain this term. Pages containing terms like paraffin or alcan that are equivalent to saturated hydrocarbon will now appear. We will also be able to discern a page about chaperons in its biochemical sense from other pages where it appears with other senses.

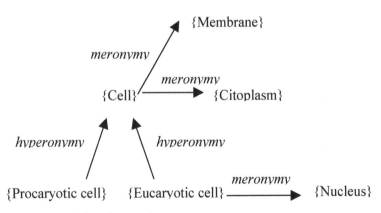

Figure 1. Main relations in WordNet

Now that the formalisms for our project have been established, the way they are being used in our framework will be explained in more detail. It is our intention to apply the concepts of user interface adaptivity into the web application context at different levels.

3. FRAMEWORK DESCRIPTION

3.1. Capturing Navigational Aspects

When a user enters our web site, he can see the application window divided into two frames. On the left side, there is a smaller frame, where the suggestions are shown, while the rest of the window is the main frame, where the visited pages are loaded.

A suggestion is simply a list of links to all documents in our site that are related, at a given degree, with the last ones the user has visited. We do not pretend at this moment to do global searches in the Internet, but only to work in a concrete site context. This idea could be useful for web sites with a large number of documents, where it is difficult to browse due to the amount and heterogeneity of the topics. Thus, when a user arrives to our web site, a cookie is created that stores all the themes, which have appeared in the consulted documents as well as the frequency of appearance. When the user accesses a new document, the frequencies of appearance of all themes in the document that match his profile are refreshed, and the new themes are added to the profile. At any time, a list of documents matching his profile is shown to the user. The server that looks for the metadata of our web site documents performs this. We could have included DC labels into some documents, like, for example, in HTML pages through XML, but we have chosen a uniform treatment for all the possible documents. So every document must be accompanied with its description in a separate XML document. Thus, these files are read in the server to obtain the list.

```
0 @9169@ WORD_MEANING
 1 PART_OF_SPEECH "n"
 1 VARIANTS
  2 LITERAL "eucaryote cell"
   3 SENSE 1
   3 STATUS 99
 1 INTERNAL_LINKS
  2 RELATION "has_hyperonym"
   3 TARGET_CONCEPT
    4 PART_OF_SPEECH n
    4 LITERAL "cell"
     5 SENSE 1
```

Figure 2. A file containing ontological information

Notice, however, that we are not looking for a lexical equivalence, but rather for a certain semantic relation degree. To get it, there is an ontological information base, consisting of a data file set and its respective query function set. As you may observe in Fig. 2, these files are divided into text blocks, each one containing the description of a synset. In the block header, we can find the synset terms, and, in a sequential way, a relationship list where the synset appears.

3.2. Managing Ontological Information

Since a synset is enough structured, through an appropriate interface, we can obtain the semantic support that our model needs. On Table 2, all the interface methods are shown. In this table, we can see the methods defined to manage this ontological information. The first ones, through a convenient relationship, allow us the browsing of the semantic tree (remember Fig. 1) and obtaining reachable terms by any length branches. Nonetheless, the two last ones are really of a special interest to us. Let us focus on them:

- *Closeness*: quantifies the semantic closeness of two terms. This method calculates the distance between the tree nodes and the relevance of the relationships used. It is invoked to choose the best-tailored sense in a context (where this function gets the highest value).

- *Sense_of*: establishes the sense of a term within a context (a list of unknown sense terms). Thus, this function allows jumping from the lexical unit used at metadata level to the semantic unit needed to access the ontology. This step is necessary if we want the phases to be independent. Thus, when a new document is added, and its subjects are written, it is not necessary to know the ontology. The temporal information stored about the session is also semantic in-formation. Then, to match new pages into the profile, we must make a conversion how they relate between themselves to achieve goals.

There is also a term closeness scale to be introduced. We define closeness degree 0 when two terms match lexically. Degree 1 is used if the terms are synonyms, degree 2 if they are joined by one-step of the first relationships, and so on. This mechanism allows configuring the web site to work at different precisions, because the respective functions have degree parameters.

This interface allows using our ontology to interpret document metadata and to extract their semantic information. Sometimes, an isolated metadata can still have semantic ambiguity, but then, our ontology allows solving it through the context.

Function	Returned Value
Ret_dir_rel	Set of terms related to a given one through a relation in a single step
Ret_relationed	Set of terms related to a given one through a relation in any number of steps
Return_relationed	Starting from a term and its sense, all terms related through a list and degree
Is_relationed_s	Are two terms related through a relation (in any number of steps)?
Has_common_ancestor	Starting from two terms, their senses and a relation, it determines if they have a common ancestor
Synset	Set of terms of a synset
Sense_set	Set of senses of a term
Unique_sense	Is a term monosemic?
Closeness	Closeness function
Sense_of	Sense of a term from a context

Table 2. Ontological information query functions

3.3. Exploiting Information

As told before, the server is the one that can explore the web site document features. We are interested in obtaining the descriptive theme set for each document. It is possible to quantify the user's interest in the document, starting from this term list, and through the tools studied. We could say that we have software agent aided navigation [20].

From this perspective, an automaton maintains an updated list of links to help the user to reach his objectives in a handy and efficient way. When a page matches some user interest themes, this page is proposed in the left frame. We must give priority to the most tailored links, even showing only the best ones.

We included some mechanisms to quantify page closeness to all the user-consulted themes, but perhaps, these themes are not equally relevant. In a way, we must be able to study user behavior, because not all the stored information is equally useful at a given moment. On the other hand, during a same session a user may consult on different thematic areas. Therefore, different behavioral patterns are created in a same navigation session, getting different areas of the global ontology. This, and other factors, must be studied in more detail for tailoring possible user interest evolutions.

4. CONCLUSIONS

At the beginning of this paper, we considered the application of principles of user interface adaptivity to the web application area. We affirmed that this was not an easy task due to the great number of features involved in this kind of applications. Thus, when we began to analyze the way in which our prototype puts our ideas into practice, we assumed certain restrictions. These restrictions affect the number of accessible documents (we work just in a controlled web site), and the complexity of the user profile (we only store a limited set of visited themes), and allow us to aid the user through an intelligent navigational session by means of an adaptive interface. Nevertheless, there is still much work to do in our attempt to provide the user with useful information through a guided interface. The analysis carried out on the first prototype has allowed, as expected, to study the features incorporated to the user model, the limitations, and some hints to improve our initial intentions.

ACKNOWLEDGEMENTS

This work is supported in part by the Spanish Junta de Comunidades de Castilla-La Mancha PBC-03-003 and the Spanish CICYT TIN2004-08000-C03-01 grants.

REFERENCES

1. Chan, P. A non-invasive learning approach to building web user profiles. *Proceedings of the KDD-99 Workshop on Web Analysis and User Profiling*, pp. 7-12, 1999.
2. Cueva, J.M., González, B.M., Aguilar, L., Labra, J.E. and del Puerto, M. (Editors). *Proceedings of the International Conference on Web Engineering*, ICWE 2003, Lecture Notes in Computer Science 2722, 2003.
3. Dix, A., Finlay, J., Abowd, G. and Beale R. *Human-Computer Interaction*. Prentice-Hall, 1998.
4. Dublin Core Metadata Initiative. http://www.dublincore.org
5. EuroWordNet Consortium. http://www.illc.uva.nl/EuroWordNet

6. Fernández-Caballero, A., López-Jaquero, V., Montero F. and González, P. Adaptive interaction multi-agent systems in e-learning/e-teaching on the web. *Third International Conference on Web Engineering*, ICWE 2003, Lecture Notes in Computer Science 2722, pp. 144-153, Springer-Verlag.

7. Fons, J., García, F. J., Pelechano, V. and Pastor, O. User profiling capabilities in OOWS. *Proceedings of the International Conference on Web Engineering*, ICWE 2003, Lecture Notes in Computer Science 2722, pp. 486-496, 2003.

8. Google. http://www.google.com

9. Klamma, R., Hollender, E., Jarke, M., Moog, P. and Wulf, V. Vigils in a wilderness of knowledge: metadata in learning environments. *Proceedings of IEEE International Conference on Advanced Learning Technologies*, ICALT 2002, pp. 519 -524, 2002. IEEE Computer Society, Los Alamitos, CA.

10. López-Jaquero, V., Montero, F., Molina, J.P., Fernández-Caballero, A. and González, P. Model based design of adaptive user interfaces through connectors. *10th Workshop on Design, Specification and Verification of Interactive Systems*, DSV-IS 2003, Lecture Notes in Computer Science 2844, pp. 245-257, 2003.

11. López-Jaquero, V., Montero, F., Fernández-Caballero, A. and Lozano, M.D. Towards adaptive user interface generation: One step closer to people. *Proceedings of the 5th International Conference on Enterprise Information Systems*, pp. 97-103, 2003.

12. Macías, J. A. and Castells, P. Tailoring dynamic ontology-driven web documents by demonstration. *Proceedings of the 6th International Conference on Information Visualisation - International Symposium of Visualisation of the Semantic Web*, page 535. IEEE Computer Society, 2002.

13. Olsina, L., de los Angeles M., Fons, J., Mara S. and Pastor, O. Towards the design of a metrics cataloging system by exploiting conceptual and semantic web approaches. *Proceedings of the International Conference on Web Engineering*, ICWE 2003, Lecture Notes in Computer Science 2722, pp. 324-333, 2003.

14. On-To-Knowledge: Content-driven Knowledge-Management through Evolving Ontologies. http://www.ontoknowledge.org

15. Resource Description Framework (RDF). http://www.w3.org/RDF

16. Tamura, Y. Domain-oriented approach to the reuse of learning knowledge: An overview. *Proc. of IEEE International Conference on Advanced Learning Technologies*, ICALT 2002. IEEE Computer Society, Los Alamitos, CA.

17. The Maryland Information and Network Dynamics Lab Semantic Web Agents Project. http://www.mindswap.org/

18. The Semantic Web Community Portal, Markup Language and Ontologies. http://www.semanticweb.org/knowmarkup.html

19. Wahlster, W., Lieberman, H. and Hendler, J.A., *Spinning the Semantic Web: Bringing the World Wide Web to its Full Potential*. The MIT Press 2003.

20. Weiss, G. (Editor). *Multiagent Systems: A Modern Approach to Distributed Artificial Intelligence*. The MIT Press, 2000.

21. WordNet: A Lexical Database for the English Language. http://www.cogsci.princeton.edu/~wn

Newspaper Archives on the Semantic Web

P. Castells[1], F. Perdrix[2], E. Pulido[1], M. Rico[1], J. M. Fuentes[1],

R. Benjamins[3], J. Contreras[3], E. Piqué[2], J. Cal[2], J. Lorés[4], T. Granollers[4]

[1]Universidad Autónoma de Madrid Campus de Cantoblanco, Tomás y
Valiente 11, 28049 Madrid
{pablo.castells,estrella.pulido,mariano.rico,chema.fuentes}@uam.es
[2]Diari Segre S.L.U. C/ Del Riu nº6, 25007 Lleida
{fperdrix,epique,jcal}@diarisegre.com   [3]iSOCO, S.A. c/
Fca. Delgado 11 – 2º 28100 Alcobendas – Madrid
{rbenjamins,jcontreras}@isoco.com
[4]Universitat de Lleida C/ Jaume II nº69, 25001 Lleida
{jesus,tonig}@griho.net

1 Introduction

The introduction of information technologies in the news industry has
marked a new evolutionary cycle in journalistic activity. The creation of
new infrastructures, protocols and exchange standards for the automatic or
on-demand distribution and/or sale of information packages through
different channels and transmission formats has deeply transformed the
way in which news industry players communicate with each other. One
interesting consequence of this technological transformation has been the
emergence, in very few years, of a whole new market of online services for
archive news redistribution, syndication, aggregation, and brokering.
Newspaper archives are a highly valuable information asset for the widest
range of information consumer profiles: students, researchers, historians,
business professionals, the general public, and not the least, news writers
themselves. Providing technology for news archive construction,
management, access, publication, and billing, is an important business
nowadays.

The information collected from everyday news is huge in volume, very
loosely organised, and grows without a global a-priori structure. This ever-
growing corpus of archived news results from the coordinated but to much
extent autonomous work of a team of reporters, whose primary goal is not
to build an archive, but to serve the best possible information product for

267

R. Navarro-Prieto and J. L. Vidal (eds.), HCI Related Papers of Interacción 2004, 267-276.

immediate consumption. Reporters are often assisted by librarians and archive specialists, who help classify, index, and annotate news as they are sent to the archive, using special-purpose archive management software. But in addition to this, powerful search and navigation mechanisms are needed for information consumers to find their way through. Current technology typically provides keyword-based search, browsing facilities inside newspaper issues, and, in online newspapers, navigation through static hand-made hyperlinks between news materials.

A wide margin remains yet for taking advantage of the possibilities offered by the digital medium to exploit a newspaper archive. Aspects that can be improved include: a) keyword search falling short in expressive power; b) weak interrelation between archive items: users may need to combine several indirect queries manually before they can get answers to complex queries; c) lack of a commonly adopted standard representation for sharing archive news across newspapers; d) lack of internal consensus for content description terminology between and among reporters and archivists; e) lack of involvement of reporters in the archiving process. We believe the emerging Semantic Web technologies [1] provide a good approach to overcome these limitations.

The Neptuno project (see http://nets.ii.uam.es/neptuno) has been set up to apply Semantic Web technologies to improve current state of the art in diverse aspects of the production and consumption of digital news. This paper presents the results achieved in the first phase of the project, which focuses on the construction, management and exploitation of a newspaper archive. The goal of this work is to develop a high-quality semantic archive for the Diari SEGRE newspaper where a) reporters and archivists have more expressive means to describe and annotate news materials, b) reporters and readers are provided with better search and browsing capabilities than those currently available, and c) the archive system is open to integration in potential electronic marketplaces of news products.

According to these goals, a platform has been developed whose main components are:

- An ontology for archive news, based on journalists' and archivists' expertise and practice, and integrating current dominant standards from the IPTC consortium [2].
- A knowledge base where archive materials are described using the ontology. A DB-to-ontology conversion module automatically integrates existing legacy archive materials into the knowledge base.
- A semantic search module, where meaningful information needs can be expressed in terms of the ontology, and more accurate answers are supplied.

- A visualisation and navigation module to display individual archive items, parts or combinations of items, and lists or groups of items.

The Diari SEGRE reporters will be the primary users of the archive exploitation functionalities. A version for the general public is planned as a future extension of the project.

The rest of the paper is organised as follows. The next section describes the creation and management of the newspaper library with the technology previously in use at the Diari SEGRE. After this, an overview of the online newspaper archive industry and current technologies is given. Section 3 describes the definition of an ontology for the Neptuno project, and Section 4 explains the search and visualisation functionalities for the knowledge base. Section 5 describes the platform architecture and the construction of the knowledge base from current archive news databases, providing some implementation details.

2 Online Newspaper Archives

The elaboration of news within a mass media group like Diari SEGRE is fed by diverse information sources, among which in-house newspaper archives are a must. These digital archives are a constant reference for background information search, or browsing related news, in order to complement, clarify, or help place in a certain context the new information a journalist is writing.

Most press media nowadays have massive information repositories based on relational database systems, with special-purpose software to manage their contents. The Diari SEGRE newspaper may publish over a hundred news and some fifty photographs everyday, which are automatically uploaded into the digital archive of the newspaper. The archive consists of a database, JPEG image files (published photos), and PDF files (newspaper pages). The archive currently contains all the issues of the newspaper since July 1995 to date. Milenium Arcano, one of the most popular content management platforms in the news sector in Spain and Portugal, is used to manage the archive. Arcano provides functionalities for archive update, manual documentation, and content search.

The news archival process is done by the documentation department, according to the criteria of experts in this department, and the possibilities (and limitations) of the software platform, classifying news using a hierarchical thesaurus, in endless evolution, of available concepts for contents annotation. On the other side, journalists consume this archived information when they need to inform themselves on subjects, histories or events, often under strong time constraints, and with limited beforehand archive system knowledge to be sure how to formulate their queries and information needs.

Today virtually all press media published on the web have a public access system to their news archive through the web. While a few newspapers keep providing free archive access, in the last few years paid access, by pay-per-view or periodical subscription, is becoming prevalent. Diari SEGRE itself has a service of this kind. Online archives usually provide searching and browsing facilities for archive news, which, in their advanced modality, allow queries by section, date, heading, lead, body, author, type of content (text, photography, graphic, animation, audio, video), etc. These applications suffer, at a smaller scale, from the same problems and limitations as the ones highlighted by the Semantic Web perspective: no support for conceptual search; extensive ad-hoc implementation efforts are required for integration with other archives or external information systems; platforms are not open to unforeseen extensions; rigid browsing facilities; no explicit notion of the semantics conveyed by archive documents. The aim of our project is to achieve or enable specific improvements by introducing ontology-based semantics, and exploiting this to provide better and/or novel functionalities in a news archive management system, following and/or improving existing proposals from the Semantic Web field, and contributing our own.

3 An Ontology for a Newspaper Library

The first step in the development of the Neptuno project has been the definition of an ontology to represent and process news information. After evaluating the available languages and standards for ontology definition, we have chosen RDF [3], currently the most mature, stable and widespread standard in the latest projects and developments in the Semantic Web area.

The level of detail of domain semantics in our ontology stops at the definition of generic categories by topics and subtopics, such as "politics", "immigration", "economy", "trade", "stock market", or "sports", as will be described next, but does not include specific classes and entities for these areas, such as "political party", "suffrage", "judge", "lawyer", "sentence", "sportsman", "theatre play", or "music group", nor the instances of these entity types. The creation of a knowledge base for these entities, that would completely take in the potential informative coverage of a mass media, exceeds the capacity of any single organisation willing to undertake such an endeavor. On the other hand, the utility of a partial collection, more feasible to construct, is difficult to justify.

Our first observation, when considering the reuse of existing ontologies and standards in this field, is that as of now no proper journalistic ontology has been published, as far as we are aware. In this sense our work is a contribution to the growth of the Semantic Web and publicly available ontology collections. With respect to other kind of controlled vocabularies, different standards have been developed in the area of journalism, such as NewsML [4], NITF [5], XMLNews [6], the IPTC subject reference system [2], and PRISM [7]. After evaluating all these standards, we have adopted the IPTC Subject Reference System, transforming it into an RDFS class hierarchy, as a thematic classification system for news archive contents.

Diari SEGRE has a database in which information about news, photographs, graphics and pages is stored. Newspaper contents are classified everyday by archivists using the Milenium Arcano tool. The criteria used for this classification are basically two: the section to which the contents belongs (Sports, Economy, ...) and the topics they deal with. For the latter classification a thesaurus is used that has been elaborated incrementally over time among all archivists, and that is frequently updated as new needs arise.

The ontology to represent the archives of Diari SEGRE has been built by using the Protégé ontology editor [8]. Some of the concepts in this ontology correspond to tables in the existing database, such as News, Photograph, Graphics and Page. All these concepts are subclasses of the Contents concept. In addition, contents are classified by subject following the IPTC subject classification hierarchy. This classification replaces those by section and category in the thesauri that were used so far by documentalists. A mapping has been established between the old thesaurus categories and those in the IPTC hierarchy.

4 Semantic Query and Semantic Navigation

The defined ontology serves to enrich the existing news archive contents with explicit semantic representations, giving rise to a semantic knowledge base. The added value of this enrichment pays-off with the possibility to develop advanced exploitation modules like, in Neptuno, a semantic query module, and a system for ontology visualisation, both integrated in a semantic portal.

4.1 Semantic Query

With respect to search, the availability of semantic information in the knowledge base allows the user to formulate more precise and expressive user queries, and implement a system that is able to use conceptual elements to match information needs against archive contents. Most existing search systems today are keyword/based: the user introduces the relevant words, and the search engine retrieves all the documents that contain them.

Occurrences of words are sought in documents, without taking into account:

- The meaning of words (they may have multiple).
- The relation between words in the query.

Which can result in the following problems:

- The system may return many documents with low relevance for the original query.
- It is the user's responsibility to open each document to check its relevance.

This may result in users not finding the sought information even when it exists, or on the other extreme, an information overload due to the large number of documents returned.

A semantic search engine [9] has knowledge of the domain at hand. The availability of a domain ontology that structures and relates the information according to its meaning allows the implementation of a search system where users can specify search criteria in terms of modelled concepts and attributes. The results are presented in a structured form including only the requested information. Contrary to traditional search systems where the answer consists of whole documents, where the user has to find manually the sought information, semantic search systems can return only the requested information.

The search module in Neptuno has been developed following these principles of semantic search. Moreover, the module combines direct search by content classes and class fields, with the possibility to browse the IPTC taxonomy, according to which archive news and documents are classified. The combination is twofold. On the one hand, search by fields is restricted to the IPTC categories selected by the user. On the other, Neptuno shows the list of categories to which the results of a search belong. The user can navigate directly to them, or select them to narrow down the search successively.

4.2 Visualisation

Despite the advantages that semantic models provide to retrieve information, one of the problems of these models is supplying a readable and understandable presentation for the end-user. In the model design and construction phase, the expressive value of the model is valued, and no visual or aesthetic aspects are taken into consideration. The main purposes for building ontologies are to provide semantic content for intelligent systems. The knowledge models are designed to offer the appropriate information to be exploited by the software. No visualisation criteria are used to build an ontology and often the information is not suitable to be published as it is. For example, it may happen that concepts have too many attributes, or relations are represented as first class objects so that the navigation becomes tedious, or concepts to be shown do not always correspond to modelled ones.

In our case, modelling of concepts and relations in the newspaper archive ontology has not been restricted by publication criteria, as could be the number of attributes of a concept, number of instances, or existence of auxiliary concepts for the representation of relations. There is a need to differentiate between what is going to be modelled from how it is going to be visualised. That is why we introduce the concept of Visualisation Ontology [10]. This ontology, called publication schema, allows organising the concepts and attributes in order to be published in the portal. The visualisation ontology represents publication concepts as they should appear in the portal. It does not duplicate the content of the original ontology, but links the content to publication entities using an ontology query language. This way one ontology that represents a particular domain can be visualised through different views. The visualisation ontology has two predefined concepts:

- Publication Entity: encapsulates objects as they will be published. Any concept defined in the visualisation ontology will inherit from it and should define these attributes:
  - o XSL style-sheet associated to the concept that translates its instances to HTML.
  - o Query that retrieves all attribute values from the original ontology.

- Publication Slot: Each attribute that is going to appear on the web should inherit from this concept. Different facets describe how the attribute will appear on the page.
  - o Web label: The label that will appear with the value.
  - o RDQL: reference to the query used to retrieve the attribute value.
  - o Link : When the published value should perform some action on mouse click (link, email, button, etc.), the action is described here.

Portal elements are described as children of the Publication Entity and their instances are defined according to the languages the entity will be published in (labels in English, Spanish, etc.), or the channel (the transformation style-sheet can translate into HTML, WAP, or just XML). In this case, the news library is exported in HTML format.

5 Architecture and Implementation

The current version of the Neptuno platform is an extension of previously working systems at Diari SEGRE that does not interfere with technology and procedures previously in use. The manual creation of ontology instances, associated to several hundred thousands news accumulated over the last nine years in the Diari SEGRE archive, would unquestionably be the best way to warrant the highest quality of the introduced semantics, but also an out of proportion, unfeasible work, out of any reasonable cost/benefit balance. For this reason Neptuno includes a module that populates the ontology with instances that are extracted automatically from the Arcano database, by using a mapping tool from JDBC/ODBC databases to RDF [11].

The manual creation of instances for new informations and photographs stored in the newspaper archive, at a regular daily pace, from the deployment of Neptuno onwards, is indeed a feasible goal in the future. The introduction of new semantic documentation tools requires, however, a careful work of analysis, design, testing and balancing of the additional burden that such tools may impose on archivists. Meanwhile, we have decided not to interfere with the current environments with which the Diari workers interact, and to generate new instances everyday by the same automatic procedure as used for old materials, without altering the newspaper production pace.

The contents search and visualisation modules operate directly on the knowledge base in RDF. The user poses search requests through a web interface in which (s)he selects the contents class to be searched (News, Photograph, Graphics, or Page), and specifies keywords for the desired fields (heading, author, section, date, subject, etc.) in the selected class. This information is sent to the Neptuno server where the request is formalised as an RDQL query. This query is run on the knowledge base and returns a list of resources (instances) that satisfy the query constraints.

The list of resources is sent to the visualisation module, which generates an web page where the found instances are displayed in an abbreviated and clickable form. When the user selects an instance, the visualisation module finds the class to which the instance belongs, selects the corresponding publishing entity, and generates a web page where the resource details are shown according to the principles described in the previous section.

6 Conclusions and Future Work

A newspaper archive is a fundamental working tool for editorial teams, and a potentially marketable product towards different kinds of consumers through diverse distribution channels. The size and complexity of the stored information, and the time limitations for cataloguing, describing and ordering the incoming information, make newspaper archives a relatively disorganised and difficult to manage corpus. In this sense, they share many of the characteristics and problems of the WWW, and therefore the solutions proposed in the Semantic Web vision are pertinent here.

The work developed so far represents an application experience of Semantic Web technologies in a real setting, making novel contributions to several of the undertaken aspects: definition of ontologies in a specific domain, semantic search and exploration functionalities, development of a user interface to interact with the knowledge base, transition from a working system with traditional technologies to a semantic-based platform.

Other goals we are considering from this point are the integration of new sources (external newspaper archives), contents types (text, audio, video) and languages (Spanish and Catalan), the enrichment of contents description through automatic methods of text and multimedia analysis, and the automatic adaptation to multiple devices and access channels. We also intend to improve the achievements so far by, for example, increasing the precision of the search system by defining ranking algorithms, increasing its expressiveness with more advanced interfaces, and carrying out a methodological revision of the representation and classification systems (ontology) currently used in the knowledge base.

7 Acknowledgements

This work is funded by the Spanish Ministry of Science and Technology, grants FIT-150500-2003-511 and TIC2002-1948.

References

1. Berners-Lee, T., Hendler, J., Lassila, O.: The Semantic Web. Scientific American (2001).
2. IPTC Subject Reference System & NewsML Topicsets, http://www.iptc. org/metadata
3. Lassila, O., Swick, R.R.: Resource Description Framework (RDF) Model and Syntax Specification. W3C Rec. 22 Feb. 99. Available at http://www. w3.org/TR/REC-rdf-syntax
4. IPTC NewsML, http://www.newsml.org
5. IPTC News Industry Text Format (NITF), A Solution for Sharing News, http://www.nitf.org
6. XMLNews, XML and the News Industry, http://www.xmlnews.org
7. Pub. Requirements for Industry Standard Metadata (PRISM), http://www. prismstandard.org
8. Noy, N.F., Sintek, M., Decker, Crubezy, M., Fergerson, R.W., Musen, M.A.: Creating Semantic Web Contents with Protege-2000. IEEE Intelligent Systems 16(2) (2001) 60-71
9. Guha, R., McCool, R., Miller, E.: Semantic search. 12th International World Wide Web Conference (WWW2003), Budapest, Hungary (2003), 700 – 709
10. Contreras, J., Benjamins, V.R., Prieto, J.A., Patón, D., Losada, S., González, D.: Duontology: an Approach to Semantic Portals based on a Domain and Visualisation Ontology. KTWeb.
11. Bizer, C.: D2R MAP -A Database to RDF Mapping Language. 12th International World Wide Web Conference (WWW2003). Budapest, Hungary (2003)

Learning among equals: the use and analysis of KnowCat system to support group work

Cobos, Ruth & Pifarré, Manoli.

Universidad Autónoma de Madrid, Spain & Universidad de Lleida, Spain.

Introduction

The sociocultural approach of the process of teaching and learning highlights the relationship among the development of mental processes of subjects and the characteristics of cultural, historic and institutional scenes in which they take part. Differences in the social and cultural organisation among various societies will produce changes in the development of individuals' psychological processes. These processes do not mature spontaneously, their construction require personal interaction. From this perspective, the social mediation of someone else, of cultural tools (instrumental and symbolic ones) and of entities and social organisations are the main variables to explain the individual development [13].

The use of symbolic tools allows us to process in different ways the information that comes to us from our surroundings, transforming therefore our cognitive capabilities. In Salomon, Perkins and Globerson's words, working with an intelligent tool like a computer *has effects in "what" a student does, "how" he/she does it and "when" he/she does it.*

The students' learning results and the student's cognitive changes can be explained by the different processes implicated in the use of a symbolic tool [9]. Thus, it is necessary to know the general and specific characteristics of the tool in order to design the best educational context that takes profit of its characteristics in favour of the student's learning.

In this line of work, our study departs from the design and the analysis of a specific teaching and learning proposal at the university education that is offered by the KnowCat system. KnowCat is a groupware system that allows us structuring and constructing collaboratively knowledge in a thematic specific space.

In this paper, firstly, we expose a summary of the systems that can help us supporting the collaborative teaching and learning processes. Secondly, we present the main characteristics of the KnowCat system. Also, in this section, we introduce the educational experiences accomplished with Psychopedagogy's students of Universidad de Lleida (UdL) using the

R. Navarro-Prieto and J. L. Vidal (eds.), HCI Related Papers of Interacción 2004, 277-287.

collaborative work system –KnowCat. Thirdly, we analyse the learning results obtained in these experiences. And, finally we expose the main conclusions of our work.

Systems for Collaborative Learning

The students' knowledge acquisition development has social nature [12]. It is very important to facilitate the learning process and to provide media for supporting interaction, awareness information and collaboration among the members of collaborative learning communities.[14].

There are several tools and systems for collaborative learning and teaching. They are called Computer Supported Collaborative Learning environments or system –or CSCL systems for short–. They can be classified in different ways. Next, we can find two approaches.

a) Jermann *et.al.* [5] classify CSCL systems in the following three types: "Systems that Reflect Actions", such as GroupKit, NCSA Habanero, CuseeMe or Microsoft NetMeeting; "Systems that Monitor the State of Interaction", such as HabiPro, MarCO or EPSILON; and "Systems that Offer Advices" such as DEGREE (it will be explained later), Group Deader System, GRACILE or iDCLE.

b) Martínez *et.al.* [10] offer the following classification: "Learner-model oriented" systems, such as GRACILE or COLER; "Interaction oriented" systems, such as EPSILON or MarCO; and "Participatory perspective" systems, such as TAGS.

Collaborative learning is a social activity that involves a learners' community who share knowledge and acquire new knowledge, this process is known as "social construction of knowledge" [6]. From this point of view, CSCL systems have in common the following features [4]:

First, a space for the learners' community where they can exchange ideas and knowledge, using several collaborative tools provided to help them in their group work.

Second, the knowledge is generally structured by topic. The units of knowledge are besides documents, are also exercises, studies, questions-answers, etc.

Next, we can find some examples of this type of systems. The first one is WISE *(http://wise.berkeley.edu)*. It is supported by the National Science Foundation (NSF). Its purpose is to provide to learners a didactic collaborative tool, by which students can learn by designing and debating solutions to respond to scientific controversies of the moment.

The two following systems deal with student knowledge expressed in form of "ideas". The DEGREE system (acronym for Distance education Environment for GRoup Experiences), developed by the UNED (*National University for Distance Studies*, Spain), which allows users to exchange ideas and contributions in order to reach agreements to write a document together [2]. The CSILE system (*Computer Supported Intentional Learning Environments*), developed by Scardamalia and Bereiter of the Ontario Institute for Studies in Education, Toronto *(http: //www.ed.gov /pubs /Ed ReformStudies/EdTech/ csile.html)*.

The KnowCat system (acronym for "Knowledge Catalyser") has been developed by the group GHIA at Universidad Autónoma de Madrid (UAM) [3]. KnowCat is a distributed non-supervised system for structuring knowledge and its purpose is enabling the crystallisation of collective knowledge as the result of user interactions. The main aim of this system is generating quality educational materials as the automatic result of the interaction of students with the materials, by catalysing the crystallisation of knowledge.

Finally, we have to mention adaptive systems for learning in Internet. Some examples of these type of systems are: TANGOW (Task-based Adaptative learNer Guidance On the Web), which has been developed by the group GHIA at UAM. TANGOW is a CSCL platform for delivering Internet-based courses *(http://www.ii.uam.es/esp/investigacion/tangow /present.html)*. These courses are structured by means of Teaching Tasks and Rules. Another example is WebDL (Web-based Distance Learning) which has been developed by the U.N.E.D *(http://www.ia.uned.es/personal /elena/webdl/index.html)*. WebDL allows us to adapt information resources and services to users.

KnowCat: the system use analyse the learning and teaching processes

During the last two decades, one can find many issues that study the incidence of the mediation of the computer both in the processes of interaction among equals and in the result of learning. The main working hypothesis that has guided the planning of these studies is that the intrinsic characteristics of the computer allow to define it as a highly interactive tool that can mediate and increase the power of the interaction among equals and can also promote collaborative learning [13][7].

In spite of the potential benefits of the improvement of student's learning, interaction processes among equals and the mediation of the computer in these processes; the works of revision and of meta-analysis of this research only show partial and inconsistent correlation among learning, computer mediation and interaction processes among equals [16].

Different arguments can be defended in order to explain the diversity of results obtained with the use of a computer. We highlight the specific features of the interaction among equals. Different authors indicate the features and the type of the assistance that the students exchange during the execution of a task as a relevant variable in order to explain the learning promoted by the interaction among equals [8][17] In this sense, these studies show, firstly, the assistance that the students offer each other can come from different level of elaboration and complexity. Secondly, the students' knowledge acquisition increase when the assistance provided is more elaborated and contains relative information about the task contents, about the process and about the main strategies to solve the task. And, finally, the highly elaborated assistance benefits the students who provides and who receives said assistance.

Several further educational research studies with similar educational aims have been motivated by the conclusions of the previous mentioned contributions. Among these studies, one can emphasise on the ones which analyse the main variables to solve a task (i.e. the task of the resolve of a mathematical problem, of the writing of an argumentative text, and note-taking processes). In these studies, guidelines, questions, aspects to be considered, etc., are designed in order to improve the strategies to solve the concrete task [8][15]. These guidelines have two objectives: on the one hand, to teach in an explicit way relevant strategies in order to solve the task, and on the other hand, to enrich the processes of giving and receiving assistance among equals. Furthermore, the interaction among equals deals with relevant aspects of the task and its realisation.

Our study is framed by this line of work. Concretely, the main aim of our work is to enrich the processes of giving and receiving assistance among equals with the use of the KnowCat system.

The main aim of KnowCat system is enabling the crystallisation of collective knowledge as the result of user interactions –without an editor managing the task–. The system is based on the concept of "Knowledge Crystallisation" supported by virtual communities of experts [1].

KnowCat provides us the building of places where one can find the relevant knowledge about an area or topic. With the word "relevant" we are referring to quality knowledge about the area. These places are called "KnowCat sites" or KnowCat nodes. One can access to a KnowCat site through a specific URL with a Web browser.

KnowCat organises the knowledge in the form of a tree structure. The root of this tree is the main topic of the knowledge area or KnowCat node. Each node of the *knowledge tree* represents a topic and contains two items: a set of mutually alternative descriptions of the topic (a set of addresses of Web documents) and a refinement of the topic (a list of other KnowCat nodes that can be considered the "subjects" of the current topic). All documents are competing for being the best description of the topic.

The documents may receive annotations –or notes for short–. A note reflects the knowledge of the note author about the information represented in the annotated document. For instance, a note may be a suggestion, comment, opinion or notice. The author of a document may contribute with another document version of his/her document.

In our work, we have used these notes as help messages –the previous mentioned assistance– that are offered to the students for improving their writing documents. Concretely, we have used KnowCat to enhance the learning processes of Psychopedagogy's students of UdL.

Basically, in our work we have used KnowCat in two types of activities:

a) Generating knowledge of quality on different topics of two subjects of the studies of Psychopedagogy: "Learning Strategies" and "Psychopedagogy Intervention in Children with Development Upsets". This knowledge construction came from the reading of papers and from professor's lectures.

b) Resolving of practical cases. In the resolve of these cases the students had to manage the generated knowledge from the lecture classes and from the reading of specific issues.

In both activities, we had used the notes of KnowCat as help messages among equals, which are offered for thinking over their learning processes and for improving their learning. This objective has been reached by the following three main instructional actions:

Firstly, the teacher and students analysed together about the principal variables that have an effect on the note-taking processes as a learning tool at the University.

Secondly, teacher and students elaborated together a guideline about the more relevant aspects to take into account in the note-taking processes. Concretely, this guideline motivates the students to think about how to elaborate, organise and personalise their ideas in the note-taking processes [11].

Thirdly, the students use this guideline to evaluate and to help to their classmates for improving their documents.

Experiences and results

KnowCat has two main applications: one of them is the generation of quality educational materials as the result of student interactions with the materials; another application of the system is the generation and the maintenance of collective knowledge of a researcher group.

We have tested KnowCat during the last six years with several students' communities at UAM and UdL (*http://knowcat.ii.uam.es/tool/eng/*). As result, there are several knowledge areas that may be consulted in Web address.

In the next sections we are going to explain the two experiences –and the results obtained– that have been made with students at UdL.

1. Experience: Learning Strategies

The knowledge area "Estrategias de Aprendizaje" or "Learning Strategies" (*http://knowcat.ii.uam.es/estrategiasAprendizaje/*) have been created by students enrolled in the subject called "Learning Strategies".

The main objective of this experience was to evaluate if the use of notes may be seen as assistance among students in the task of improving their document. We wanted to test the following hypothesis: if a document author takes into account the received notes in the creation of a new document version of his/her annotated document, the new document version will be improved.

This knowledge area started with a knowledge tree composed by five topics. The students had to accomplish three phases: Firstly, each student had to select a topic and add a relevant document on the selected topic. This document could be a Web document from another author. Then they had to vote for the best document and to add three notes to several documents in that same topic. At the end of this first phase, we had a crystallised document (the best description of the topic in terms of users' opinions) in each topic and the no-crystallised documents were removed from the system.

Secondly, they had to contribute with an own document about the selected topic (taking into account the crystallised document). Moreover, they had to vote to one document of the topic and to add three notes to other documents. In this case, they could give their opinion (with votes and notes) of not only the crystallised document in the first phase but also of the new ones.

Finally, the students had to write a new document version from their own documents.

In both experiences –the actual and the following one–, we have took out the following note types:

"Explanation" type: it is useful for doing clarifications about some parts of the document.

"Support" type: it is useful for approving the document.

"Review" type: it is useful for suggesting to add, remove or change some parts of the document. More specifically, there are "addition" type (for suggesting to add something), "delete" type (for suggesting to delete something), and "correction" (for suggesting to change something) type.

The instructor of the subject evaluated the original documents written by the students and the new document versions. The 82% of these document versions received better evaluation by the instructor in comparison with the previous documents. The authors of these documents took into account the greater part of received notes, in fact, the author who took into account all the "review" notes ("addition", "delete" and "correction" ones) contributed with a remarkable improved document version. We can corroborate this fact because the instructor evaluated their document version with greater values than their previous ones.

With this experience we have corroborated that a document may be improved taking into account the received "review" notes. Moreover, in both experience –the actual and the following one–, we have corroborated that the use of document annotations is useful for motivating document authors in generating new document versions.

2. Experience: Psychopedagogy Intervention

The knowledge area "Intervención psicopedagógica" or "Psychopedagogy Intervention" *(http://knowcat.ii.uam.es/IP/)* was created by the students enrolled in the subject called *"Psychopedagogy Intervention in Children with Development Upsets"*. There were 23 students, 18 students used KnowCat to learn the contents of the subject and 5 students did not use the system.

The objective of this experience was to evaluate if the use of KnowCat supporting the construction of collaborative knowledge has an effect on the result of learning. In this experience, the students used KnowCat to write in a collaborative way two types of documents:

First, documents about specific themes about the subject. The students wrote a document about the more relevant ideas of a concrete theme. The students had common information to elaborate this document: readings from teacher lectures. The students shared their documents in KnowCat, the classmates contributed to help the author of the document to improve it with notes. The notes were about the content of the document, about the organisation and about the relationship among the main ideas of the document. These notes were useful to motivate the document author to re-elaborate it and improve it.

Second, documents with the resolve of practical cases. The students wrote a report of a concrete case. In this report, the students should plan and justify the lines of their educational intervention to improve the pupil's problems. Again, the students shared and checked these reports in a collaborative form using KnowCat.

We have tested the results of the learning of the university students. The test consisted of 4 questions, three of them were about theoretical points and in the last one the students had to solve a practical case. This test has been accomplished by the 23 students (18 students had used KnowCat and 5 students had not used KnowCat).

A statistical analysis of results has come true. Comparing the total punctuation of the test, the results evidence that the students that have used KnowCat obtain better results, and statistically significant, than the students that have not used this information-technology tool [AVAR factorial mixtio (2x2 intra), F (1,21) = 9.494 p = 0.0057].

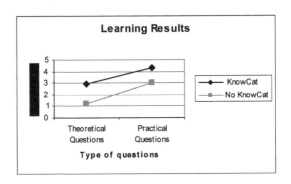

Fig 1. Comparison between results obtained in the test by the students who have used KnowCat (upper line) and who have not used it (lower line).

If we compare the results obtained by the students in the different questions of the test, we noticed that the students that have used KnowCat get better results than the students that have not used KnowCat in theoretical as well as practical questions.

Conclusions

KnowCat facilitates the processes of giving and receiving assistance among equals. Educational research gives evidences that these processes are indispensable for explaining the learning that results from the interaction among equals. The use of notes is useful for the mentioned processes.

We have accomplished two educational experiences with Psychopedagogy's students of Universidad de Lleida. In both experiences, we have corroborated that the use of document annotations is useful for motivating document authors to write new document versions. Furthermore, in the first experience, we have corroborated that a document may be improved taking into account the received notes

Working with KnowCat increases the awareness of students' learning processes. From our point of view, this fact can have an effect on the development of metacognitive abilities. These abilities have been indicated in educational investigations as responsible for effective learning.

In our opinion, the fact that KnowCat may mediate in the students' development of metacognitive abilities, may explain the better results which we have observed in the case of our students. Moreover, we want to highlight the fact that the students that have used KnowCat solve more satisfactory practical cases. As a conclusion, the students that have used KnowCat are able to use their knowledge in a more flexible way and are capable to apply this knowledge for solving new posed problems.

Acknowledgements

The KnowCat system is partially funded by Spanish National Plan of R+D (project number TIC2002-01948).

During 2003, the KnowCat system has been tested and improved in the frame of two projects of teaching innovation programs. One of them supported by UAM, and the another one supported by the University, Research and Networking Department, Catalonia Government (project number: UNI/3611/2002).

References

[1]   Alamán, X., Cobos, R. (1999) KnowCat: a Web Application for Knowledge Organization. In: Lecture Notes in Computer Science 1727, Chen, p.p., *et.al.* (eds). Springer, 1999: pp. 348-359.

[2]   Barros, B. (1999). Aprendizaje Colaborativo en Enseñanza a Distancia: Entornos Genérico para Configurar, Realizar y Analizar Actividades en Grupo. Tesis Doctoral, Departamento de Inteligencia Artificial de la Universidad Politécnica de Madrid.

[3]   Cobos, R. (2003). Mecanismos para la cristalización del conocimiento, una propuesta mediante un sistema de trabajo colaborativo. Tesis Doctoral. U. Autónoma de Madrid.

[4]   Cobos, R., Esquivel, J., Alamán, X. (2002). IT Tools for Knowledge Management: A Study of the Current Situation. Journal of Novática and Informatik/Informations, special issue on Knowledge Management and Information Technology, Vol. III, no 1.

[5]   Jermann, P., Soller, A., Muehlenbrock, M. (2001). From Mirroring to Guiding: A Review of State of the Art Technology for Supporting Collaborative Learning. Procs. of the First Conference ECSCL, Maastricht, The Netherlands, pp. 324-331.

[6]   Jonassen, D., Mayer, T., McAleese, R.A, (1992). Manifiesto for a Constructivist Approach to Uses of Technology in Higher Education, in Designing Environments for Constructive Learning, Duffy, Lowyck, Jonassen (eds), Springer-Verlag. pp. 231-247.

[7]   Kanselaar, G., Erkens, G., Jaspers, J., Schijf, H. (2001). Computer supported collaborative learning. Teaching and Teacher Education 17, pp. 123-129.

[8]   King, A. (1997). Ask to think-tel why: a model of transactive peer tutoring for scaffolding higher level complex learning. Educational Psychologist, 32 (4), 221-235.

[9]   Martí, E. (1992). Aprender con ordenadores en la escuela. Baracelona: ICE/Horsori.

[10]   Martínez, A., Marcos, J.A., Garrachón, I., Fuente P. de la, Dimitriadis, Y. (2002). Towards a data model for the evaluation of participatory aspects of collaborative learning. Procs. of the CSCL 2002. Boulder, Colorado, USA.

[11]   Monereo, C. (coord.) Barberà, E., Castelló, M., Pérez, M. LL. (2000). Tomar apuntes: Un enfoque estratégico. Madrid: A. Machado.

[12]   Pifarré, M., Sanuy, J. (2000). El diseño de contextos educativos mediados por ordenador y el aprendizaje de contenidos procedimentales de matemáticas en la ESO. Infancia y Aprendizaje, 19, 2000: pp. 87-100.

[13]   Salomon, G., Perkins, D. (1998). Individual and social aspects of learning. Review of Research in Education, 23, pp. 1-24.

[14]   Schlichter, J., Koch, K. Chengmao, X.(1998). Awareness The Common Link Between Groupware and Communityware. Community Computing and Support Systems, Ishida, T. (ed), Springer Verlag, pp. 77–93.

[15]   Shaw, J. (1997). Cooperative problem solving: using K-W-D-L as an organizational technique. Teaching children mathematics, 3 (9), pp. 482-486.

[16] Susman, E. B. (1998). Cooperative learning: a review of factors that increase the effectiveness of cooperative computer-based instruction. Journal of Educational Computing Research, 18 (4), pp. 303-332.

[17] Webb, N. M., Troper, J. D., y Fall, R. (1995). Constructive activity and learning in collaborative small groups. Journal of Educational Psychology, 87 (3), pp. 406-423.

Group Learning of Programming by means of Real Time Distributed Collaboration Techniques

Crescencio Bravo[1]

Miguel Á. Redondo[1]

Antonio J. Mendes[2]

Manuel Ortega[1]

[1]Departamento de Informática, Universidad de Castilla-La Mancha
[2]Departamento de Engenharia Informática, Universidade de Coimbra

1 Introduction

This approach of Pair Programming is popular in the business sphere, mainly in organizations using eXtreme Programming (XP). In this kind of task, two programmers design software together in the same computer, working collaboratively in the same algorithm, design or programming task. The situation is identical to the aforementioned case of teaching practical programming. The Pair Programming model has demonstrated to be beneficial in students of programming. Quantitative and qualitative studies show that the use of this approach in the lessons of Programming Fundamentals improves the students' learning, increases their satisfaction, reduces their shared frustration and decreases the number of bugs in the programs developed [10].

But when it is not possible for two students to be physically together, computer technology can support collaboration at distance. Thus, the concept of computer Collaborative Programming arises. Collaborative Programming is the application of collaborative strategies and computer support to Pair Programming. This allows, not only two, but three or four users to work in group. Previous studies [7, 11] indicate that Collaborative Programming does not only accelerate the problem solving processes, but rather it improves the quality of the software products. According to Johnson [5], the process of analysing and criticising software artefacts produced by other people is a powerful method to learn programming languages, design techniques and application domains. A system that

R. Navarro-Prieto and J. L. Vidal (eds.), HCI Related Papers of Interacción 2004, 289-302.

allows geographically distributed programmers to participate concurrently in the design, coding, test and debugging and documentation of a program is RECIPE (REal-time Collaborative Interactive Programming Environment) [8]. This tool allows the easy conversion of single-user compilers and debuggers in collaborative applications without modifying the executable elements (transparency) and the integration of existent collaborative editors in the system. However, it does not register the programmers' work in order to draw conclusions on their work, neither does it offer specialized tools for communication and awareness.

In spite that the computer laboratory is the natural place to carry out these works, the students not always finish them in the time scheduled, so they have to complete them in out-of-school time in their homes or in free computer classrooms. Moreover, on many occasions self-study tasks are proposed that can also be done in group. With our proposal, work at distance is allowed and motivated, optimising the time the students can spend on the subject, since sometimes they have to move to their partner's home or to the study centre to finish the exercises. A factor to take into account as an additional benefit is the motivating aspect of collaboration at distance, which offers tools to which young people are accustomed, such as chat or electronic mail. With this new approach the scenario that takes place consists in the students (two or three), at home or in their educational centre, editing together a program that solves a previously outlined problem, compiling it simultaneously, debugging it and finally making it run. To make this feasible, high speed connections facilitating synchronous interaction are required. Currently, there are a great number of DSL connections available in homes and university centres have high speed networks.

In this work we outline the exploration of these possibilities and the modelling of this kind of systems for the realization of practical exercises in programming, in Java or in any other language. This way, a Collaborative Programming system would be available, which could be used as a CSCW/Groupware system for companies as well as a CSCL system for learning in teaching centres. The paper is organized as follows: the next section is a short presentation of DomoSim-TPC, a CSCL environment used to apply its positions and part of its technological infrastructure to the kind of systems we approach; in section 3, the collaborative programming process is modelled and the components that make up these systems are described; in section 4, some aspects of the pedagogical support are considered; the next section shows a first prototype of the system; and finally, in section 6, the conclusions are drawn and future work lines are shown.

2 DomoSim-TPC: A Design Collaborative System

DomoSim-TPC [1] is an environment of collaborative learning of design in Domotics by means of complex problem solving, with which the students discuss, design and simulate in shared work areas. The system supports the whole teaching-learning process, including tools for the organization and analysis of activities on the part of the teacher.

This system proposes a semi-structured interaction model for the synchronous collaborative resolution of design problems, following techniques such as Collaboration Protocols [9] to structure the learning process, the Language/Action Perspective [12] to arrange the execution of certain tasks, and the Flexible Structuring [6] to build effective tools of communication and coordination.

A collaboration protocol describes the shared workspaces available and how the group of students can navigate along these spaces. A workspace is an area of development and exchange of information, which is independent but related to others in the system. The workspaces proposed by this system are five:

1. Design: Where the model representing a solution to the problem is built.
2. Work Distribution: Where the students distribute and organize their work defining an allocation of actions.
3. Parameter Definition: Where the general variables of the problem are defined.
4. Cases and Hypotheses: Where the students define cases and hypotheses of simulation.
5. Simulation: Where the model is simulated and the students experiment with it.

These workspaces integrate different mechanisms that support the process of design and simulation in group [2]:

− Direct manipulation mechanisms: The students design and simulate the models by means of elementary actions of direct manipulation, following the collaborative electronic whiteboard based on the object-action model.
− Communication and coordination support: While designing and simulating the solution to a problem, the students can use a Structured Chat and a Decision-Making Tool. The latter is activated by means of a button available in the Structured Chat.
− Awareness techniques: To facilitate real time collaboration, we have given great importance to awareness [4], which is the perception and knowledge of the interaction that other people carry out in a shared workspace. For that reason, tele-pointers, lists of participants and lists showing the interactions carried out are used.

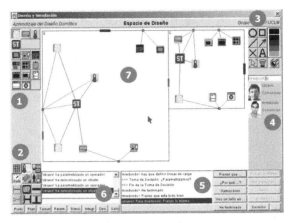

Fig. 1. Design Workspace.

In Fig. 1 the main DomoSim-TPC tool is shown: the tool supporting Collaborative Design. On the left, the operator (1) and links (2) toolbars, and on the right, the draw toolbar (3), are shown. The operators and the links relating them are the model components. The Session Panel (4), the Structure Chat (5) and the area (6) for interaction messages and errors (6) on the left of the chat can be seen. The work surface (7) contains the house plan on which the model is built. The data model that makes up the solution and the construction process that produces that model are persistent, being stored and available for the teacher's query as well as for the continuation of the work in other session. This feature differentiates CSCL systems from CSCW systems; in the former the product is as interesting as the process itself that allows building it.

3 Modelling of the Collaborative Programming Process

We will apply the structuring model of the DomoSim-TPC system and its collaboration-support mechanisms to the Collaborative Programming systems. In the programming process we distinguish several stages (source code edition, compilation and execution of object program) that will be described with a collaboration protocol. When the students use the system they carry out domain tasks, and communication and coordination tasks. The domain tasks are those related with programming. The communication and coordination tasks allow users to exchange information about the domain, to coordinate actions and to reach agreements.

3.1 Collaboration Protocol

We identify a 3-stage collaboration protocol. It is described in the graph in Fig. 2. Each stage or node corresponds to a workspace where to carry out one of the three domain-specific tasks. The main workspace is Edition/Revision, in which one user edits the source code. This workspace can also be used to revise the source code without carrying out changes in it. From this workspace, the compilation can be carried out or the execution can be directly started when the object program is available. The group's stay will be short at the Compilation workspace: the system will call the corresponding compiler and will show the compilation messages in a workspace area. Then, the students can observe the compilation results (errors messages, line numbers...), discuss on them and carry out the debugging (if there are errors) moving to the Edition/Revision workspace. If there are no errors they can access the Execution workspace. The program execution is carried out in a specific console. When finishing any of these two tasks, the group will always be located in the Edition/Revision workspace to start the process again, correcting the program if the expected results are not obtained.

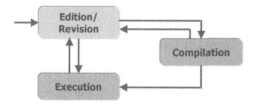

Fig. 2. Collaboration Protocol for Programming.

In Pair Programming users with two different kinds of roles are identified [10]: *driver* and *observer*. During the edition, the *driver* has the control of the interaction (keyboard/mouse) and carries out the design or coding, and the *observer* revises the work of the fellow pair member looking for bugs, considering alternatives and outlining questions. While the *driver* reflects upon his/her work, the *observer* asks for clarifications and explanations as the resolution process evolves. For the computer-supported Collaborative Programming systems we model a one-user edition task as this traditional method proposes, overcoming in this way the implementation difficulties of a synchronous collaborative editor and giving more importance to the negotiation for the turn shift in the edition role, which the students have to manage.

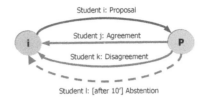

Fig. 3. Conversational graph for a proposal.

The navigation along the workspaces is organized by means of proposition mechanisms (Fig. 3). A first student makes a proposal of navigation and the fellow students (or the partner) will answer him/her in agreement or disagreement. The proposals and the reactions to them are expressed by means of buttons. When all the students agree or they abstain, the navigation to the new workspace takes place. A abstention is produced automatically by the system when a student does not answer in ten seconds, although this time setting is configurable. If no agreement is reached or no proposals are made, the group cannot work. Thus, the responsibility of moving forwards falls on the group and their participants. This same mechanism is used to manage the edition role turn shift, to carry out the compilation and to run the program execution.

3.2 Support for Domain Tasks

The domain tasks are materialized following the paradigm of interaction by means of direct manipulation based on the object-action model. In the edition, the objects are the language particles (variables, methods, classes...) or, at a smaller granularity level, the characters that are inserted or deleted in the source code. The actions are inserting, deleting, selecting, saving, cutting, pasting, etc. In the compilation and execution workspaces there are neither significant objects nor actions.

The direct manipulation is also used for the coordination tasks. The objects are the abstractions that model the proposition and communication processes: edition turn, compilation proposal and execution proposal; and the actions are those of proposing, being in agreement, being in disagreement and being absent, which will be generated if no other action is carried out.

3.3 Support for Communication and Coordination

The communication and coordination instruments are used from all the workspaces. Communication is materialised by means of a Structured Chat, which is based on the Flexible Structuring for communication proposed by Lund et al [6], which allows the exchange of text messages among the learners. This chat is structured because it offers a pre-established set of communication acts. The messages that can be sent are classified according to three criteria:

- Type of message: According to the type, the messages can be assertions, questions and answers.
- Position in the dialogue: In relation with the position the text message takes in the dialogue, there are initial and reactive messages.
- Type of adaptation: According to the type of adaptation of the message to the context, the messages can be adaptive or non-adaptive. The adaptive messages collect data from the domain tasks and generate particular messages for these situations. For example, depending on the classes, methods and variables existing in the source code, messages including these elements can be sent.

We propose the following specific messages for Collaborative Programming systems:
- Discussion messages:
  - "I think that...": assertion, initial and non-adaptive.
  - "I think so": assertion, reactive and non-adaptive.
  - "I don't think so": assertion, reactive and non-adaptive.
  - "Why...?": question, initial and non-adaptive.
  - "I don't know": answer, reactive and non-adaptive.
  - "Because..." : answer, reactive and non-adaptive.
- Messages related to domain objects: These messages have a link with the different domain objects, which are classes, methods, attributes, etc. and are manipulated mainly in the Edition workspace. Two kinds of messages are proposed:
  - "The (class | method | attribute | reserved word | variable) <object> is missed": assertion, initial and adaptive.
  - "A mistake in the (class | method | attribute | reserved word | variable) <object> can be seen": assertion, initial and adaptive.
- Free messages: To offer an additional communication functionality to the users giving them more freedom, messages with free text can be used. However, the students will be always guided during the system training in the preferential use of the structured messages, which structure the communication with semantically understandable forms suitable for the domain task and also facilitate the later communication analysis. For that reason, the chat registers the last five free-text

messages sent, which saves keying time and focuses the students' attention in a small set of messages. In certain experiences or in different moments this kind of messages could not be available in order to enforce the students to use the other two kinds of messages: structured and object-related.

Although it is possible to use audio and video channels during any collaborative activity, including programming, the textual structured communication has an advantage with respect to audio and video: it allows registering the communication acts so that they can be analyzed afterwards. From an audio or video stream it is difficult to extract meaningful information about the communication. However, if each chat message is stored, this log can be analyzed by means of diverse techniques. This approach has been explored in the Monitoring and Analysis Subsystem of DomoSim-TPC [1].

The coordination support is shown in the three proposition processes described which are specific to each one of the tasks or domain workspaces, which, as the navigation along the workspaces, follows the conversational graph of Fig. 3. The utilization of actions (buttons) to represent speech acts such as to propose, to agree, etc. is inspired on the Perspective of Language as Action [12].

3.4 Awareness Techniques

In the execution of domain tasks as well as of coordination and communication tasks awareness functions are available. This support is offered by means of the following elements:

– Session Panel: This is the main awareness element. It shows a list of participants in the session. Besides the name of each participant the photo of the user is also shown in order to reduce the barrier that implies remote collaboration. Each user's name is shown in a particular color used to identify his/her interactions. These interactions will be reflected in the same color. In addition, this panel shows the state in which each user is. We propose the following states: editing, communicating, observing, compiling and running.

– Tele-pointers: Although it is not necessary to have drawing tele-pointers since there is not a collaborative whiteboard, it is really interesting to show the edition pointer of the user whose turn it is. Therefore, only a tele-pointer has to be shown. It is a text-edit cursor, which shows the area in which the user is editing or the character that is being manipulated.

- Interaction lists: There are three coordination areas: turn shift, compilation proposal and execution proposal. Each one incorporates a message list that shows the initial proposals as well as the agreement/disagreement messages, always including the message sender.
- Awareness in the communication: The Structured Chat shows a list of the messages and their author.

4 System Interventions and Process Monitoring

For the success of the programming learning task by means of program construction a suitable management of the edition turn is required. In the system modelled, the students are responsible of this management. One of the aims of this research consists in exploring which turn shift mechanisms are more productive in these situations. When the turn assignment is the users' responsibility, the limitations of a student can be overcome with the knowledge or skills of another. But so much freedom makes it possible that a student never participates, the other carrying out all the actions. An advantage of computer-supported Collaborative Programming versus Pair Programming is that the turn shift could be the responsibility of the system, so that the time would be distributed equally among all the participants enforcing them all to participate. Other negotiation mechanisms that assure participation and maximize the pedagogic benefit can be established.

Besides the structuring of the turn shift there are many other pedagogic possibilities to guide the process, based on the ideas of the Intelligent Tutoring Systems. But this is a future objective of the system. However, we consider appropriate to incorporate a function that allows the students to consult the error statistics and detect which errors they usually make in order to focus their attention in the aspects in relation to these errors and facilitate discussion on this.

The analysis of the work carried out by the students, during the experiences or when they conclude, is specially interesting in this domain. If we pay attention to a group of students at work, we can see that in each task they have a different behavior. In the Edition all of them contribute with ideas or edition actions. During the compilation they stay expectant to observe the result. When the compilation ends, above all when there have been errors, there is a reflection process which leads to their correction. Finally, in the execution, there is a common work of definition of input data and of interpretation of the output data, looking for incorrect functioning or execution errors. The behavior and work of the group, if registered in an appropriate way, can be studied with different techniques of Artificial Intelligence, such as Fuzzy Logic, Neural Networks or Genetic Algorithms, which can contribute to design a more effective system.

The group's navigation along the workspaces, the communication and the proposition processes are registered in the system. But the storage of the actions in the editor, mainly the ones relative to the correction of a programming error, is not a trivial aspect because it is convenient to associate each action with the related error. In order to do so there are two possibilities:

1. The student relates which changes in the edition correspond with which compilation errors. This makes the registration possible but makes the students work more. For this purpose a list of error messages could be made available, so that the student first selects the error to correct and then modifies the source code.

2. The system relates each error with its correction. This mechanism has an advantage: the registration is transparent to the user. However, it is complex to put it into practice. A first approach is based on the line numbers in which errors occur and on the line numbers in which the changes are carried out. But in this case, it is necessary to take into account that the line number of a error can change when other error has been corrected (if lines are deleted or inserted), that other corrections or improvements not coming from any error can be made, and that certain errors produced in a line can be corrected in other different lines.

To facilitate this second possibility and to register the produced errors correctly it is necessary to define how the error lines and the error types are shown in the specific compiler used. This is necessary since the system is independent of the language used. The language should simply have a compiler and an interpreter or virtual machine. This definition will be carried out using a configuration function.

5 The COLLEGE System

COLLEGE (COLLaborative Edition, compilinG and Execution of programs) is a system developed to support the task of group programming, as previously described. In Fig. 4 the user interface of the tool that allows users to access the system is shown. When the user is connected to the server, a tool to manage sessions is available. In this case, contrary to DomoSim-TPC, the teacher is not the one that takes charge of defining the work sessions, but rather it is the role of the students themselves. A session is defined by means of a name, a type, a file and a schedule in which the session can be carried out. The file contains a formulation of the problem to be solved that will be available to consult from COLLEGE. The students can see the participants connected to a session by clicking on the session in the list.

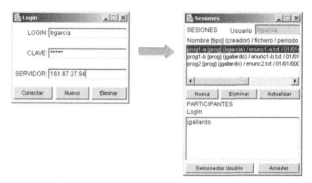

Fig. 4. Login and session management in COLLEGE.

Fig. 5 shows a work session with COLLEGE. The areas for Edition/Revision task (1), and Compilation and Execution tasks (2), as well as the three areas for the proposition processes (3, 4, 5), the Session Panel (6) and the Structured Chat (7) can be seen. In the figure the students are elaborating a program to solve second degree equations. When the code has been compiled and some errors have occurred, the students start discussing with the aim of solving them. Once the program has been finished and the students have agreed on running it, the execution console is activated in the way shown in Fig. 6 (1). The compilation and execution tasks use the same console. During the execution an area for entering data is available (2) and the Structured Chat can also be used.

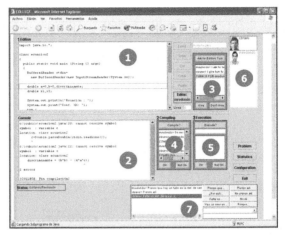

Fig. 5. A Collaborative Programming session in COLLEGE.

Fig. 6. Console for program execution.

The system is developed in Java, and operates following a client/server model on TCP/IP networks to facilitate its use on the Internet/intranet. The synchronization subsystem operates on the Synchronization Infrastructure for Collaborative Systems (ISSC), developed by our research group starting from the Java Shared Data Toolkit (JSDT)©, which presents a centralized communication architecture.

6 Conclusions and Future Work

The COLLEGE system aims to be a means to investigate behavioural aspects in the work of edition, compilation and execution of programs in group, as well as a support system to the programming learning, so that improvements in the teacher/learning of this discipline can be introduced. In its development we have applied the models and architectures that proposes DomoSim-TPC and taking advantage of the technological infrastructure built in this project. COLLEGE structures the programming task by means of Collaboration Protocols, and combines the realization of domain tasks by means of direct manipulation with collaborative support for communication and coordination based on the Flexible Structuring and the Perspective of the Language as Action.

This system is currently being evaluated. Before being used for the teaching of programming in Java, it is being used in the construction of programs to practise aspects related with the subject area of protection and security of information (as a groupware system). Once the first results have been processed, which will allow us to improve the system, COLLEGE will be used in the practical classes of the subject of Programming Foundations. To do so, we are defining experiences with students from the Universities of Castilla – La Mancha (Spain) and Coimbra (Portugal). We have randomly arranged two sub-groups of students and we have defined a library of problems with increasing complexity. The first sub-group will solve the problems in a traditional way, following the Pair Programming approach. The second sub-group will solve the same problems both individually and in pairs using the COLLEGE system. Then, in the first stage, the solutions and the work carried out by the students in the sub-groups will be studied using statistical calculations. With this data we expect to confirm the hypothesis of improvement of the programming learning process.

With respect to future work, we are collaborating with the University of Coimbra to link COLLEGE with the OOP-ANIM system [3], which allows learners to visualize an animated representation of the execution of a Java program. OOP-ANIM is a single-user tool, and it will be transformed into a collaborative tool in a simple way using the ISSC.

At a more general level, we are outlining the aim of approaching tasks characteristic of software engineering, as structural or dynamic modelling, taking advantage of the ideas and results obtained in the present investigation and in the DomoSim-TPC system. Specification techniques allowing users to make the developed components more flexible applicable to different domains, tasks and situations will be used.

Acknowledgements

This research work has been supported in part by the Red Iberoamericana de Informática Educativa (RIBIE) and the Universidad de Castilla - La Mancha (Spain).

References

1. Bravo C (2002). Un Sistema de Soporte al Aprendizaje Colaborativo del Diseño Domótico Mediante Herramientas de Modelado y Simulación. Ph.D. thesis, Universidad de Castilla - La Mancha
2. Bravo C, Redondo MA, Ortega M, Verdejo MF (2002). Collaborative Discovery Learning of Model Design. In: Cerri SA, Gourdères G, araguaçu F (eds) Intelligent Tutoring Systems. LNCS, Springer, Berlin, pp 671-680
3. Esteves M, Mendes AJ (2003). OOP-Anim, a system to support learning of basic object oriented programming concepts. In: Proceedings of CompSysTech' 2003 - International Conference on Computer Systems and Technologies. Sofia, Bulgaria
4. Gutwin C, Greenberg S (1997). Workspace Awareness. In: CHI'97 Workshop on Awareness in Collaborative Systems. Atlanta, Georgia, USA
5. Johnson PM (1998). Reengineering Inspection: The Future of Formal Technical Review. Communications of the ACM 41:49-52
6. Lund K, Baker MJ, Baron M (1996). Modelling dialogue and beliefs as a basis for generating guidance in a CSCL environment. In: Proceedings of the International Conference on Intelligent Tutoring Systems. Montreal, Canada, pp 206-214
7. Nosek JT (1998). The Case for Collaborative Programming. Communications of the ACM 41(3):105-108
8. Shen H, Sun C (2000). RECIPE: a prototype for Internet-based real-time collaborative programming. In: Proceedings of the 2nd Annual International Workshop on Collaborative Editing Systems. Philadelphia, Pennsylvania, USA
9. Wessner M, Hans-Rüdiger P, Miao Y (1999). Using Learning Protocols to Structure Computer-Supported Cooperative Learning. In: Proceedings of the ED-MEDIA'99 World Conference on Educational Multimedia, Hypermedia, Telecommunications. Seattle, Washington, Usa, pp 471-476
10. Williams L, Upchurch RL (2001). In Support of Student Pair-Programming. In: ACM SIGCSE Conference for Computer Science Educators
11. Williams LA, Kessler RR (2000). All I really need to know about pair programming learned in kindergarten. Communications of the ACM 43(5)
12. Winograd T (1988). A Language/Action Perspective on the Design of Cooperative Work. In: Greif E (ed) CSCW: A Book of Readings. Morgan-Kaufmann

A Proposal of Design for a Collaborative Knowledge Management System by means of Semantic Information

Jaime Moreno Llorena[1] and Xavier Alamán Roldán[2]

Dpto. de Ingeniería Informática, EPS Universidad Autónoma de Madrid
28049 Madrid, Spain
[1]Jaime.Moreno@uam.es and [2]Xavier.Alaman@uam.es

Introduction

Everyone agrees that the introduction of information and communication technologies, the Internet and the Web has caused an information overload. Users have progressed from merely keeping a small amount of information to having so much that it is too extensive and difficult to manage, and less useful than could be hoped for. From different fields of investigation (Knowledge Management, Information and Data Mining, Semantic Web, and so on) solutions for this problem are being looked for, but the solutions found are not applicable to all the cases.

An interesting idea for finding a solution to this problem within the Internet context is to use network characteristics to solve the problems that it causes. As for the more limited case of the network knowledge management systems, a solution could be to use the characteristics of the elements involved in the knowledge management (user's community, knowledge, and network) and to take advantage of the residual power from the activity of people, services and other entities that interact with those systems. This is the approach which this paper focuses on.

The technologies needed to prove this hypothesis could be not found in an only knowledge area, but they could be searched in the integration of ideas from many different research fields that coincide in the Semantic Web area. The five knowledge fields that are going to be considered in this paper are Knowledge Management, Human Computer Interaction (HCI), Computer Supported Cooperative Work (CSCW) [13], Information and Data Mining, and Semantic Web [4].

KnowCat [1], that stands for Knowledge Catalyser, is an original system for knowledge management over the Web, which proposes a different

R. Navarro-Prieto and J. L. Vidal (eds.), HCI Related Papers of Interacción 2004, 303-315.
© 2006 *Springer. Printed in the Netherlands.*

management procedure in relation to other approaches that is based on the collaborative work of a virtual user's community [14]. Its approach is closely related to the aforementioned hypothesis, because its main goal is to facilitate the crystallisation of collective knowledge as the result of user interaction. Moreover, this system unites many of the characteristics from other more general environments and provides an ideal platform for putting such hypothesis into practice, demonstrating its usefulness for solving the aforementioned problems in this particular context.

During the last few years, experiments have been carried out with KnowCat in several Spanish universities. These pilot schemes have provided evidence of the benefits of the KnowCat approach, and the ability of the system to manage knowledge without supervision by means of users' interactions [7]. At the same time it has been possible to obtain other interesting conclusions [2][8]. Furthermore, this has enabled us to identify new research areas, which fall into a wide range of knowledge fields aforementioned. This paper discusses some of these new research areas and their initial results [18].

The Semantic KowCat System

To put these ideas into practice, a new system called "Semantic KnowCat" (SKC) has been designed which:

- Follows the KnowCat philosophy, and exhibits its general characteristics and its most important functionalities [7].
- Its purpose is to add some new functionalities:
- To integrate system nodes in networks, SKC Networks;
- To provide different simultaneous ways to organize, access and present the knowledge;
- To provide a way to make a particular monitoring of each user activity and the activity of each entity that interact with SKC.
- Applies ideas from the different knowledge areas mentioned above:
- Information and Data Mining and Semantic Web, to analyze activity registers, documents and knowledge structure, and to enrich knowledge managed by the system;
- Semantic Web, Human Computer Interaction, Adaptative Hypermedia and Computer-Supported Cooperative Work postulates, to increase and to make knowledge management easier, in a collaborative, automatic and non-supervised way;

- Semantic Web and Agents, to establish and to keep links between SKC nodes over the Internet in order to integrate them in networks.
- Replaces the system architecture to make the aforementioned possible.

In the proposed approach, knowledge management is fundamentally based on the user interaction with the knowledge. Such management is made as transparent as possible for the users and should be a side effect of user's use of the knowledge. This is a challenge for the HCI field for several reasons. In one hand, each user has to be able to work with the knowledge according to the ontology that better adapts to him. In the other hand, every user has to be able to work with the whole knowledge in the system, independently of the ontologies used by him and the rest of the users. Furthermore, the system has to observe and to analyze the user's activity in order to obtain information to enrich and manage the knowledge. Finally, the system has to be able to show the enriched knowledge in an appropriate way for the situation, point of view and preferences of each user.

The general functional requirements of the system are briefly shown in the following Use Case model summary (see Figure 1).There are five actors for SKC. Firstly, the System User (SU) represents the human user who interacts with the system for working with the knowledge that it manages. Secondly, the Remote Agent (RA) corresponds to the agents that interact with SKC in representation of other instances of the system (SKC nodes) over the Internet. Thirdly, the Remote Monitor (RM) illustrates the system monitor, which takes data about user activity and provides information about system activity. Following this, the Analysis Module (AM) is the module that interacts with SKC's core for enriching the knowledge managed by the system. Finally, the Crystallization Module (CM) is the module that interacts with SKC's core for selecting the knowledge managed by the system.

RM is a component of the system itself like AM and CM. Each system instance has a RA, which as well as interacting with the system itself, it does so with the agents of others SKC instances over the Internet. These four entities are considered as actors, because they interact with the system's core independently and automatically. This approach makes it possible to capture part of the internal system's requirements.

The names of most of the use cases in the diagram are self-explanatory; however, some of them may need clarification.

The System User (SU) needs to select and to visualize the knowledge which it can use and which the SKC manages. Moreover, SU need to manage the contents that it puts in the system and its personal configuration. However, not all the administrative operations could be done by the SU itself, these are the not delegated operations. The system provides a mechanism for requesting these kinds of operations and the monitoring they carry out. Finally, the SU can manifest its consideration regarding the contents put in the system by other people.

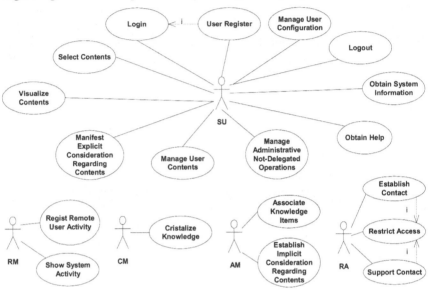

Fig. 1. Use Case Diagram for the SKC system

The Remote Monitor (RM) takes information about user activity on the client side and gives him information about system activity. The system uses that information source for establishing the implicit users' consideration regarding the contents that they manage.

The Analysis Module (AM) analyzes system contents and the activity registers of both user and system, to obtain new information that enriches the knowledge managed by SKC. This module deals with two main tasks: automatically linking knowledge elements, with the objective of organizing knowledge in different ways and making its management easier; and establishing the implicit users' consideration regarding the contents that they manage, using their activity registers.

In general, the architectural design (see Figure 2) is built around Ontologies [12]. These represent the management system knowledge and all the model entities needed to do this. To organize this Knowledge, the user's community can establish as many ontologies as they consider appropriate. The System's Model Entities are also ontologies. They are defined during the system design, deployment and configuration. At the same time, the system is composed of four fundamental active modules: the Data Base Manager, the Analyze Engine, the Catalyze Engine and the Interaction Module, which includes the system interfaces.

The Data Base Manager makes possible to manage the ontologies [15] that describe the knowledge and the models of all the system elements. In this way, the data repository is constituted by five Data Bases (DB). Firstly, User DB gathers the models of individual user and different kinds of associations between them. Secondly, Knowledge DB gets together all the models of documents and knowledge graphs. Thirdly, Presentation DB is composed of the models of interlocutors and patters needed for knowledge presentation. Following this, System DB contains the models of system, nodes and network. Finally, Register DB is the data repository of system and its elements activity.

The Analyze Engine tries to obtain new knowledge to enrich the existing knowledge already available, and to show up new information to the Interaction Module and the Catalyze Engine. In order to achieve this purpose, it takes care of the system knowledge review as well as it deals with the analysis of the activity register of the system and its interlocutors. The information obtained by the Analyze Engine is applied in most of the System's Model Entities.

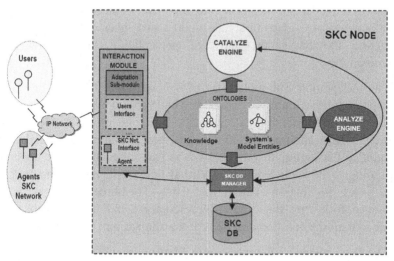

Fig. 2. General architecture of the SKC system

The Analyze Engine is performed by many demons, with configurable tasks, each one devoted to examining a part of the knowledge or the system elements and log, working on the Data Base mentioned before. It works in the same way as the spiders that index the Web [3], but uses, in this case, the ontologies that describe the system and the knowledge elements. The engine has a Control Unit that establishes the operation parameters depending on the system conditions. This engine activity works in the background.

The Analyze Engine applies Information and Data Mining techniques for the knowledge and registers analysis. In the first case, it uses procedures based on vectorial models [6][19][21]. In the second case, it employs methods from Web Usage Mining [6][11][20].

The Catalyze Engine deals with the selection of the knowledge that the system manages, taking into account the users' consideration regarding it and the total information available in the system. Catalyze is a relative concept in SKC, involving an object and a context. The Catalyze Engine, like the Analysis one, works in the background, has a Control Unit, uses the ontologies for covering the instances of the classes kept in the database and has many configurable demons, each one focusing on a particular catalysis context.

The Interaction Module (see Figure 3) supports two communication interfaces through an IP Network, one for the Users and the other for the other SKC Nodes by means of the SKC Network Agents [9][10]. Both interfaces use an Adaptation Sub-module that takes care of adapting the contents, the navigation and the presentation to the interlocutor characteristics.

The Adaptation Sub-module is of special interest within the Human Computer Interaction (HCI) context. This Sub-module has a three layers design, as in Martins' [16] approach, with one process in each layer: Filtering, that chooses the documents that compose the final virtual document; Packaging, that decides which parts of each of these documents are going to be included in this virtual document; and Formatting, that establishes the final format of the result. The three processes work in sequence following the order of presentation and use a database with models of all the questions needed for the adaptation.

The fundamental differences from Martins' approach are in the use of three new models, Virtual Content Model, Session Model and Interlocutor Model, and in the use of ontologies as a support for the adaptation. The

Sub-module (see Figure 3) applies to six models in the whole adaptation process:

- The Interlocutor Model [5] represents the entities that interact with the system through the interfaces. The User and SKC Network Agent models support it, because in the proposed design there are only two interfaces. If there were more interlocutors, the Interlocutor Model would take into account the corresponding models. This model is used in the three adaptation processes.
- The Virtual Contents Model determines the knowledge elements combination in replay to a request for some of them. For example, when a user requests a document, the system replays to the whole document or part of it, but usually together with a selection of knowledge elements that the system considers appropriate to combine, such as links to other documents, or references of other users working with the original document at this time. Actually, the system manages Knowledge Elements, but it usually shows them combined in Virtual Contents. This model is used in the two first adaptation processes.
- The Package Model establishes what parts of each of knowledge elements, which are selected for a Virtual Content, are going to be in the answer. Following the previous example, when a user requests a document, the system returns a Virtual Content with the full text of this document, but only the URLs of documents related to it.
- The Terminal Model represents the medium used in the communication with the interlocutors. The system has to consider terminal characteristics for establising which parts of each of knowledge elements are going to be shown and how. Imagine that the system has audiovisual documents with different versions for different band lines. This model is only used in the Packaging Process.
- The Format Model determines the final presentation of the result. In the case of user interface, the presentation format is usually a Web page, but could be a spreadsheet file or an image file. When the interlocutor is an agent, the presentation format is usually a data interchange file like XML. This model is only used in the last adaptation process.

- Finally, the Session Model is a representation of the system status and interlocutors temporary preferences, which are not included in the Interlocutor Model. The Session Model is used throughout the adaptation process.

The five first modules are in the Presentation Data Base and the last one, Session Model, is in the System Data Base.

The three processes included in the sequence used by the "Adaptation Sub module" to carry out its work (see Figure 3) are the following, presented in order of intervention:

- Filter Process decides which content elements from the system, as documents, vertex or graphs, are going to be included in the Virtual Content. Virtual Content [17] is a combination of documents that the system uses to answer the content questions from the interlocutor.

- Package Process establishes which sections from the contents elements determined by the Filter Process have to appear in the Virtual Content. That will serve to answer the content request that begins the process.

- Format Process determines how the answer of the emitted request will be present. In order to do that, it establishes the format to present the Virtual Content as an HTML page, or an XML file, or a PS file, etc.

The SKC nodes use agents [9][10] to be integrated making networks, SKC networks. SKC nodes are stand-alone, and each one has a Network Agent SKC that is responsible for establishing and keeping links with other SKC nodes over the Internet. These links are not all the same. All of them maintain basic information exchange that supports the SKC Network existence over the Internet, but only some of them are also devoted to exchanging data related with the managed domain knowledge. This happens when a SKC Node finds other with similar subject. At the same time, the agents are devoted to restrict the access to the information in their respective nodes.

Whenever a SKC node is created and connected to an IP network, it publishes a Web page with the meta-information necessary for other SKC nodes that can establish communication with it. If the new node location is not visible from the Internet, it is necessary to indicate where to find other accessible nodes. Furthermore, the new node tries to register its Web page with the most important Search Engines. Every SKC node attempts to find new nodes, using the information provided for it at the creation time or searching in search engines if it can access to them. Whenever a SKC node finds a new one, tries to make contact with it. Each SKC nodes periodically tries to communicate with the rest of the nodes in the SKC Network. In each communication between SKC nodes, the nodes involved update their own existing nodes databases. When several times in a row it is not possible to make contact with a particular node, this is considered missing.

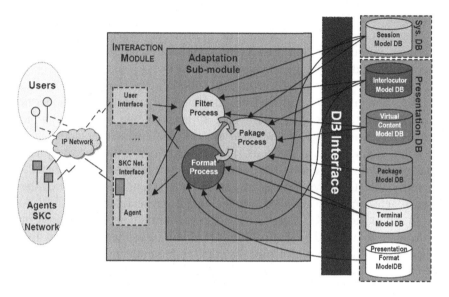

Fig. 3. Interaction Module of the SKC system

Summary and Conclusions

One of the undesirable effects produced by the introduction of information and communication technologies, the Internet and the Web, has been the information overload. Solutions for this problem are being looked in different research fields, such as Knowledge Management, Information and Data Mining, Semantic Web, etc.

An interesting hypothesis for finding a solution to this problem in the network knowledge management systems context is to use the characteristics of the elements involved in the knowledge management, the user's community, the knowledge and the network, and to use residual power from the activity of people, services and other entities that interact with them.

KnowCat (KC) is an original system for knowledge management over the Web, which facilitates knowledge management as the result of the user's community interaction without supervision. This approach is closely related to the proposed hypothesis and provides a good starting point.

Semantic KnowCat (SKC) is the new system proposed for proving this hypothesis, which integrates the KnowCat approach and ideas from several research fields: Knowledge Management, Human Computer Interaction, Computer-Supported Cooperative Work, Information and Data Mining and Semantic Web.

The SKC system will manage the information overload problem in a specific environment, but this system may be a paradigm for many other network-based knowledge management systems.

This paper has stemmed from the authors' experience with the KC system obtaining some ideas from the knowledge areas aforementioned that coincide in the Semantic Web. It presents the design of a new unattended knowledge management system, SKC, which includes several original characteristics: the coexistence of different ontologies to present the same knowledge domain; model of the system entities, register its activity and its analysis; automatic interaction among the system entities; and adaptation of the knowledge access and its presentation.

In conclusion, SKC suggests a suitable environment for research into information overload to find solutions for knowledge management without supervision by means of a user's virtual community interaction over the Web. SKC also seems to be a feasible way to prove the proposed hypothesis.

Foreseeable and Future Work Study

Furthermore, to try to demonstrate the proposed hypothesis, the purpose of this research is to obtain three kinds of results:

- A new system Semantic KnowCat (SKC) with KnowCat (KC) functionality extended. This will allow continuity of the research regarding the unattended knowledge management.
- To align the unattended knowledge management approximation introduced by KC with emergent and convergent areas of research: Semantic Web, Hypermedia Adaptative, The Knowledge Management and the Data and Information Mining.

This article leaves the following questions for future research: completing new systems development and determining the experiments and field tests needed to prove the new environment and the proposed postulates.

The users' tests are especially important, because the approach proposed in this paper is essentially based on users' interaction with the system. Two categories of experiments are considered: some of the experiments will be carried out in a laboratory, where an experts group will observe how users do some activities with the system; a second group of experiments will be field proves, to test the system as support for learning activities. In both cases, we will try to obtain empirical data about system operation, users' subjective impressions of system use and their satisfaction grade. The tests will be carried out at the beginning of, during and at the end of the development process, and their results will be used to refine the system and in its final validation.

Acknowledgements

Some part of the KnowCat system and the research work presented here, has been financed by the Science and Technology Ministry with the project ARCADIA (TIC2002-01948).

During 2003, KnowCat system has been exploited by two educational innovation projects:

- "Plataforma KnowCat para la gestión colaborativa de materiales docentes en red", which has been financed by the Universidad Autónoma de Madrid
- "L'ús d'un entorn web específic com a eina per elaborar, estructurar, compartir y optimitzar el nou coneixement construit pels alumnes universitaris a partir de la presa d'apunts", financed by the "Departamento de Universidades, Investigación y Sociedad de la información de la Generalitat de Catalunya" (UNI/3611/2002).

During 2004 and 2005, KnowCat has been exploited by the educational innovation project named "Aprendizaje activo y tutelado en la generación colaborativa de materiales docentes en la Web con la asistencia del sistema KnowCat", which has been financed by the Universidad Autónoma de Madrid.

References

[1] Alamán, X., Cobos, R. *KnowCat: a Web Application for Knowledge Organization*. In Procc. World-Wide Web and Conceptual Modeling (WWWCM'99). París, Francia. Noviembre, 1999. En: Lecture Notes in Computer Science 1727, Chen, p.p., et.al. (eds). Springer, 1999:pp. 348-359.

[2] Alamán, X., Cobos, R., Moreno, J. *Una propuesta para la gestión colaborativa del conocimiento*. In Procc. of the Workshop: Investigación sobre nuevos paradigmas de interacción en entornos colaborativos aplicados a la gestión y difusión del Patrimonio cultural, COLINE'02. Granada, Spain, November 11-12, 2002.

[3] Baeza, R., Ribeiro, B. *Modern Information Retrieval*. Addison Wesley, 1999.

[4] Berners-Lee, T. http://www.w3.org/2000/Talks/1206-xml2k-tbl. 2000.

[5] Brusilovsky, P. *Methods and Techniques of Adaptive Hypermedia*. En: Brusilovsky, P., Kobsa, A., Vassileva, J. (eds.), Adaptive Hypertext and Hypermedia. Kluwer Academic Publishers, 1998, pp. 143.

[6] Chang, G., Healey, M., McHugh, J., Wang, J. *Mining the World Wide Web: An introduction search approach*. Kluwer Academic Publishers, 2001.

[7] Cobos, R. *Mecanismos para la cristalización del conocimiento, una propuesta mediante un sistema de trabajo colaborativo*. Tesis Doctoral. Universidad Autónoma de Madrid, 2003.

[8] Cobos, R., Pifarré, M., Alamán, X. *Aprendizaje entre iguales en la red: Análisis de la asistencia del sistema KnowCat en el trabajo en grupo*. V Congreso Internacional de Interacción Persona-Ordenador. Lleida, España (2004).

[9] d'Inverno, M., Luck, M.. *Understanding Agent Systemas*. Springer, 2001.

[10] Franklin, S., Graesser, A . *Is it an agent, or just a program?: A taxonomy for autonomous agents*. In
J.P. Müller, M.J. Wooldridge, and N.R. Jennings, editors, Intelligent Agents III-Proceedings of the Third International Workshop on Agent Theories, Architectures, and Languages, Lecture Notes in Artificial Intelligence, volume 1193, pages 21-35. Springer-Verlag, 1997.

[11] Garofalakis, M. N., Rastogi, R., Seshadri, S., Shim, K. *Data mining and the Web: Past, present and future*. In Proceedings of the WIDM99 Conference, pages 43-47, Kansas City, Mssouri,1999.

[12] Gruber, T. R. *A Translation Approach to Portable Ontology Specifications*. Knowledge Acquisition, 5(2), pp. 199-220, 1993.

[13] Grudin, J. *Groupware and Social Dynamics: Eight Challenges for Developers*. Communications of the ACM, 1(37), pp. 92-105, 1994.

[14] Grudin, J. *CSCW: History and Focus*. IEEE Computer, 27(5), pp. 19-26, 1994.

[15] Hjelm, J. *Creating the Semantic Web with RDF*. Wiley 2001.

[16] Martins, L. C., Coelho, T. A. S., Barbosa, S., D. J., Casanova, M. A., Lucena C. J. P. de. *A Framework for Filtering and Packaging Hypermedia Documents*. In The 2nd Adaptive Hypermedia and Adaptive Web-Based Systems (AH2002), Málaga, Spain, 2002. Proceedings pp 275-283.

[17] Milosavlejevic, M., Vitali, F., Watters, C. *Workshop on Virtual Documents, Hypertext Functionality and the Web* at the Eighth International World Wide Web Conference. Toronto, Canada, May 1999. Actas disponibles en: http://www.cs.unibo.it/~fabio/VD99/index.html.

[18] Moreno, J. *Una Propuesta para la Gestión de Conocimiento Colaborativa Mediante Información Semántica.* Proyecto de Investigación. Universidad Autónoma de Madrid, 2003.

[19] Salton, G. *Automatic Text Processing : The Transformation, Analysis, and Retrieval of Information by Computer.* Addison-Wesley, Reading, Massachusetts, 1989.

[20] Srivastava, J., Cooley, R., Deshpande, M., Tan, P. N. *Web usage mining: Discovery and applications of usage pattern from Web data.* SIGKDD Explorations, 1(2):1-12, 2000.

[21] Yang, Y., Pierce, T., Carbonell, J. *A study on retrospective and online event detection.* In Proceedings of the 21st Annual International ACM SIGIR Conference on Research and Development in Information Retrieval, pages 28-36, Melbourne, Australia, August 1998.

Contextualized Argumentative Discussion for Design Learning in Group

Miguel A. Redondo, Crescencio Bravo, Manuel Ortega

E. S. Informática. University of Castilla – La Mancha
Paseo de la Universidad, 4.13071 Ciudad Real (Spain)
{Miguel.Redondo, Crescencio.Bravo, Manuel.Ortega}@uclm.es

Introduction

The learning of experimental subjects involves the realization of practical works [8]. However, the material necessary to carry out these assignments is usually expensive and in many cases it is not adequately provided. This problem gets worse with the difficulty to bring the student closer to real situations, to replicate accidents and to simulate those chaotic situations which may happen in the real world. In order to soften this problem by means of the use of technology, we have developed a distributed environment with support for distance learning: DomoSim-TPC [2]. This system is a telematic environment for the collaborative learning of domotics design.

Collaborative learning environments commit the learners in the realization of cognitive and meta-cognitive activities promoting the development of shared knowledge. In these environments technology provides mechanisms for the use of information, realization of distance activities, organization and structuring of these activities, etc. In particular, DomoSim-TPC provides support to diverse collaborative tasks in which the approach on the discussion model is important for bringing the student closer to real situations and reaching the commitment of the participants in the problem resolution.

In this article we describe the dialogue model that adopts the system for the task called *Collaborative Planning of Design* [8] and some experimental results which provide an idea of the global effectiveness and efficiency of this system. First, we situate the concept of online conversation. Next, we describe in depth the characteristics of the discussion process adopted in our system during the aforementioned task. Then, we present the results of some experiences developed with

R. Navarro-Prieto and J. L. Vidal (eds.), HCI Related Papers of Interacción 2004, 317-327.
© 2006 *Springer. Printed in the Netherlands.*

DomoSim-TPC. Finally, we highlight the most important conclusions that have been obtained with this work.

Dialogue and discussion models

Many systems that offer support for collaborative tasks base great part of this support on the use and integration of a tool for online conversation. To refer to this conversation type, terms such as "dialogue", "discussion" and, simply, "conversation" are frequently used. However, some significant differences exist among them. We should have in mind these differences mainly when our objective is to achieve constructive models of dialogue that serve as a nexus for the users that interact with other users using a system based on the information and communications technologies. The word conversation comes from the Latin "convertere" and it can be interpreted as "turn distribution". Jenlink and Carr [5] identified three main purposes of a conversation: the negotiation or exchange of information in the framework of the resolution process of a problem; the criticism of the work of others, while hiding your own; and the creation of new knowledge from a more general point of view and with a scientific approach.

These authors suggested a taxonomy to differentiate four conversation types: Dialectics, Discussion, Dialogue and Design. Dialectics is centred on the logical structure of an argument. Discussion appears in a forum where many people can defend their individual positions locating them in a specific context. Dialogue is centered on the construction of the semantics through multiple shared perspectives. It constitutes a form of construction of a community to converse. "Messages" are located in this type (distribution lists, newsgroups [3], etc.). Design is usually the main objective of the conversation and it is centred on the creation of something new. According to Isaacs [4], it goes beyond the presentation of personal opinions, the participants' transformation and the capacity to listen and to ask on perspectives and points of view different from personal vision.

Discussion and *Dialogue* are very pragmatic, but *Dialogue* is less common. *Dialectics* and *Design* are more disciplined conversation forms. All of them can be appropriate, depending on the purpose of the conversation.

Discussion in DomoSim-TPC

Considering the objective which motivated the development of the DomoSym-TPC system and the tasks that it supports, our choice is located between the *Discussion* and the *Design* concepts. The model that the system incorporates is inspired in the work style that the learners follow in face-to-face activities in a traditional laboratory. The students carrying out practicals of domotical design usually work in groups of two or three people on a panel in which they distribute work, criticize, justify and explain the actions that they carry out and the design decisions that they make. The students propose and discuss their modelling work, receiving constructive feedback from the rest of the members of the group. Additionally, this process is carried out with the surveillance of the teachers or coordinators of the group. They outline problems and assign tasks, supervise development, propose instruction methods and evaluate the achievements left unattained.

To incorporate this mode of working on a telematic environment it is necessary to have a tool for the discussion on a problem (topics) or on the possible solutions to the problem. This tool should facilitate that those learners responsible for the resolution of each section in an activity can present and justify a solution proposal before the rest of the participants. Therefore, these participants should interact with the contributions and proposals being able to carry out diverse actions. For example: to visualize them for their study and analysis; to modify them creating other alternatives or proposals; to request explanations; to issue comments; to clarify doubts on the resolution mechanism; etc.

In order to materialize this mode of working we adopt a discussion model inspired in the Topic-based Conversation related with the tasks that the learners have to solve to build a certain design model [7,11]. Thus, the discussion process is characterized to be a social task in which the participants in an activity reflect on the work that they carry out. They collaborate, exchange ideas, propose resolution mechanisms, argue, justify, refine their contributions and acquire new knowledge, always in the context of a specific topic. This is called *Argumentative Discussion*. Furthermore, as it is located around a specific topic we describe it as contextualized. In the next section, we describe the main characteristics of the tool supporting it.

Characterization of the dialogue elements

Using the new technologies, the materialization of the previously introduced discussion process is especially important to provide a high degree of realism. For this, we use an approach based on work spaces. We can point out that in this situation we should consider three different but related spaces: (a) definition space; (b) elaboration space and (c) communication space. We want to point out that the domain in which we work can be modelled for automatic processing using techniques to determine the characteristics and qualities of the products elaborated [7, 9]. This is an important aspect to consider in order to relate the work spaces and, therefore, to achieve the contextualization.

To structure the actions of the communication space we have organized the types of the participants' interactions in several categories. These categories present a high degree of generality and independence of the specific domain in which we work. We consider as contribution an intervention of the participants or of the system which is related with other contributions in the discussion process. We make a first classification to distinguish contributions of *specification, elaboration* and *communication*.

The *specification* contributions have as their origin the definition space and their purpose is to define the characteristics of the activity and the problem to be solved. These contributions are generated in an automatic way and they indirectly start from the specification of the activity and the problem formulation, which is defined by the teacher [9]. The elaboration *contributions* are built in the elaboration space and they are associated to properly structured design plans [6]. These plans become a solution proposal to a design problem and they constitute the specific context of the discussion. The *communication* contributions are an extension of the proposals in [1], and their origin is located in the space communication. Their objective is to facilitate the criticism and justification of *elaboration* contributions or of specific parts of these *elaboration* contributions [7].

Refining the previous classification we identify the following as *specification* contributions: *activity, epigraph* and *epigraph-in-agreement*; as *elaboration* contributions: *proposal, counterproposal* and *proposal-in-agreement*; as *communication* contributions: *question, explanation, comment, system-comment* and *agreement*. These last types of contributions are described below.

Specification contributions:
- The *activity* represents the work that the teacher has proposed to the group. It will always be the first contribution and will be generated in an

automatic way as a consequence of the activity definition that the teacher carries out.

- The *epigraph* or section represents each of the subproblems in which an activity is structured. It is directly related to the tasks (problem resolution) that the participants will carry out and, therefore, to those that the participants will have to propose solutions to. They are generated at the moment when the teacher proposes the activity. The number of epigraphs of each activity depends on the problem and of their application domain. They are generated in an automatic way after processing the information of the problem [9].

- When an alternative solution for an epigraph has been proposed and it has agreement of the members of the group, then an *epigraph-in-agreement* is generated. The solution is the proposal reached jointly by the group.

Elaboration contributions

- A *proposal* represents a strategy or design plan that a participant has built and, later on, he/she has proposed as solution to an epigraph. It can also represent a solution outline that the teacher proposes to cause a reflection to search mistakes, to detect any aspects susceptible of being improved, etc. In synthesis, a design plan [6] is a sequence of actions in the way:

    ```
    <item>::=<id><time><action><prevAction>
    ```
    where,
    ```
    <action>::= <type><area><plan><object>
    <prevAction>::=<id>
    ```
    <id> is an action identifier, <area> makes reference to an management area or organization of the services in a domotical installation, and <type> is the kind of the action (insert, link, etc.).

- The *counterproposals* are proposed of design refining some aspect of a proposal. They are always submitted as an alternative to a proposal. However, the proposals are submitted as solutions to an epigraph.

- When a design proposal has the agreement of all the participants in the discussion it becomes a *proposal-in-agreement*. This represents the solution to an epigraph and it is associated to an *epigraph-in-agreement*.

Communication contributions

- When a request of an explanation on the content of a contribution is expected you can send a *question*. This kind of contribution usually requires to be answered with a comment or with an explanation. They can include links to the actions of a proposal (or counterproposal).

- A *comment* is a contribution with textual content that you can use to explain certain aspect in other contribution. It can also include links to the actions of a proposal.
- The *explanations* are dedicated to be the answer to previously outlined questions. Although, according to the viewpoint of the participant responsible, the one that proposes the activity, they can be used for other objectives. As in the previous cases they can be related with the actions of a proposal.
- To show and to reflect the view-point on a contribution (generally proposals or counterproposals) *agreement* and *disagreement* contributions are used.
- When the system has to intervene in an explicit way in the discussion process, it sends a *system-comment*. When all the members of the group are in agreement with a proposal, the system analyzes the proposal [7] and if it is correct it consolidates this as a solution of the group (for the epigraph). If the proposal was not correct, the system sends comments indicating or standing out some characteristics of the proposal that should be improved. In addition to this, the system also sends comments when it observes that the proposals which the students discuss are not improving. For this, we say that the discussion process is *guided* [10].

The relationships among these categories are not fixed in a permanent way by the system. For each activity, some restrictions and different relationships can be established, generating very different conversational graphs. For example, you can make a question to be always answered by means of an explanation, the submission of questions to be prohibited; etc. [10].

Organization and representation of the information

To organize the contributions that are generated during the process of discussion we start from the idea proposed in [1] and a hierarchical structure is used. This structure is represented by means of an inverted tree, where the node root is the definition of the activity and in the following level there are nodes for each section in which the activity is divided. The nodes of the following levels represent the contributions carried out by the participants as a consequence of the discussion and argument in search of a solution in agreement. This structure is named *Outline of the Discussion Process*. We name this structure as Outline of the Process of Discussion and Argument. The branches/edges of the tree can be expanded and contracted to facilitate the browsing of the discussion process followed by the participants. Also, it is essential to establish relationships between the nodes of the structure and their contents, and in this way to contextualize the discussion. We define four kinds of relationships between the nodes and the contents:

1. Dialogue. They relate a contribution with other contributions. These relationships allow the organization and representation of the evolution of the discussion process. That is to say, they define the hierarchical structure by means of which this process is represented.

2. Content. They relate a dialogue contribution with its content. This content will be hypertextual. This is, the text can contain links to design proposals (contextualization relationships).

3. Design. They relate an elaboration contribution with the actions or items included in a design plan. This plan has been previously elaborated with PlanEdit [6].

4. Contextualization. They establish relationships between dialogue and elaboration contributions. That is to say, they allow the insertion of references in the text from a dialogue contribution to the content of an elaboration contribution. They are materialized including, in textual contributions, links pointing to design proposals. What is more, considering the structuring of the work domain [7], they can be built by mean of links to specific actions of a design proposal.

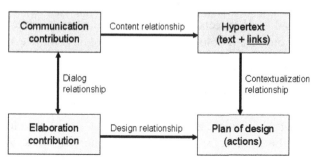

Fig. 1. Contributions and relationships in the discussion of the design decisions.

The contextualization relationships should be established by the user in an explicit way, while the rest are generated in an implicit way when a new contribution is added. Figure 1 shows an outline synthesizing these kinds of relationships and contributions affected. These relationships are implemented using a framework that allows the management of links between elements of the elaboration and communications spaces [10].

An experiment with students

Next we present the results of an experiment in which we intended to obtain some data to confirm that our position can be effective for the group learning of domotics design. Thus, we randomly chose several students of Secondary Education without any knowledge of domotics design. We taught Domotics to these students. For this, we followed the protocol that we have outlined and we used DomoSim-TPC and PlanEdit. Next, we tried to determine if the students have learned specific aspects of the domain and techniques of group work. Thus, we have carried out an experiment in a real context in which twelve students were involved. They were all beginner students of Domotics.

The experiment was structured in several phases. In the first phase we asked the users to answer some questions relative to design procedures (*pre-test*). From this test we could infer conclusions on the low level of knowledge they had about the design, mainly with problems of high complexity. Next, we proceeded to give some master classes where theoretical concepts relative to the elements and design procedures used in Domotics were presented.

The twelve students were organized in six groups of two (G1 to G6) and they were proposed to carry out five design activities (A1 to A5). The complexity of each activity was progressively increasing. Thus, the first activity studied local aspects to some management area, while the last ones approached complex problems in the scope of a complete building, this way increasing the number of tasks to carry out as well as the difficulty level. The help offered by the system in each activity was progressively decreasing, in contrast to the evolution of the increasing level of complexity. With the registered data we center on studying the evolution of the quantity of design work (or modelling work) developed in each activity and the number of errors made during this work. As errors we consider those mistakes observed in the final solutions and those situations in which the system intervened to avoid the realization of inappropriate design actions.

In order to graphically represent the previous information we define a parameter named *Quantity of Design Work* (QDW). This is expressed as the number of design proposals built with PlanEdit in an activity multiplied by their average size (measured in number of design actions). In the same way, we have defined the *Number of Errors* (NE) made as the number of suggestions of the system during the elaboration process plus the number of mistakes observed in the final solutions the students have built.

In order to illustrate how the ability of the participants increased during the realization of this experiment we put the two previous parameters together. That is, we express the Ability of the participants in function of QDW and NE. Thus, we obtain a representative value of the ability, which we normalize and represent in the graph shown in figure 2. In this figure, we can observe how the ability of all the participants was progressively increasing when they got engaged in new activities, although these were more complex.

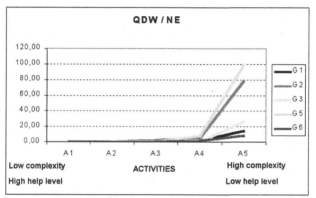

Fig. 2. Evolution of the ability in function of QDW and NE.

In the last phase, we carried out a test (*post-test*) to determine if the students would be able to manage real situations and with authentic materials. We visited a laboratory where advanced installations of automation of services for buildings were being developed. The students immediately identified the elements that were being manipulated in this laboratory with the ones integrated in our tool. They began to discuss on how they should be installed and connected to reach diverse objectives. It was remarkable that the students adopted work mechanisms similar to the ones previously used.

Conclusions

In this paper, we have described the characteristics of the discussion process to build a design satisfying a specification. The main characteristic of the model that supports the discussion process is the possibility to establish relationships (links) between discussion and elaboration spaces. This characteristic is named *Contextualized Discussion*. This discussion model has been implanted in the DomoSim-TPC system. We have carried out several experiences with this system demonstrating their effectiveness and efficiency from a global viewpoint.

Currently, we are developing a project, named CoPlan, with the Universities of Castilla-La Mancha in Spain and Coimbra in Portugal to apply the concept of Collaborative Planning of Design to the learning of programming. This concept is based on the discussion model described in this paper. Also, we think this model and the architecture which supports it can help us to determine influences between communication and elaboration spaces and the result of this process.

Acknowledgements

This work has partially been supported by the University of Castilla-La Mancha, the Junta de Comunidades de Castilla – La Mancha and the Ministerio de Ciencia y Tecnología in the projects CoPLAN, PBI-02-026 and TIC2002-01387.

References

1. Barros, B., (1999). Aprendizaje Colaborativo en Enseñanza a Distancia: *Entorno Genérico para Configurar, Realizar y Analizar Actividades en Grupo*. Phd: AI Department. U. Politécnica de Madrid.
2. Bravo, C., Redondo, M.A., Bravo, J., Ortega, M., (2000). DOMOSIM-COL: A Simulation Collaborative Environment for the Learning of Domotic Desgin. *Inroads - The SIGCSE Bulletin of ACM*, vol. 32 (2), pp.65-67.
3. Herrmann, F., (1995). Listserver communication: The discourse of community-building. Indianapolis. *Proc. of the CSCL'95 Conference*.
4. Isaacs, W.N., (1996). The process and potential of dialogue in social change. *Educational Technology*, 36 (1), pp. 20-30.
5. Jenlink, P., & Carr, A.A., (1996). Conversation as a medium for change in education. *Educational Technology*, 36 (1), pp. 31-38.
6. Redondo, M.A., Bravo, C., Ortega, M., Verdejo, M.F., (2002). PlanEdit: An adaptive tool for design learning by problem solving. In P. De Bra, P. Brusilovsky y R. Conejo (Eds.), *Adaptive Hypermedia and Adaptive Web Based-Systems*. LNCS 2347, pp. 560-563. Springer-Verlag.
7. Redondo, M.A., (2002). *Collaborative planning of design in simulation environments for distance learning*. ProQuest Information and Learning. USA.
8. Redondo, M.A., Molina, A.I., Bravo, C., Bravo, J., Ortega, M., (2003). Planificación colaborativa y ubicua para el aprendizaje del diseño en el sistema Domosim-TPC. *Proc. of the 4th Conf. of the AIPO (I2003)*. U. Vigo.

9. Redondo, M.A., Bravo, C., Bravo, J., Ortega, M., (2003). Organizing activities of problem based collaborative learning with the DomoSim-TPC system. En M. Llamas, M.J. Fernández y L.E. Anido (Eds.), *Computers and Education: Towards a Lifelong Learning Society.* Kluwer Academic Publishers.

10. Redondo, M.A., Bravo, C., Ortega, M., (2004). Discusión Argumentativa Contextualizada y Monitorizada para el Aprendizaje en Grupo del Diseño. *Proc. of 5th Conf. of the AIPO (Interacion 2004)*, pp. 358-364.

11. Savery, J., & Duffy, T., (1996). Problem based learning: An instructional model and its constructivist framework. In B. Wilson (Ed.), *Constructivist learning environments: Case studies in instructional design.* Englewwod Cliffs, NJ: Educational Technology Publications. pp. 135-148.

A Mechanism For Developing
User Interfaces

Francisco Montero, Víctor López-Jaquero, María Lozano, Pascual González

Grupo de Investigación LoUISE ,
Universidad de Castilla-La Mancha, Albacete – España
{fmontero, victor, mlozano, pgonzalez}@info-ab.uclm.es

1 Introduction

User Interface is the part of the system that receives the input from the user, and presents information to him/her. Strictly speaking, the user interface includes both hardware and software components, although in the context of software design, it refers to the software that manages the interaction with the user.

Nowadays, we have many devices and theirs associated programming languages. To handle this diversity, service providers must either devote considerable resources to the development of multiple alternative user interfaces, each specialized for a particular delivery context, or they must develop more flexible user interfaces able to cope with the diversity of devices.

In this paper we introduce a design pattern-based framework as a solution for flexible user interface development. This framework is a model-based user interface development environment (MB-UIDE) where a hierarchical structure is identified. This structure consists of a meta level, where MB-UIDE platform-independent models are located, and a base level where platform dependent models are hosted. This hierarchical structure shapes a reflective architecture, where a clear separation of concerns between platform-independent an dependent features is introduced.

This paper is organized into three further sections. Section 2 presents relationships between independent and dependent components in user interfaces. Section 3 presents our framework: a reflective-MB-UIDE that can be implemented using design patterns. How these patterns can be used is described too. Finally, section 4 presents conclusions and future challenges in UI design.

R. Navarro-Prieto and J.L. Vidal (eds.), HCI Related Papers of Interacción 2004, 329-336.
© 2006 *Springer. Printed in the Netherlands.*

2 User interfaces: configuration *vs.* appearance

Reality is the configuration of any substance, material or spiritual. Therefore, the definition of reality is found in the substance and configurations of existence. To find out whether reality is made of substance or configuration an example is used: a clay model is a good test for this purpose. The question then is, is reality in the substance?. A model of a search form can be made of a different appearance, and it still represents a search mechanisms. So the reality is not in the appearance.

The question then is whether the reality is in the configuration. When the configuration is changed, the reality changes. Therefore, the reality is in the configuration. This definition is adequate for both material and spiritual substance. It is accurate for thoughts in the mind, for that which is observed and for that which is communicated.

Truth is an attempt to properly represent the characteristics of unified reality. Thus, its proper definition is the communicated representation of unified reality.

In UI design, the same analogy can be found. Is UI functionality or just a presentation?. Developers often see the functionality of a system as separate from the UI, with the UI as an add-on. Users, however, do not typically make distinctions between the underlying functionality and the way it is presented in the UI. To users, the UI is the system. Therefore, if the UI is usable, they will see the entire system as usable.

User interface is often thought of as referring only to how screens look. But because users see the UI as the system, this is a too narrow definition. A broader definition of UI includes all aspects of the system design that influence the interaction between the user and the system. It is not simply the screens that the user sees, although these are certainly part of the UI. The UI is made up of everything that the user experiences, sees and does with the computer system.

2.1 Separation of concerns in UI development

In our paper, the main goal is to *improve UI architectures* bridging the gap between Software Engineering and UI development. *Separation of concerns* is used in our paper to introduce a comparison with the actual tendency in user interface development. This separation is a basic principle in software development and the connection between these worlds is achieved by abstraction and reification mechanisms. Fig. 1 and Fig. 2 introduce similar interaction components, but in Fig. 1 abstract interaction objects are used and in Fig.2 concrete interaction objects are used.

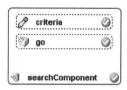

Fig. 1. Search component
specified in an abstract
notation

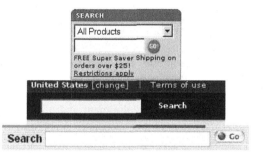

Fig. 2. Search component appearances for different
websites (Amazon, IBM and Palmtops)

Obviously, in our proposal many references on usability patterns are being used (e. g. [1], [15], [17], [3], [16], [8]). In fact, in Fig. 2 an interaction pattern has been used (*Search*). However, design patterns [2] are used also in UI development (e. g. [10], [11]). At this moment, usability patterns are not much different from guidelines. Although guidelines have been proved useful to improved user interfaces design, they present some flaws mostly related with the way they are applied, where the experience of the developer is a critical factor in applying them in the right way. Thus, from a developer point of view, diagrams and notations can be considered to overcome the limitations of guidelines application ambiguity, to improved user interfaces design experience for both novice and expert designers. These diagrams and notations should be provided in abstract terms, representing general solutions expressed in notation that is platform and modality independent. Concrete references should be used to provide different examples on how this general solution can be applied. These examples can be generated by compiling or transforming [4] diagrams, following Model-Driven Architecture (MDA) [7] recommendations.

2.2 Human-Computer Interaction: Model-Based User Interface Development Environments

Model-Based User Interface Development Environments (MB-UIDEs) provide a context where declarative models can be constructed and related, as part of the interface design process [12, 14]. MB-UIDEs use an explicit, largely declarative representation capturing application semantics and other knowledge needed to specify the appearance and behavior of an interactive system. The goal of the MB-UIDE is to identify reusable components of a UI and to capture more knowledge in the model, while reducing the amount of new procedural code that has to be rewritten for each new application. In a MB-UIDE we can find several typical models: domain, task, presentation, dialog, user, etc., many of these models are platform-independent.

Nowadays, we have many user interfaces description languages (UIDL) and by using them we can work at an abstract user interface (AUI) level. The AUI model separates a user interface into concrete and abstract components, so that a number of concrete user interface styles may be specified for a single abstract user interface. The AUI notation is an executable specification language used to define the abstract user interface. By only specifying abstract interaction once, the development and maintenance costs will be reduced and the interaction semantics consistency of an interactive system will be held across multiple concrete user interfaces.

Domain, task and abstract user interface model are platform independent models that can be used to describe an application in a platform-independent manner. A domain model is an object model of a problem domain. Elements of a domain model are domain classes, and the relationships between them. The user-task model is a representation of the tasks the user can perform through the interface. These tasks can be carried out by the system, the application, or the user. The presentation model is a view of the static characteristics of an interface, notably its layout, organization, and attributes such as fonts or colors. Finally, the user model is not designed to be a model of the mental state of the user at a particular time during the interaction, but it defines the types of users of the interface and the relevant attributes for the user interface of those users. Its main purpose is to influence interface generation to build user interfaces that best fit each user/group characteristics.

3 Our framework

In our framework [5, 9] MB-UIDEs and reflection, work together. Reflection has been proposed as a solution to the problem of creating applications able to maintain, use, and change representations of their own designs [6, 13]. Reflective systems are able to use self-representations to extend, modify, and analyze their own computation.

A reflective architecture yields such a degree of flexibility that allows designers not only to extend a language by itself, but also to adapt and add functionality to existing systems in a transparent way. Reflection has been used in several domains, such as concurrent programming, distributed systems, artificial intelligence, and expert systems. Not only functional requirements can be achieved by using computational reflection, but also not functional requirements, such as usability, can be achieved.

In reflective architectures, components that deal with the self-representation and the application reside in two different software levels organized in a hierarchical manner: *metalevel* and *base level*, respectively.

Two processes, abstraction (bottom-up transformations) and reification (top-down transformations), occur between the levels of this hierarchy. We have adopted the word reification to indicate the inverse operation to abstraction. Abstraction implies a many-to-one transformation from the many possible variants to a single invariant form. Reification, on the other hand, implies *not* a one-to-many transformation, which would potentially produce an infinite variety of variants, but rather a one-to-one-of-many transformation, although the exact variant that is generated could be any one of the infinite variety of variant forms. These processes, abstraction and reification, are implemented by using design patterns from [2].

3.1 Abstraction process

The state of an object is a combination of the current values of its attributes. When you call a *set-* method, you typically change an object's state, although an object can change its own state as its methods execute too.

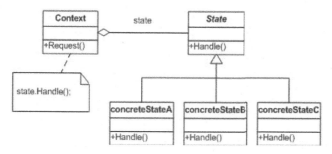

Fig. 3. State pattern structure

Objects are often discussed in terms of having a state that describes their exact conditions at a given time, based upon the values of their properties. The particular values of the properties affect the object's behavior. In this sense, *Context* in Fig. 3 is our application described in a platform-independent manner, that is, in *Context* we can find task, domain and presentation in an abstract way. In *State* we can find concrete presentation associated with each different device as different devices families we are taking into.

At base level, the Decorator Pattern is used for adding additional functionality to a particular object as opposed to a class of objects. It is easy to add functionality to an entire class of objects by subclassing an object, but it is impossible to extend a single object this way. With the Decorator Pattern, you can add functionality to a single object and leave others instances of the same class unmodified. Decorator pattern is used at our base level to add additional functionality to a concrete presentation by reusing concrete interaction objects functionality without using inheritance (Fig. 4).

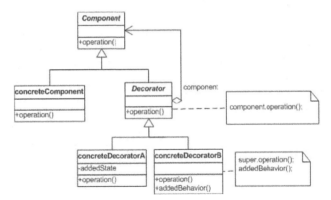

Fig. 4. Decorator pattern structure

Fig. 4 shows several classes located at our base level. These classes are related to concrete interaction objects (CIOs) in different devices (*concreteComponent*), and *Decorator* classes are associated with additional functionality that can be added dynamically to CIOs.

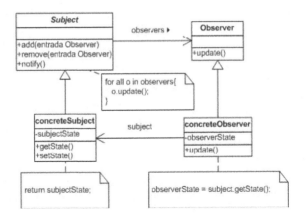

Fig. 5. Observer pattern structure

3.2 Reification process

The Observer pattern [2] (Fig. 5) allows one object (*Observer*) to watch another (*Subject*). The Observer pattern allows the subject and observer to form a publish-subscribe relationship. Through the Observer pattern, observers can register to receive events from the subject. When the subject needs to inform its observers of an event, it simply sends the event to each observer.

A causal connection, between base and meta level, is implemented using Observer pattern. *Subject* classes are models located at meta level and *observer* classes are platform-dependent descriptions of our application, that is to say, concrete interaction objects.

4 Conclusions and future works

In our everchanging world, information technology is being embedded into more and more everyday items, and many persons are increasingly getting reliant on electronically delivered information, this information is delivered by means of a great diversity of devices with which individuals access these electronic services. Abstraction and reification are efficient tools to address the problem of the development of flexible user interfaces. This paper presented different design patterns that are successfully applied in user interface development under a model-based user interface development environment. Future works will include use this approach to implement applications with different interaction degrees. Non-functionality requirements, such as usability, and design patterns is just another challenge.

Acknowledgements

This work was supported by the Spanish CICYT project TIN2004-08000-C03-01 and the PCB-03-003 project from the Consejería de Educación de la JCCM.

References

1. Fincher, S. *The Pattern Gallery.* from http://www.cs.ukc.ac.uk/people/staff/saf/patterns/gallery.html

2. Gamma, E., Helm, R., Johnson, R., & Vlissides, J. *Design Patterns: Elements of Reusable Object-Oriented Software.* Reading, Massachusets, US: Addison-Wesley. 1994

3. Graham, I. A Pattern Language for Web Usability. Addison Wesley. 2002. http://www.wupatterns.com/

4. Limbourg, Q., Vanderdonckt, J., Michotte, B., Bouillon, L., López-Jaquero, V. USIXML: a Language Supporting Multi-Path Development of User Interfaces. Design, Specification and Verification of Interactive Systems 2004, DSV-IS 2004. Hamburg, Germany, July 11-13

5. López-Jaquero, V., Montero, F., Molina, J.P., González, P. , Fernández-Caballero, A. A Seamless Development Process of Adaptive User Interfaces Explicitly Based on Usability Properties. 9th IFIP Working Conference on EHCI-DSV-IS 2004. Springer Verlag, 2004

6. Maes P. Concepts and Experiments in Computational Reflection. In *Proceedings of OOPSLA '87*, ACM Sigplan Notices, p.147-155, Orlando, Florida, 1987

7. Model-Driven Architecture (MDA). http://www.omg.org/mda/

8. Montero, F., Lozano, M., González, P., Ramos, I. A first approach to design web sites by using patterns. In Proceedings of the First Nordic Conference on Pattern Languages of Programs (VikingPLoP, 2002), edited by Pavel Hrusby and Kristian Elof Sorensen. 2003

9. Montero, F., López Jaquero, V., Molina, J.P., González, P. An approach to develop User Interfaces with plasticity. Design, Specification and Verification of Interactive Systems 2003, DSV-IS 2003. In *DSV-IS 2003*. Springer Verlag, LNCS 2844, 2003. Madeira, Portugal June 4-6, 2003

10. Noble, J. GOF Patterns for GUI Design. In *Proceedings of the European Conference on Pattern Languages of Program Design*. Irsee, Germany. 1997

11. Rossi, G., Schwabe, D., Lyardet, F. User Interface patterns for hypermedia applications. Proceedings of the working conference on Advanced visual interfaces. 2000

12. Schulungbaum, E. Model-based user interface software tools – current state of declarative models. Graphics, visualization and usability centre, Georgia Institute of Technology, GVU Tech #96 #30. 1996

13. Smith, B.C. Reflection and Semantics in a Procedural Programming Language. PhD thesis, MIT, 1982

14. Szekely, P. Retrospective and challenges for model-based interface developments. In: Bodart, F., Vanderdonckt, J. (eds.) Design, Specification and Verification of Interactive Systems. 1995

15. Tidwell, J. UI Patterns and Techniques. http://time-tripper.com/uipatterns/index.php

16. van Duyne, D., Landay, J., Hong, J. The Design of Sites.Addison Wesley, 2003

17. van Welie, M. Patterns in Interaction Design, 2004, accessible at http://www.welie.com

A notation for Goal Driven Interfaces Specification

A.L. Carrillo-León, J. Falgueras-Cano, A. Guevara-Plaza
Dept. of Computer Science and Artificial Intelligence
University of Malaga-Spain
{carrillo, juanfc, guevara}@lcc.uma.es

1 Introduction

Although *direct manipulation with WIMP (Windows, Icons, Menus and Pointer) elements* is currently the most extended user interface paradigm in use, there are still many users that need a training and learning period, manuals and/or expert support to become efficient users. We present here a new and alternative style of interaction: *Goal Driven Interaction* (GDI).

GDI was meant to become the interaction style of choice for applications where the main priority is ease of use and minimal learning time for a user to interact with the program, even if sacrificing speed in task achievement, the ability of running parallel tasks and other advantages of *WIMP interfaces* [5].

GDI's main philosophy is to guide the user in a hierarchical and progressive way through the whole interaction process, not only as far as the tasks and goals approach are concerned, but also about the sequence of steps to follow or the choices that can be made at any given moment to achieve those goals. Therefore, GDI can be considered in between *direct manipulation with WIMP elements* and *assisted interaction* [5], combining characteristics of both.

Two aspects are considered fundamental for the success of GDI and the interfaces supporting them. The first of them is the fact that their specification and design process can be carried out based on main interface engineering techniques and methodologies, as those based on tasks hierarchical analysis [7,5], whose importance, usefulness and other advantages are widely recognized. Nevertheless, even the most adequate, Kieras's notation, NGOMSL [8], needs to be adapted and extended, and that constitutes the main aim of this paper. A second fundamental aspect would be the possibility of using a software tool that would automate the process of generating a basic prototype. To that end we have developed the GDIST tool [4] that apart from facilitating the specification task, generates a user interface prototype.

337

R. Navarro-Prieto and J. L. Vidal (eds.), HCI Related Papers of Interacción 2004, 337-344.

2 Fundamentals of GDI

The fundamentals of GDI trace back to the works of Newell and Simon [9] about the mechanism of human reasoning for problem resolution. Their vision of problem solving (as in GDI) was based in the breaking up of the main or general goal in a hierarchical tree of sub-goals whose branches would have different lengths depending on the degree of their fragmentation into sub-goals. The leaves of the tree would be elementary sub-goals reachable by means of basic information processing.

Based on these works, Card, Moran and Newell [1,2] developed the most important of the existing cognitive models, the Human Processing Model, whose initial paradigm (as in GDI) consisted in conceiving the interaction as a problem resolution task, and described a psychological model of humans formed by three interactive systems: perceptive, motor and cognitive, each one would have their own memory and their own processor. The perceptive system manages external stimuli, the motor system controls the actions, and the cognitive system provides enough knowledge to connect both.

This vision of the user as an information processing system, allows for the formalization of all the activities (both physical and mental) that take part in that task, and gave origin to the methods for modeling, specification and evaluation of the user interface that are widespread today, the GOMS (Goals, Operators, Methods, and Selection rules) methods [6], that allow, among other things, for the description of the sequences of behavior and knowledge that the user needs to have to correctly interact with the system. The models themselves are framed in the set of techniques that allow for a hierarchical task analysis, as their main goal is the decomposition of those tasks so that the resolution method can be followed step by step.

Therefore, and given that a user interface GOMS model includes the knowledge the user must have (the tasks that can be carried out with it, and the procedures that need to be followed to carry them out in a satisfactory way) and regarding their hierarchical and temporal structure, the aim of GDI is to preclude the user from having to devote time to acquiring such knowledge. It would let the interface provide gradually the user with such knowledge, and guide the user at the same time as the interaction process is being developed, always following the goal hierarchy defined in the process of interface specification that the analyst has carried out (using the *notation* we present) in the analysis and design stage.

To that end, the user interfaces based in this kind of interaction will need an area (as seen in Fig 2) called *Goals Driver Window* (GDW) [3,4], that will be the place where the user will be presented with either the *steps* of the *method* to be followed or the different *alternatives* to *choose* from, to satisfy the specific *goal* at any given moment, according to the goal hierarchy tree defined in the analysis and specification process.

These are the basic concepts in the GDI. Moreover, as we will later detail, the method steps should be executed in a sequential manner. An indicator will have to show which is the step the user needs to accomplish at any given moment to complete the method correctly and the system will only allow the user to carry out that step (to that end, the user will have to click on it) That will be the initiation of a new sub-goal (associated to another method or selection) or performing an elementary action.

The GDW will be the main mechanism for interaction in these interfaces, as it is the area where users will be guided gradually through the defined goals hierarchy while allowing the user to access the different functionalities in the system, becoming a substitute (or alternative) to the typical menus, toolbars and those elements in WIMP interfaces, that are not necessary in GDI. A small area in the interface should be devoted to showing the *active goals hierarchy* at any given time, i.e. the goals hierarchy users had to follow to arrive from the initial objective to specific ones.

3 Definitions and notation for GDI specification

As starting point for the specification of GDI we have considered the most adequate, although it also must be adapted and extended, the Kieras NGOMSL (Natural GOMS Language) methodology [8]. Reasons in favor of this election are: the existence of a good and extensive literature, practical construction methods [8,7] that can be used to a great extent, but above all is their closeness to the user's natural language. This is very important because it will allow us to generate the main parts of the user interface, (i.e. the complete contents of the GDW) in a nearly direct way, starting from a specification carried out with this notation, which in any case, needs minor adaptation and extension.

Now we will define concepts and elements present in this kind of interaction, and the appropriate notation for its specification.

- A *goal* (as in NGOMSL) is any purpose or intention the user has, any task the user wants to carry out. The analyst will need to identify all the objectives the user tries to accomplish, organizing and structuring them in a time hierarchical manner.
- An *action* (an *operator* in NGOMSL) will be any activity or task (cognitive, perceptive or motor) which will not be specified in great

detail, either because it is a primitive or elementary action, (as *hit-a-key*, or *insert-an-ATM-card*) or because it is a high level action, i.e. a task that users will be able to carry out on their own.

- Each goal that has been identified by the analyst, will need to be associated with either a ***method*** or description of the *steps* sequence that users will need to follow to accomplish such objective (which is the most frequent case), or a *selection* (as we will see later)

The steps the method is composed of, will have to be carried out or executed in a sequential manner, as they appear. Each one of them will consist of, or imply, the initiation of another more specific goal, or the realization of an *elementary action* or a *high level* one. It is convenient to keep the number of steps in a method to a minimum, and if there is more than six or seven the appropriate procedure would group the steps under new sub-goals.

The specification of a method should have the following format:

```
Method for: <goal>
 [cancelable   [disable if <condition_for_the_system>]
               [effect <effect_on_the_system>] ]
    1)  <step_1>
        . . .
    i)  <step_i>
        . . .
    n) Return with goal accomplished
            [effect <effect_on_the_system>]
```

where <step_i> (for i from 1 to *n*–1) can consist of:

```
<step_i>  =    make <action>
            |  accomplish <goal>
            |  decide: if <condition_for_user>
                       then goto <step_#>
            |  goto <step_#>
        [disable if <condition_for_the_system>]
        [effect <effect_on_the_system>]
```

The `cancelable` clause is optional. It allows the user to cancel the current method and return to the "father" one. It will always be enabled and could be considered as another step in that method. The `disable if` and `effect` clauses, will be explained later.

All methods should end in a last step that indicates that the goal has already been reached or satisfied, and after which we will return to the father goal, which will be expressed by the elementary clause: `Return with goal accomplished`.

The rest of the steps (from 1 to $n-1$) can picked out from the following set:

accomplish <goal>   It expresses the need of initiating a new sub-goal before the currently be finished.
make <action>   Tells users that they must carry out a specific action, elementary or high level.
decide: if <cond_for_user> **then goto** <step_#>   Expresses an elementary mental action, in which the user has to evaluate a condition. If true, he will have to jump to step_#, and if false, he will continue to the next step. Therefore it can express a conditional jump within a method.
goto <step_#>   Marks an unconditional jump to another part of the method.

Optionally the clause **disable if** can be added to each step that should need it, last one excepted. It must be followed by "a condition for the system", generating a *conditional* step. This condition will not be evaluated by the user, but by the system once it is running. That will imply that it examines one or several internal states. If true, the associated step will appear disabled preventing the user to access it, and the control flow will go to the next one. Finally, each step could include the **effect** clause followed by the description of the "effect on the system" that this step should generate.

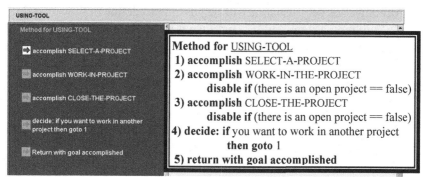

Fig. 1. GDW offering a method (and its corresponding specification)

In Fig. 1 we show in a simple way what the content of a GDW would be. In this sample the goal is achieved following a *method* (obtained from the specification that we also include on the right) that has two *conditional steps*.

- *Selections* play here a similar role to *Selection Rules* in NGOMSL. In general we define a *selection* when several methods can accomplish a goal. Also is necessary to create a *selection* when a general goal (for example, carrying out a bank transaction) involves the accomplishing of one goal between several specific goals (checking if there enough available funds, funds withdrawal, making deposits, etc.)

A selection has the following format:

```
[For the system >] Selection for: <goal>
  [ cancelable  [disable if <condition_for_the_system>]
                [effect <effect_on_the_system>] ]
    a) <option_a>
    ...
    n) <option_n>
```

and where any `<option_i>` will be of the following kind:

```
if <condition> [then accomplish <goal>]
        [disable if <condition_for_the_system>]
        [effect <effect_on_the_system>]
```

A selection will be built by as many mutually excluding options as necessary, generally between two and six, being quite convenient to avoid a higher number. Each one of them is associated with a condition that users must assess. Once the user knows which option is the appropriate, he must initiate the associate goal, that again will be satisfied by another method or selection. We must remark that later, once that goal is met, it will not be possible to go back to that selection, but to its previous method, the one that directed the flow to that selection.

Although not very usual, it will be possible to define options that do not imply initiating a goal, but just producing a determinate "effect on the system". In such case, the options will not include the `accomplish` clause, but the `effect` clause.

As it is the case with the steps in a method, it will be possible to express *conditional options*. Such kind of alternatives should be disabled if the system verifies that the condition after the **disable if** clause is true. It is also possible to define *options with effect* that could modify the system's state. To that end, we will have to include the **effect** clause. Fig. 2 shows samples of these two types of alternatives.

Generally these selections will be meant for the user to make. The user will be in charge of evaluating the selection and actually carrying it out. Nevertheless, during the interaction process, there might arise the need of showing the user either method, but determined by a system state and not by the user. In these cases we will say that they are *selections for the system* (for the program). That is, the system will be in charge of evaluating the conditions (mutually excluding), and depending on which one is true, divert the flux towards the corresponding goal. To indicate that a selection belongs to that kind, we have to start its specification with the clause **For the system.**

The **cancelable** clause could be used only if it is a selection for the user to make. It will have the same purpose that it has in a method: it will make it possible to cancel that selection and return to a method one step previous in the hierarchy. We can consider this as another alternative in this selection. It can also be accompanied by the disable if and/or effect clauses.

In Fig. 2 we show two samples of selections: a) a *cancelable selection with effect*, and with an option that only produces a determinate effect on the system, b) a *cancelable selection* with a *conditional alternative*.

In [4] we can examine a complete example of the specification of a GDI interface.

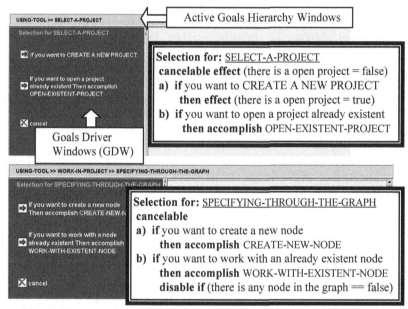

Fig. 2. Two samples of GDW (and its corresponding specifications)

4 Conclusions

It has been presented a new style of interaction: *Goal Driven Interaction*. In the special cases in which the interaction is oriented to specific tasks, taking into consideration the cost of training periods and mastering of generic user interfaces, this new kind of interaction more simplified can be the best election. In addition, the development of both a specifications language and an automatic prototyping tool has confirmed the viability of this GDI methodology.

One of the necessary further steps is the extension of our GDI specification language, building in it a higher semantic content, including the style of the widgets the user could be accustomed to and widening and adapting our interface to the cultural localization of the application. To this end a great deal of work is currently being carried out to incorporate the widgets characteristics as additional annotations in the specification of the actions. The possibilities in this field are immense.

References

1. Card S, Moran T, Newell A.: Computer text-editing: An information processing analysis for a routine cognitive skill. Cognitive Psychology, 12, 32-74.
2. Card S., Moran T., Newell A.: The Psychology of Human-Computer Interaction. Hillsdale, New Jersey: Erlbaum.
3. Carrillo A., Guevara A., Gálvez S., Caro. J.: Interacción guiada por objetivos. Actas del congreso Interacción 2002, pp 68-75. ISBN: 84-607-4501-5.
4. Carrillo A., Guevara A, Falgueras J: Notación para la especificación de interfaces IGO. Actas del congreso Interacción 2004, pp 178-185. ISBN: 84-609-1266-3.
5. Falgueras J.: Modelado y evaluación automática cooperativa de la usabilidad de interfaces de usuario. Doctoral thesis. Dept: Computer Science and Artificial Intelligence. University of Malaga (2000).
6. John B.E., Kieras D.E.: Using GOMS for User Interface Design and Analysis: Wich Technique? ACM Transactions on Computer-Human Interaction, Vol3, No.4, December 1996, pp 287-319.
7. Kieras D.: Task Analysis and the Design of Functionality. In A. Tucher (Ed.) The computer Science and Engineering Handbook. Boca Raton, CRC Inc, pp 1401-1423. (1997).
8. Kieras D.: A Guide to GOMS Model Usability. Evaluation using NGOMSL. In M.Helander & T. Landauer (Eds.), The handbook of human-computer interaction. (Second Edition) Amsterdam: North-Holland, pp 733-766.
9. Newell A., Simon H.: Human Problem Solving. Prentice-Hall.

Modelling Interactive Systems: an architecture guided by communication objects

Camila Cordero Mansilla, Ángel de Miguel Artal, Eladio Domínguez Murillo, Mª Antonia Zapata Abad

Dpto. de Informática e Ingeniería de Sistemas, Universidad de Zaragoza
Campus Pza. San Francisco, Edif. Matemáticas

Introduction

Several methods have been proposed in the literature for modelling Interactive Systems [5, 6, 7, 8, 14, 15, 16, 18]. Most of them start with the task modelling process at a certain level of abstraction and the model is progressively refined in subsequent steps until the user interface is developed. This refinement process is performed adding new aspects not previously considered to the model obtained at a certain level.

In order to perform this refinement process, authors, in general, take into account different aspects which can be grouped into those related to the domain of the problem, the tasks, the dialogue and the presentation [7, 14, 18]. The methods proposed by such authors distinguish, in general, three levels among which the elements representing the quoted aspects are distributed.

The proposals differ one from another by the method proposed and, in particular, by the different ways in which they group the four aspects mentioned above. For example, an architecture composed of three levels is considered in [7]: the *Domain* level, in which the data structure and the use that the actors make of them are reflected; the *Task-Dialogue* level, offering the support for the tasks and the information flow between them; and the *Presentation* level, in which the elements that compose the interface are specified.

On the other hand, in [14], although an architecture is not proposed, a review of several proposals is made and it agrees with [7] in relation to the levels to be considered: the Domain level, called the Application level in this case, the Task-Dialogue level and the Presentation Level.

The way in which the modelling problem is tackled and the way in which the different aspects are grouped are the main differences between the proposal shown in [18] and those previously mentioned. In [18] a new architecture is not proposed, but a method for each aspect under consideration.

R. Navarro-Prieto and J. L. Vidal (eds.), HCI Related Papers of Interacción 2004, 345-357.

The proposal consists of a method for the modelling of the domain and the tasks, another for the dialogue and a third for the interface development.

Finally, we would point out that in [5] a method is offered which starts with the task modelling and the dialogue activities are subsequently extracted from tasks. The resulting process is very close to that proposed in [18] with regard to the grouping of the user interface aspects.

From our point of view, the way of grouping proposed in [7] and [14] leads to a structure with levels too far away one each other, in term of the degree of abstraction. This is the reason why our proposal introduces a new level between the task-dialogue level and the presentation level, being in this way closer to those proposed in [5] and [18].

The main difference in our proposal is the criteria for the modelling process at this new level, which has been made possible due to the communication object notion. This will be introduced in the next section as part of the description of our proposed architecture for the modelling process of interactive systems.

Modelling architecture and communication objects

In order to present our architecture, we start from that proposed in [7]. Our proposal retains the *Domain* and *Presentation* levels with the same meaning as that proposed in [7]. At the Domain level, we model the user goals and the objects of the system. The model obtained at the Presentation level is the closest to the interface being constructed.

The main difference of our proposal is related with the Task/Dialogue level, considered in [7] as a unique level. From our point of view, this level as introduced in [7] and [14] is too far from the Presentation level in terms of abstraction.

Hence, we consider it convenient to distinguish two levels between the Domain and the Presentation levels:

- The *Tasks* level, in which those tasks that the users will need to perform to achieve his/her goals are represented.;

- The *Interaction Activities* level, in which the user-computer interaction activities performed by means of communication objects are modelled.

This differentiation is close to that proposed in [5] and [18]. However, the use of the communication object notion during the modelling process is the main difference with these proposals.

The architecture we propose is intended to be a reflection of the steps we consider must be followed during the user interface modelling process, and the notion of communication object will be a great help in this process.

The final purpose is to obtain a system to help the user to achieve his/her goals. Taking this into account, we propose the Domain level as the first level within our architecture, in which, as we have said previously, the user goals and the system objects are modelled.

Once the goals have been established, we should detail what the user must do to reach these goals, that is, the general user tasks must be fixed. These tasks will be modelled at the Task level of our architecture and we propose to use the UML activity diagrams [10] to model them.

The tasks modelled at this level are independent of any tool or system that could be used to reach the goals associated with the tasks. The perspective used to model at this level is the problem we are trying to solve. We look at the problem and the goals, analysing what the user must do to reach these goals, without taking into account the system during the modelling process.

Once the task modelling process has finished, we must turn our sights towards the system being modelled in order to find out how this system will help the user to perform those tasks.

It is generally accepted that, between user and system, a communication process will be established, during which the user wants to reach his/her goals. The system must provide a way of making such communication possible. Therefore, during the modelling process we should think about the artefacts that user and system use to communicate, and it is at this point when the communication object notion appears. We define communication object as

an object, independent of the user interface type, containing information and that it is offered by the machine mainly with the goal of establishing a communication between user and system.

It must be noted that a communication object is independent of the media used for the communication process, whether this is a computer screen, a speaker or something else. A communication object is also independent of the way in which the communication is presented, which may be, for example, a windows-based user interface or a command line-based user interface.

It is also important to notice that the communication object notion is at a different degree of abstraction from that where the abstract interaction object (AIO) [1, 11, 12] is found. In fact, the AIO notion is used at the presentation level while the communication object is used at the Interaction Activity level. During the modelling process, from our perspective, one or more of the communication objects will be transformed into one or more AIOs.

For example, we could consider that we are modelling an orders management system in which, by entering a customer ID, all the orders of that customer can be looked up and new orders added.

As it will be shown in the following section, we model the interactions between user and computer using the Activity diagrams of UML [10], extended with a set of stereotypes developed by our group. These stereotypes have the aim of typifying a set of interaction activities that are very usual in the interaction process between a user and an information system. Each one of these defined stereotypes is a primitive *communication object*.

During the modelling process that we propose, the user-computer interaction activities that are necessary to reach a certain goal are detailed. A refinement process is performed until reaching the degree of detail considered necessary.

At this point of the process, and keeping to the Interaction activities level, one of the following alternatives must be chosen:

- Each one of the communication objects will be implemented using an AIO;

- Several communication objects will be implemented using a single AIO.

In the first case, we could decide, for example, that the communication object offered to the user to enter the ID of a customer could be implemented using an AIO of the type "Form" and that the communication object used by the system to inform the user that an ID doesn't exist could be implemented with an AIO of the type "Message". In the second case, we could decide that all the communication objects used to establish a communication between user and system could be implemented using a single AIO of the type "Master-Detail".

Considering these cases, we realize that if we want to obtain a more gradual modelling process, we should introduce two new levels in the architecture.

Let us consider the first case, where we have decided that every communication object will be implemented with a different physical object. In this situation, the model we would obtain could be understood as a representation of the relations between communication objects.

Turning now to the second option, according to which all the communication objects of a model will be implemented using a single AIO, the model we would obtain could be understood as a representation of the relations between objects that are part of a single interaction object. These relations between communication objects will be noticed, from the user perspective, as a change in the state of the interaction object that contains them.

This is why we consider it appropriate to distinguish two sublevels within the Interaction Activity level during the modelling process:

- the *Inter-Object Interaction Activity* level, in which, from a user perspective, the result of the interaction activity will be a change of object to interact with; and,

- the *Intra-Object Interaction Activity* level, in which, from a user perspective, the result of the interaction activity will be a change of the state of the object offered by the system to interact with.

This division of the interaction activity level into two sublevels (due to the use of the communication object notion) is not, to our knowledge, present in any other proposals [6, 7, 9, 12, 14, 17, 18].

In the next section we will detail, using an example, the modelling process proposed for the architecture described. Although we consider every level of the architecture as important as the rest, all being part of a gradual process to model the interface, we will explain in detail the process of modelling the inter-Object Interaction Activities because it is this level which distinguishes our contribution. For the other levels of the architecture, we propose, at the moment, to use the different techniques proposed in the literature for modelling any of the aspects quoted as, for example, using class diagrams and use case diagrams for the Domain level, as proposed in [6, 8, 9] and the use of state machines of UML or Petri nets for modelling Intra-object interaction activities as proposed in [16, 5].

The Modelling process shown through an example

From now on, we will consider an example consisting of the modelling process of a library information system. The process will be described through the task of adding a new copy of a book. We will assume that the processes followed by users are those described below.

The person who receives the new copy of a book verifies that it is the one requested. If it is not, the book is sent back. If it is, the book is added to the catalogue as a new copy of a book. Before adding the received book, it must be verified whether another copy of the book exists in the catalogue. If it is a new book, all bibliographic data and the data specific to the copy must be added to the catalogue. If it is a new copy of a book that is already in the catalogue, it is only necessary to introduce the data about the new copy and modify the number of copies of this book.

Without going into detail, we must point out that at the Domain level the work objects are the copies of the books and that there is a main goal which is to add a new received book to the catalogue.

Moving on to the next level, the tasks associated with the process of reaching the goals must be determined. We propose, as a first step, to associate a task with each goal, representing the work that must be done to achieve it. For our example, we consider the goal 'To add received book' as the task representing the process associated with this goal (see Figure 1).

A refinement process is then initiated using the Activity diagram of UML [10] as representing language. This process continues until the desired level of detail is reached. For example, if we only look at the tasks that are necessary to reach the fixed goal, we can distinguish tasks from relations between tasks as the activity diagram in Figure 2 shows.

Fig. 1. Task related with the goal

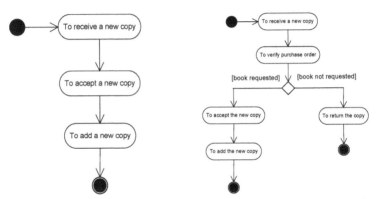

Fig. 2. Main tasks to reach the goal   **Fig. 3.** Considering tasks leading to the
of adding a new book   goal not being achieved

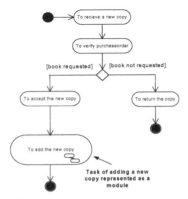

Fig. 4. Detecting complex tasks

Next, with the goal of refining the diagram even further, it is desirable to include those tasks that could lead to the goal not being achieved. So, in the case under study, the fact that a received book is not the one requested must be included (see Figure 3).

Sometimes the refining process is done with the goal of specifying complex tasks in more detail. In these situations, a more profound analysis process is required leading to a new refined activity diagram. For example, considering that the task 'To add the new copy' requires more detail, we must substitute from the model obtained at previous steps of the process, that activity that represents this task by the one representing the task as a module, as it is shown in Figure 4. In this case, a further diagram representing the refinement of the 'To add the new copy' task should be built, as the one shown in Figure 5.

It is worth pointing out that the refinement process is still at the **Task** level and, as has been described before, all tasks shown in the previous diagrams are completely independent of any application, system or tool that the user could use to perform these tasks. For example, the verification of whether an ISBN exists in the catalogue or not could be done by looking up all the bibliographical cards or using a Client/Server application to look it up in the catalogue through a web service.

The main contribution of our proposal can be found in the following steps of the process. The activity diagrams developed up to now represent the tasks

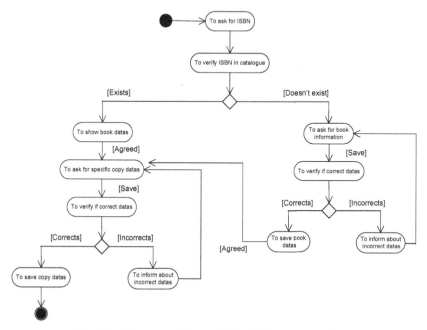

Fig.5. Refinement of the task 'To add the new copy'

that a user must perform to reach his/her goals. As has been said, these tasks have been described without taking into account any system or application that could help the user to perform them. We propose, as the next step in the process of our methodology, to distinguish the tasks that will be implemented in the system from those that will not. These decisions are dependent on the requirements of the problem [17].

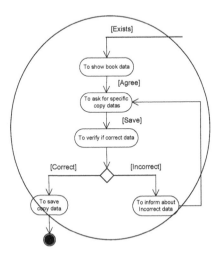

Fig. 6. Adding a new copy of a book that exists in the catalogue

For example, in the case under study, it may be decided to implement in the system being developed only the task of adding a newly received book.

The rest of the tasks, as for example 'To accept a new copy', will be maintained as intervention protocols and will not be implemented in the system. The excluded tasks will not be present in the models of the subsequent levels of the architecture.

Once the tasks to be included in the system have been determined, and taking into account that according to our proposal these tasks will be performed through communication objects, we must decide which tasks will be done through the same communication object.

Let us consider, for example, the task of adding a new copy of which other copies appear in the catalogue (see Figure 6). One could decide that the tasks 'To show book data', 'To ask for specific copy data', 'To verify if correct data', and even the task 'To inform about incorrect data', will be done through the same communication object of the system.

Once these decisions have been made, we propose a further step consisting of representing the model using the activity diagrams of UML, extended with the set of stereotypes referred in section 2. For example, based on previously taken decisions, the resulting diagram could be that shown in Figure 7.

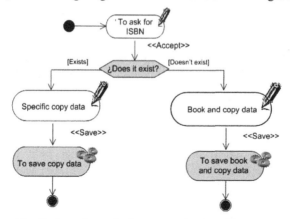

Fig. 7. Grouping tasks in communication objects

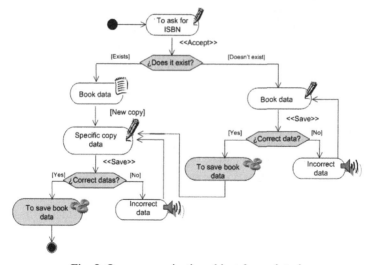

Fig. 8. One communication object for each task

In this diagram it is represented that, for example, the activity 'To ask for ISBN' is performed through a communication object of the type *'Data entry'*, so that the system, when performing this activity, will show to the user an object with all the necessary elements to enter an ISBN.

Clearly, the resulting diagram depends on the decisions taken during the process of grouping tasks. For example, Figure 8 shows the diagram obtained when it has been decided to use one communication object for each of the tasks modelled in the diagram of the previous level.

The use of the notion of communication object when we move from Task level to Inter-Object Interactive Activities level has the following advantages:

- It facilitates a more gradual, guided modelling process. It allows us to fix the degree of detail during the process, beginning at the Inter-Object Interaction Activity level. At this level we model the communication objects and relations between them leaving for the subsequent steps the modelling of the interaction activities between the elements that are inside a communication object.

- It allows us to anticipate decisions that help us afterwards at subsequent levels in the architecture. We can decide, for example, which tasks will be performed within the same communication object.

- It helps us to maintain the consistency between models from different levels of the architecture, since the decisions taken at this step of the process lead us to specific models at the subsequent levels. This is an important characteristic for the evolution of the system, because any change in any of the levels must be reflected in the others [2, 3, 4].

For example, the model shown in Figure 7 has a lesser degree of detail than the one shown in Figure 8. The objects that are modelled in Figure 7 lead us to communication objects with a great number of user-computer interaction activities inside the communication object itself, but the chosen design allows us to leave this difficulty to one side and to concentrate on relations between the fixed communication objects. Besides, the model shown in Figure 7 suggests a model at the representation level where all activities involved in adding a new copy of a book will be performed over a single interaction object as, for example, a window or a web page, depending on the technology used to implement it.

In the model shown in Figure 8, on the contrary, a system with a larger number of communication objects has been designed. If we decide to implement each communication object with a different interaction object, the model at presentation level will show a more complex navigation structure.

Which decision is to be taken depends on the problem to be modelled. The advantage of the process is that it allows the possibility of fixing in advance the communication objects to be used and developing the Inter-Object Interaction model previously.

The process continues detailing the Intra-Object Interaction activities. The technique used to model these interactions could be one of the techniques commonly used such as state machines of UML [16] or Petri nets [5]. At this point, we would be able to decide which kind of interface we will use to implement the interface modelled. The next phase would consist of designing the presentation by means of AIO and the navigation between them.

The proposed architecture as well as the models and the methodology introduced in this paper are currently being used in all the software development projects that we are carrying out with external financing. We hope that these projects will help us to make any necessary improvements to the proposed framework for modelling the user interface of interactive systems.

Conclusions and Future Work

This paper presents an architecture and a detailed example of the process followed for modelling a user interface.

The architecture offers a framework for modelling the several aspects included in a user interface. The use of Activity diagrams of UML [10] and an extension of them for modelling, respectively, the tasks and the interaction activities have been proposed. Furthermore, the notion of communication object has been introduced in the present work as criteria for changing from task level to Interaction activity level.

The process proposed shows a gradual and guided way of modelling. This process starts with the analysis of the problem to identify the tasks to be done. After a refinement process and using the communication object notion, we are able to model the Inter-Object interaction activities by means of activity diagrams extended with a specific set of stereotypes.

In future work, we intend to determine more precisely the design method shown in this paper. From the "way of modelling" [19] perspective, we will centre our efforts on the levels that have not been treated in this work (Domain level, Intra-Objects Interaction activity level and Presentation level). From the "way of working" [19] perspective, we aim to extend the method described here, offering rules and guidelines to be followed during the modelling process.

References

1. Bodart F., Vanderdonckt J. (1994) On the Problem of Selecting Interaction Objects, at Cockton G., Diaper S.W., Weir G.R.S (eds), People and Computers IX (HCI'94), Cambridge University Press, 163-178.

2. Domínguez E., Lloret J., Rubio A. L., Zapata Mª A. (2003) A MDA-Based approach to Managing Database Evolution, Proceedings of the Workshop Model Driven Architecture: Foundations and Applications, 97-102.

3. Domínguez E., Lloret J., Rubio A. L., Zapata Mª A. (2004) Elementary translations: the seesaws for achieving traceability between database schemata Conceptual Modeling for Advanced Application Domains-ER 2004 Workshops, S. Wang et al. (eds), Lecture Notes in Computer Science 3289, Springer. 377-389.

4. Domínguez E., Lloret J., Zapata, Mª A (2003) An architecture for Managing Database Evolution, Advanced Conceptual Modeling Techniques: ER 2002 Workshops, Revised Papers, LNCS 2784, Springer, 63-74.

5. Elkoutbi M, Keller R.Kin, Nielsen, M., Simpson, D. (2000) User Interface Prototyping based on UML scenarios and High Level Petri-Nets, LNCS 1825: 21st International Conference on Application and Theory of Petri Nets (ICATPN 2000), Aarhus, Denmark, Springer-Verlag, 2000. 166-186.

6. Greco de Paula M., Barbosa S. D.J., de Lucena, C. J. P. (2003) Relating Human-Computer Interaction and SoftwareEngineering Concerns: Towards Extending UML Through an Interaction Modeling Language, Workshop Closing the Gaps: Software Engineering and Human-Computer Interaction (Interact 2003). Zürich, Switzerland.

7. Griffths T., Barclay P., McKirdy J., Paton, N.W., Gray P., Kennedy, J., Cooper, R., Goble, C., West, A., and Smyth, M. (1999) Teallach: A Model-Based User Interface Development Environment for Object Databases. In Proceedings of UIDIS'99, Edinburgh, UK, IEEE Press, 86-96.

8. López-Jaquero V., Montero F; Molina J.P., Fernández-Caballero A., González, P. (2003) Model-based Design of adaptative User Interfaces trough Connectors, 10th International Workshop, DSV-IS 2003, Funchal, Madeira Islands, Portugal; LNCS 2844, 245-257.

9. Markopoulos P., Marijnissen P. (2000) UML as a representation for Interaction Design. In Paris., C., Ozkan, N., Howard, S., and Lu., S. (eds.) Proceedings OZCHI 2000, 240-249.

10. OMG (2003) UML Specification version 1.5 formal/2003-03-01, disponible en http://www.omg.org, March.

11. Paternò F., Santero C. (2003) A Unified Method for designing Interactive Systems Adaptable to mobile and stationary platform, Interacting with Computers 15, Elsevier, 349-366.

12. Paternò F., Santero C. (2002) One Model, Many Interfaces, Proceedings of CADUI 2002 (Valenciennes, France).

13. Phillips C., Kemp E. (2002) In Support of User Interface Design in the Rational Unified Process, Third Australasian User Interface Conference (AUIC2002).

14. Pinheiro da Silva P. (2002) Object Modelling of Interactive Systems: The UMLi Approach. PhD's thesis, Department of Computer Science, University of Manchester, United Kingdom.

15. Pinheiro da Silva P., Paton N.W. (2000) UMLi: The Unified Modeling Language for Interactive Applications. In <<UML>>2000, York, United Kingdom, October, 2000. A. Evans, S. Kent and B. Selic (eds.). LNCS 1939, Springer, 117-132.

16. Pinheiro P., Paton N.W. (2000) User interface Modelling with UML, Proceedings of the 10th European-Japanese Conference on Information Modelling and Knowledge Representation, Saariselka, Finland.

17. Sánchez Díaz J., Pastor O., Fons J.J. (2001) From User Requirements to User Interfaces: A Methodological Approach. CAiSE 2001, 60-75.

18. Traetteberg H. (2002) Model-Based User Interface Design. PhD's thesis, Department of Computer and Information Science, Norwegian University, Norway, 2002.

19. Wijers G. M. (1991) Modelling Support in Information Systems Development; PhD thesis, Delft University of Technology.